IMAGES
of America

SAN FRANCISCO ART DECO

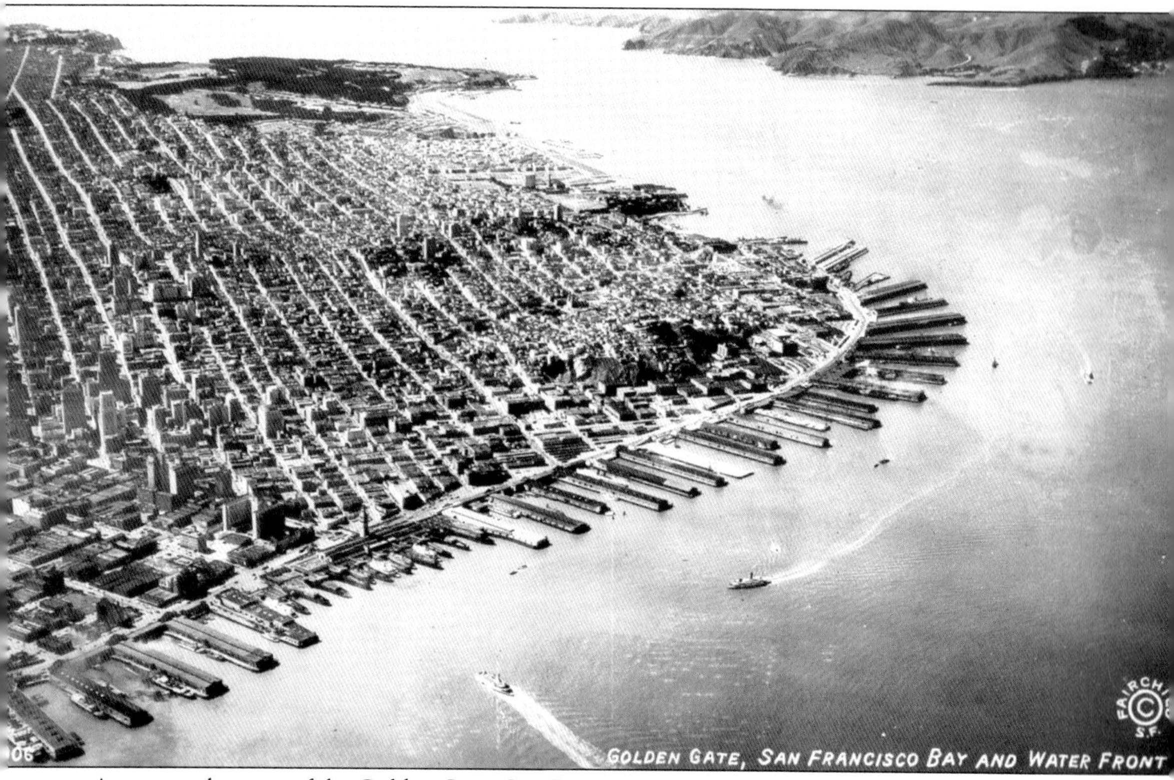

A spectacular view of the Golden Gate, San Francisco Bay, and the city's vibrant waterfront and business district can be seen in this aerial taken about 1930 for the Fairchild Company. Occupying an area of 42 square miles, with a population that would grow from 506,700 residents in 1920 to 634,500 residents in 1940, San Francisco in the Jazz Age was known for its sophisticated and modern architecture and especially for its indomitable spirit.

ON THE COVER: This is a photograph of the Roundhouse Restaurant and the Golden Gate Bridge taken in 1938. (Courtesy San Francisco History Center, San Francisco Public Library.)

IMAGES
of America

SAN FRANCISCO ART DECO

Michael F. Crowe and Robert W. Bowen

ARCADIA
PUBLISHING

ISBN 978-0-7385-4734-3

Published by Arcadia Publishing
Charleston, South Carolina

Printed in the United States of America

Library of Congress Catalog Card Number: 2006938812

For all general information contact Arcadia Publishing at:
Telephone 843-853-2070
Fax 843-853-0044
E-mail sales@arcadiapublishing.com
For customer service and orders:
Toll-Free 1-888-313-2665

Visit us on the Internet at www.arcadiapublishing.com

To my parents, Tom and Pearl, who lived through the period, and to my partner, Dan, who tells me about the period. —M. F. C.

To Brenda, with love and appreciation. —R. W. B.

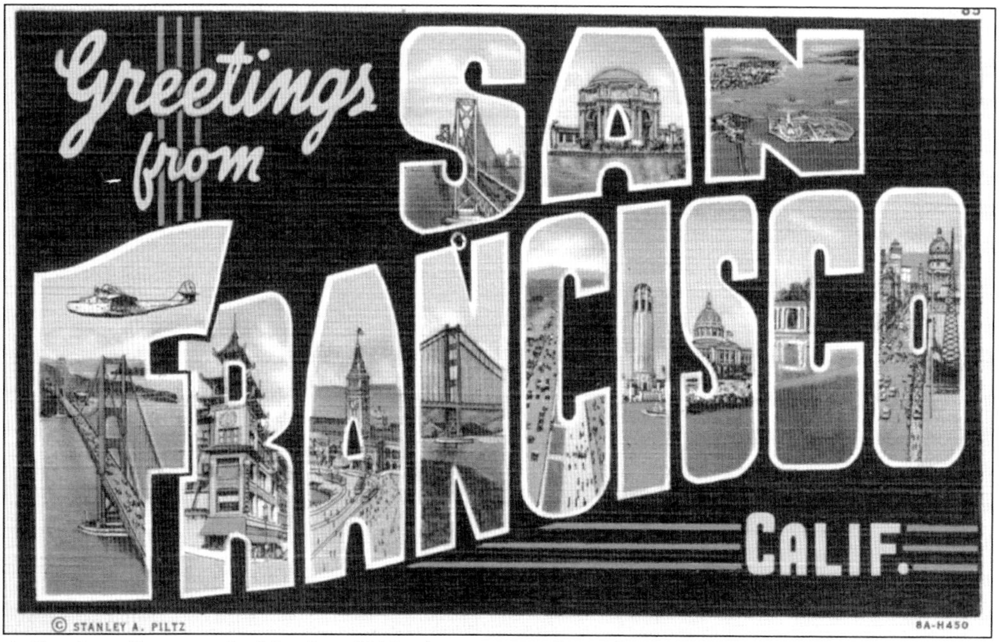

A "big letter" postcard of the late 1930s shows a popular sight in each enlarged letter, including the Bay Bridge, Golden Gate Bridge, Coit Tower, and Treasure Island—new marvels that would come to symbolize the city by the bay.

Contents

ACKNOWLEDGMENTS

We would especially like to thank our editor, John Poultney, and Arcadia Publishing for seeing the need for this book and their forbearance in guiding the project to completion. Special thanks also go to the staff of the San Francisco Public Library History Center for their speedy assistance. Photographs courtesy of the San Francisco History Center include the cover illustration and those images cited on pages 6, 15, 38, 39, 73, 77, 78, and 95. Michael F. Crowe photographs appear on pages 14 (below), 15 (above), 18, 20, 21, 22 (above), 29 (below), 30 (below), 42 (above), 43, 46–51, 53, 56–70, 75–77, 79, 109, and 125. All other illustrations not cited are from the collection of postcards, photographs, and ephemera of coauthor Robert W. Bowen.

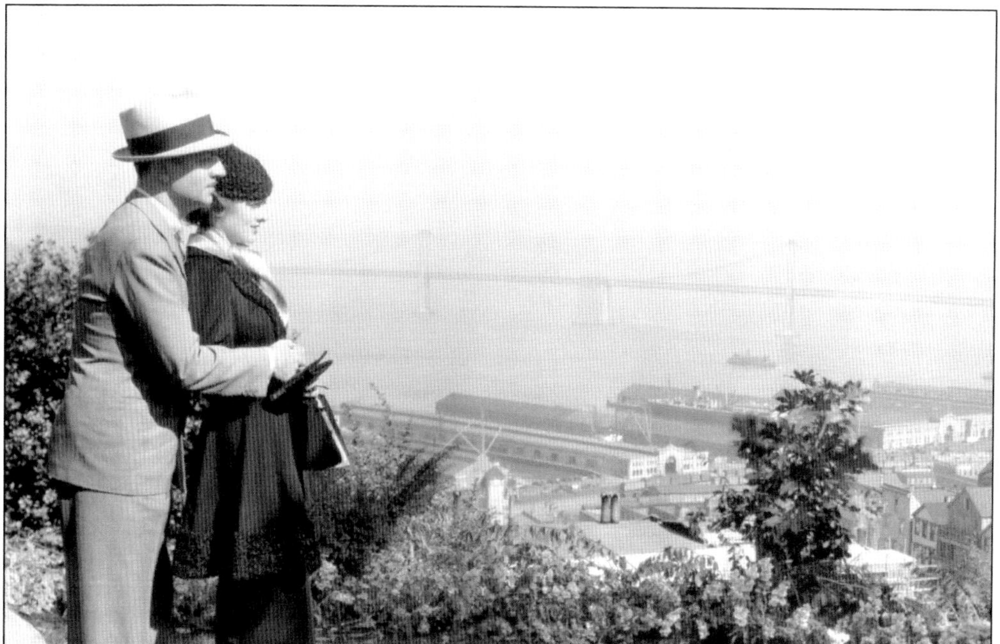

From the heights of Telegraph Hill, actors William Powell and Myrna Loy view the city between scenes from the popular MGM movie *After the Thin Man.* (Courtesy San Francisco History Center, San Francisco Public Library.)

INTRODUCTION

Art Deco—the term conjures up images of everything from skyscrapers to toasters. As a reform design movement, the Art Deco style had a significant effect on design in the United States and the world. Its early floral and cubist manifestation reflects the exuberance of the 1920s, and its later streamlining reflects the changed economics of the Great Depression.

The origins of the style lie in design reform movements and the new art movements that were developing in Europe at the beginning of the 20th century. Beginning with William Morris in England, reformers in Germany and Austria were calling for changes in the design world that would reflect the advances in technology and manufacturing to give better-designed products to an eager public. These ideas came together in Paris under the auspices of the Société des Artistes Décorateurs. They looked to the developments in artistic movements of the period such as cubism and fauvism as sources for design inspiration. They also wanted to seek new sources of inspiration and found them in the exoticism of Egypt, the Middle East, and primitive African art and textiles. Zigzigs, rays, chevrons, and other decorative elements became the new design vocabulary, replacing pointed arches, classical columns, and bracketed cornices.

This heady mix of sources were presented in 1925 in Paris at the L'Exposition Internationale des Arts Décoratifs et Industriels Modernes, held from April to October of that year. The vast exposition was meant to reestablish the preeminence of France in the design world and in the production of luxury goods. The international exhibits were heavily vetted to ensure that only items of truly modern design were presented. The exposition was meant to express the 20th century in all aspects of design from the architecture of the buildings to the items presented within the pavilions. The sources for inspiration would not be past styles or designs. Designers were encouraged to explore new color combinations, new industrial materials, and the machine image.

In the United States, the world of design lagged behind Europe. This country was untouched by World War I, and designers were still grounded in pre-war ideas. Americans in general were equally naive about modernity in design. Immediately after the Paris Exposition, American museums and department stores held special exhibits of the wares that had been presented in Paris. The intent was to create a market for these modern-looking goods. Many of the European designers came to the United States to work and educate American designers. This effort was enhanced by the changes that occurred in that most American medium—the movies.

Hollywood stars, such as Gloria Swanson, brought European designers to this country for their costumes and sets. Erte, the quintessential artist of the Folies Bergeres, worked briefly in Hollywood designing sets and costumes. It was thus possible for theater-going Americans to see these newest ideas in fashion, textiles, furniture, lighting, interior design, and luxury items regardless of where they lived. Every town had a movie theater, usually lit with neon, and so the ideas could spread rapidly, creating a tide of consumer demand.

San Francisco was part of this phenomenon. The publicity still for *After the Thin Man* depicts Nick and Nora Charles (William Powell and Myrna Loy) as characters taken from Dashiell Hamett's novels set in San Francisco. The still shows the cosmopolitan couple looking out at San

Francisco in 1936, and what they see is San Francisco becoming a modern city. Starting with the 1925 Pacific Telephone and Telegraph Building, designed by Timothy L. Pflueger, the downtown began to change with the construction of new buildings reflecting the new design aesthetic. Architects not usually associated with the style quickly adapted its principals. An example is George Kelham, who designed the main San Francisco Public Library at the civic center in 1916 and followed it later with the Shell Building in 1929. The Art Deco Shell Building couldn't be any further stylistically from the classic revival library. It is now one of the most quintessential examples of the Art Deco style.

During the period, the style was called "modernistic" or moderne. The term Art Deco was not coined until much later, probably in the late 1960s. The term is often incorrectly used to describe anything that is decorated stylistically. It did not appear in this country, as noted above, until the mid-1920s and flourished until World War II brought a halt to new construction. It should be noted that many theaters, schools, and other delayed projects were designed and planned before the war but were not constructed until afterward. As a result, some buildings constructed as late as 1950 still show evidence of the style.

After World War II, the Art Deco style swiftly fell out of favor. The International style, heralded in the mid-1930s as the only true modern architecture, replaced the Art Deco style. It too had its origins in Europe, most notably the Bauhaus. The Nazi German government closed the Bauhaus in the early 1930s, and the instructors were dispersed. Many of these architects and designers came to the United States and brought these new ideas with them. Some taught at prestigious architecture schools, educating a new generation of architects to scorn all previous periods and styles of architecture. Glass, steel, and crisp lines with no ornamentation would be the new rule. As a result of this change in taste, Art Deco buildings were neglected or demolished in the name of progress. What Art Deco structures are still here though are worth protecting and, most of all, enjoying.

One

DIAMOND JUBILEE

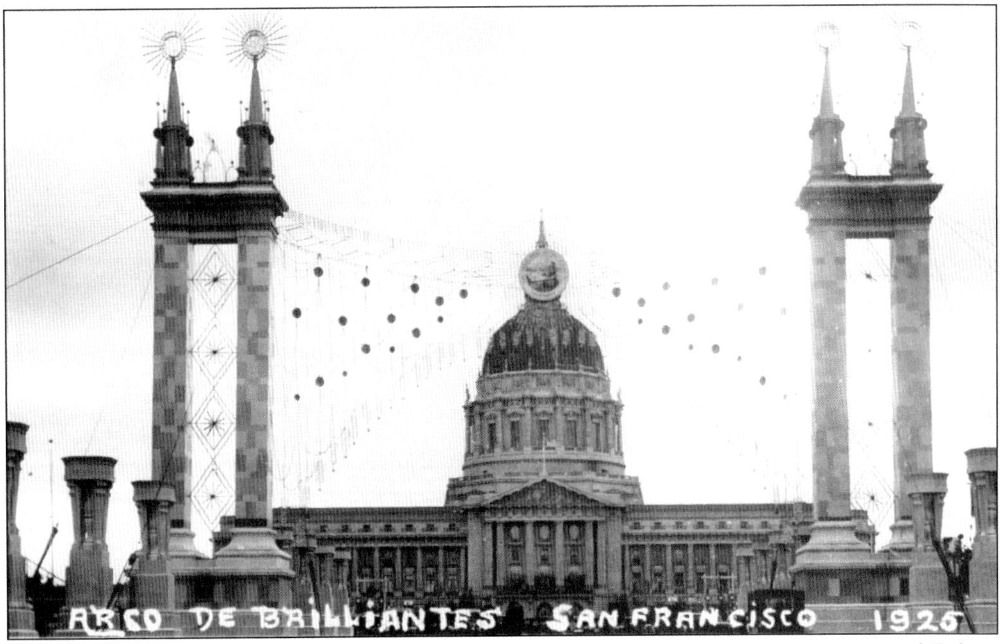

El Arco de Brillantes (the jeweled arch), also known as the Arch of Progress, spanned Fulton Street south of the main San Francisco Public Library. Forty thousand glass baubles imported from Europe, plus relics from the 1915 Tower of Jewels, decorated the arch while San Franciscans celebrated California's Diamond Jubilee from September 5 to September 12, 1925. Lawrence Walsh of the Pacific Gas and Electric Company had the idea to hold a celebration honoring California's admission into the Union and 75 years of state history. The concept won the approval of California boosters including Mayor James Rolph Jr. There would be five parades, dozens of athletic events, yacht races, automobile races, simulated air battles, banquets, and balls. Visiting sailors and soldiers were given free streetcar rides and vaudeville shows. Honored guests included Vice Pres. Charles Dawes and a Covered Wagon Baby Revue of 45 mature adults born in covered wagons while their parents were en route to California. The Diamond Jubilee not only would recognize the pioneer era but coincidentally became the symbolic event announcing the beginning of a new modern era.

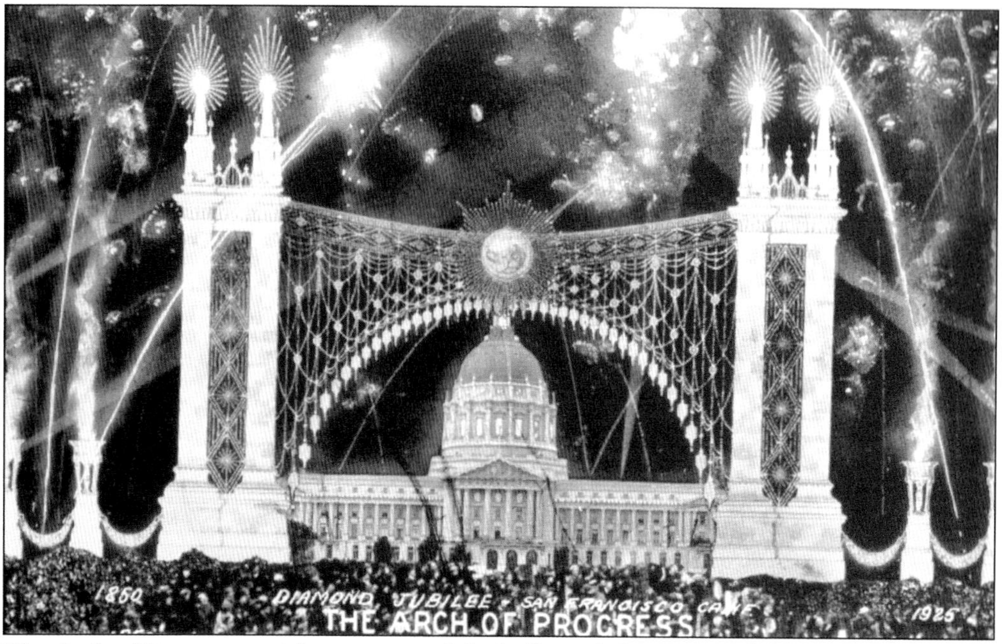

The Arch of Progress at night was part of the brilliant lighting provided for the civic center. The arch was spectacular with a constant flood of light on its iridescent jewels. On either side were cauldrons issuing jets of colored steam. Strategically placed multicolored floodlights bathed each of the public buildings in light. Illumination throughout the city was under the direction of General Electric's W. D'Arcy Ryan, who had set the standard for lighting 10 years earlier at the Panama Pacific International Exposition.

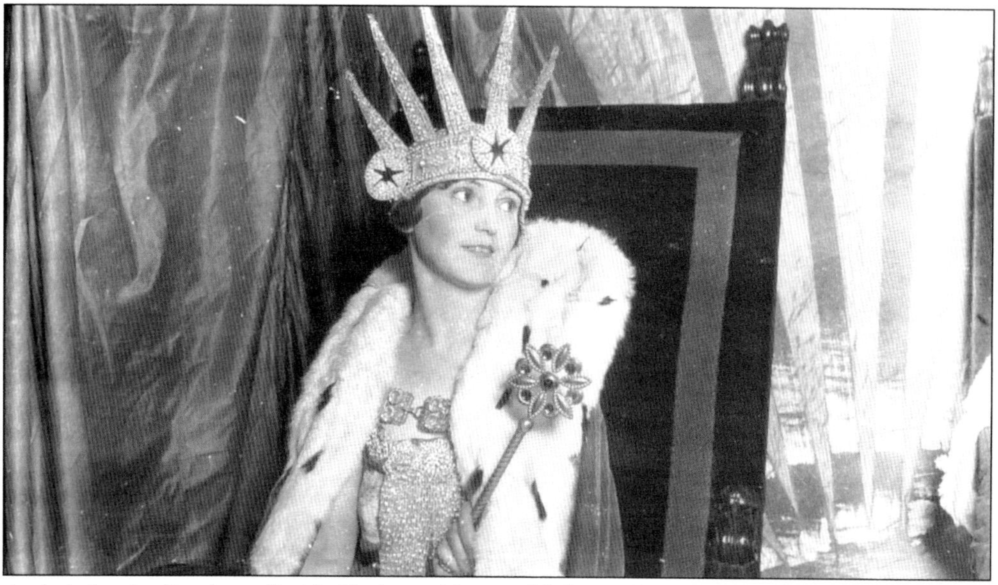

A clerk for the Southern Pacific Railway, 16-year-old Agnes Pottage was selected the Diamond Jubilee's Queen of California. At the Spanish-themed ball in Exposition Auditorium, Mayor Rolph placed a diadem on the young lady's head, saying, "I crown you Queen Agnes, and happily may you reign." The young queen presided over the grand ball, the parades, and happily was awarded a trip for two to Australia.

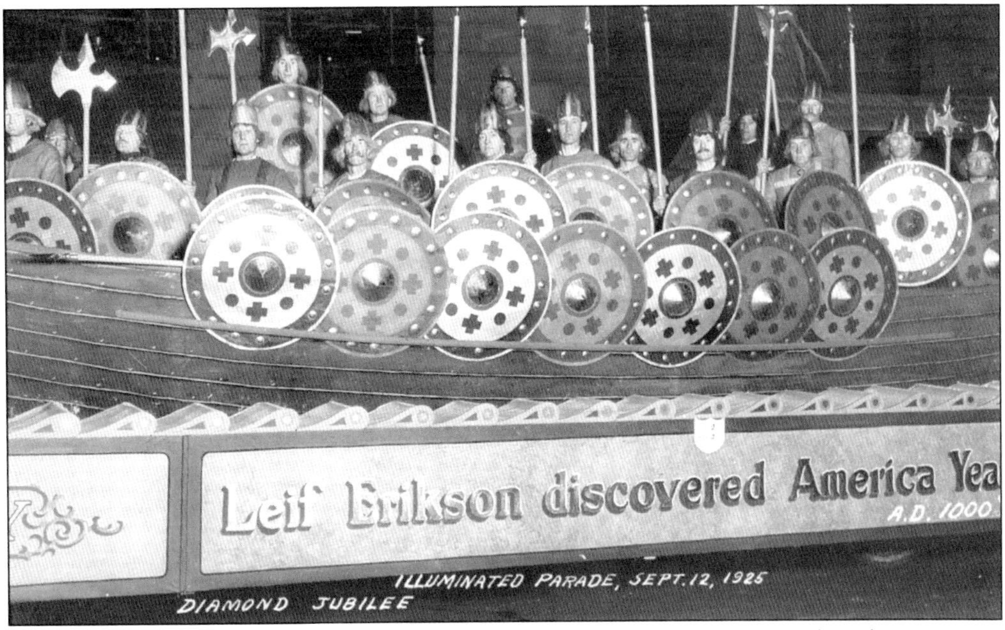

San Francisco's "Path of Gold" was the route of the Night Parade, planned as the crowning achievement in the city's parade history. Along the marching line, thousands of pounds of red, yellow, and green material were burned on the roofs of more than 100 buildings. Over 300,000 spectators viewed floats from a dozen nationalities including the Sons of Norway Viking boat. Marchers included veterans, Odd Fellows, Eagles, Knights of Columbus, DeMolay, Boy Scouts, and the Daughters of Liberty.

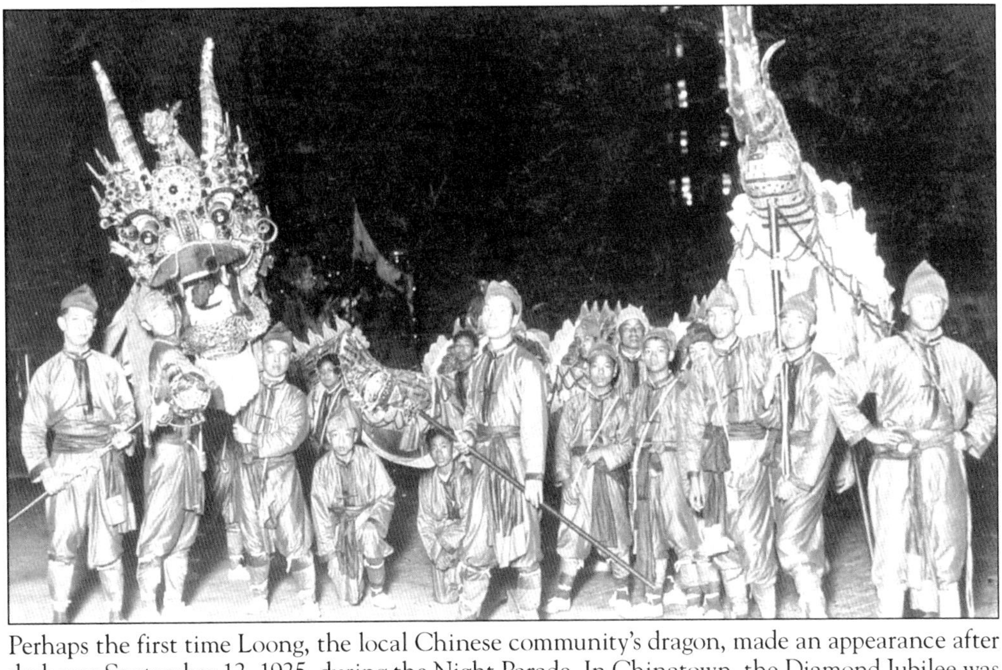

Perhaps the first time Loong, the local Chinese community's dragon, made an appearance after dark was September 12, 1925, during the Night Parade. In Chinatown, the Diamond Jubilee was also celebrated with the installation along Grant Avenue of 40 bronze streetlamps designed by W. D'Arcy Ryan in a Chinese lantern style.

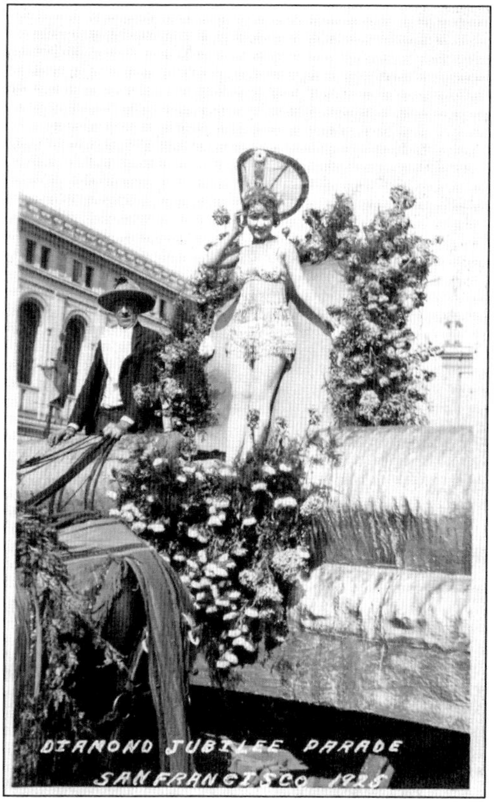

There were military parades, a Labor Day parade, and Admission Day parade. Floats celebrated California history, particularly the Spanish colonial period. During the week of the Diamond Jubilee, people were encouraged to dress in the garb of forty-niners, pirates, cowboys, 19th-century gamblers, and especially as Spanish ranchers and senoritas. Theater ushers and Shell Oil Service Station attendants dressed in the uniforms of Spanish dons.

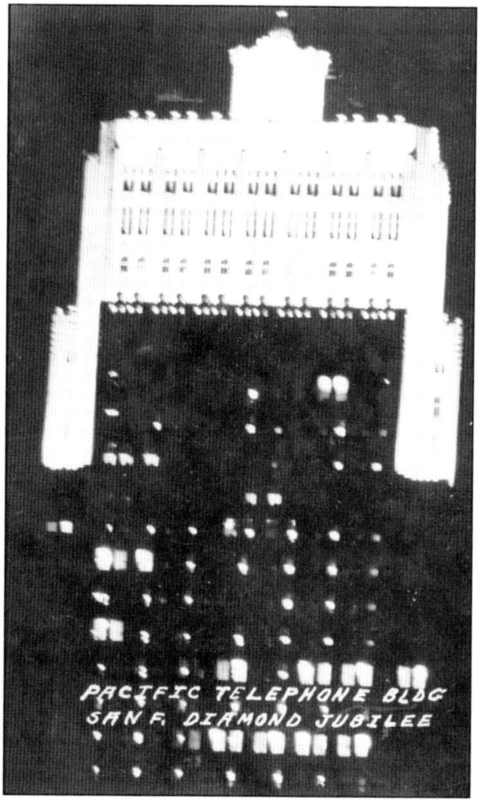

Letters were sent by the Lighting and Decorations Committee to the owners of large buildings requesting a liberal use of lighting effects and window decorations. Among the most dazzling illuminated buildings was Pacific Telephone and Telegraph's new corporate headquarters. The floodlighting was provided by 287 lamps placed on offsets of the structure to create the desired effect on the upper floors. It was described as a phantom-like spire rising out of the shadows of the sleeping city.

Two

Jazz Age Skyscrapers

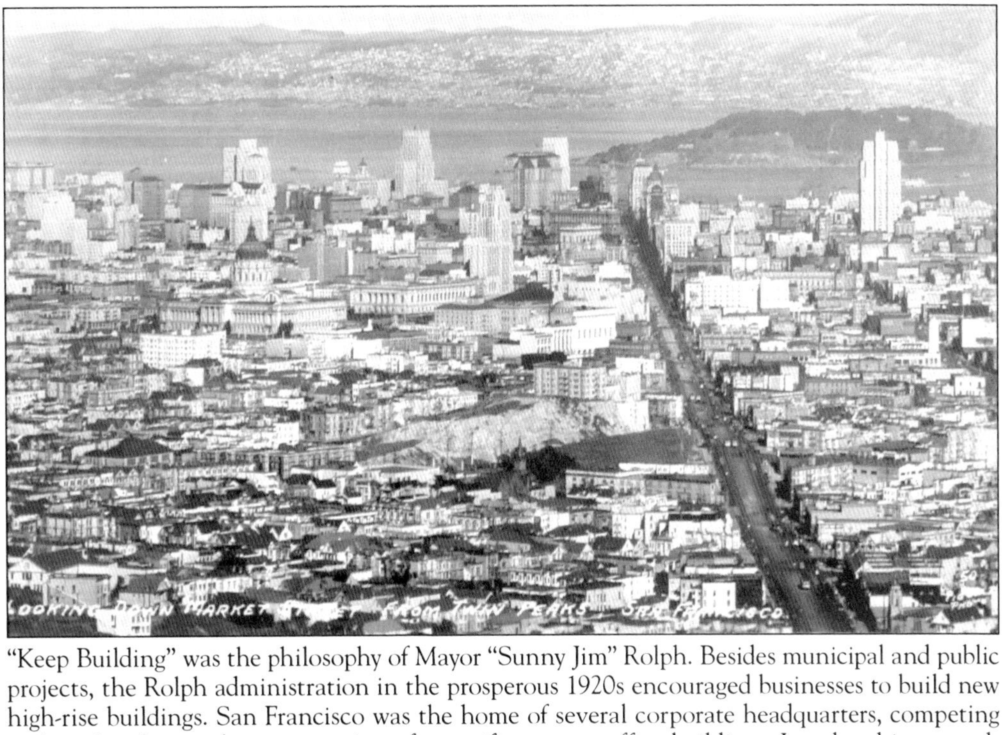

"Keep Building" was the philosophy of Mayor "Sunny Jim" Rolph. Besides municipal and public projects, the Rolph administration in the prosperous 1920s encouraged businesses to build new high-rise buildings. San Francisco was the home of several corporate headquarters, competing with each other in the construction of magnificent new office buildings. Local architects such as Timothy Pflueger and George Kelham designed most of these new structures. The Pflueger-designed Pacific Telephone Building seen in the upper right would be the tallest edifice south of Market Street for many years to come. It is considered the first of San Francisco's Art Deco skyscrapers. On the left, in the Financial District, the Russ Building, Shell Oil Building, Standard Oil Building, and several other newly constructed structures would establish a dramatic modern skyline. This was the city that newspaper columnist Herb Caen would describe as "a unique jewel gleaming on the western shore."

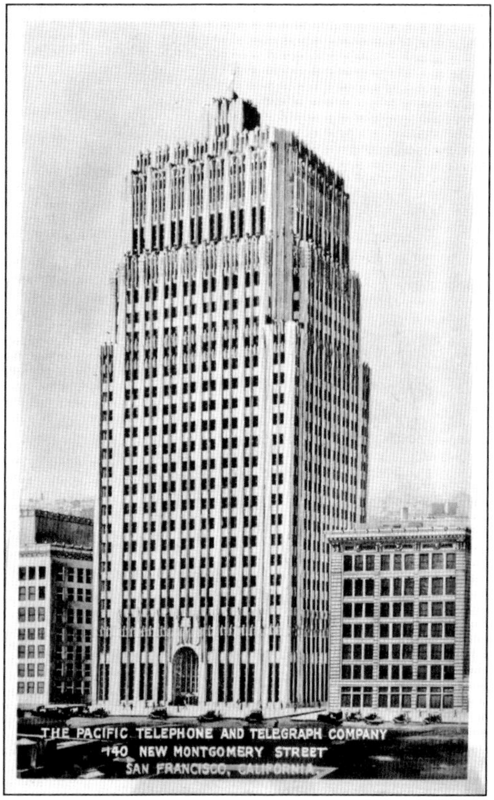

Architect Timothy L. Pflueger claimed he was inspired by the granite peaks of the Sierra Mountain Range. He was also influenced greatly by Eliel Saarinen's Chicago Tribune Tower. From the very beginning, the Pacific Telephone Building at 140 New Montgomery Street was a city landmark. Clad in nine shades of gray granite-like terra cotta at 435 feet, it was the tallest building on the West Coast. Accommodating nearly 2,000 workers, "140" was the first building to be wired for a personal telephone line at each desk.

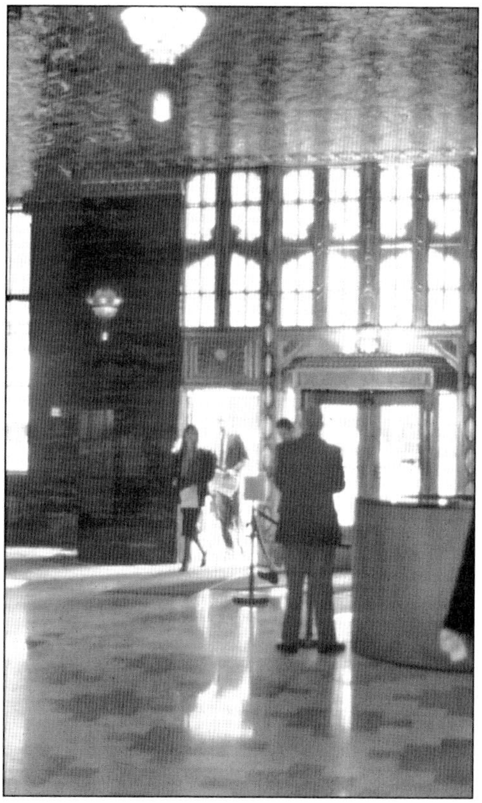

Timothy Pflueger designed a lobby at 140 New Montgomery that was an Asian fantasy. Black polished marble floors were opposite a brilliant red ceiling intertwined with black and gold designs of unicorns, phoenixes, clouds, and three-fingered hands. Complemented by windows, doors, and vertical glass panels, anyone entering the ornate first floor lobby could not help but get a sense of success and prosperity.

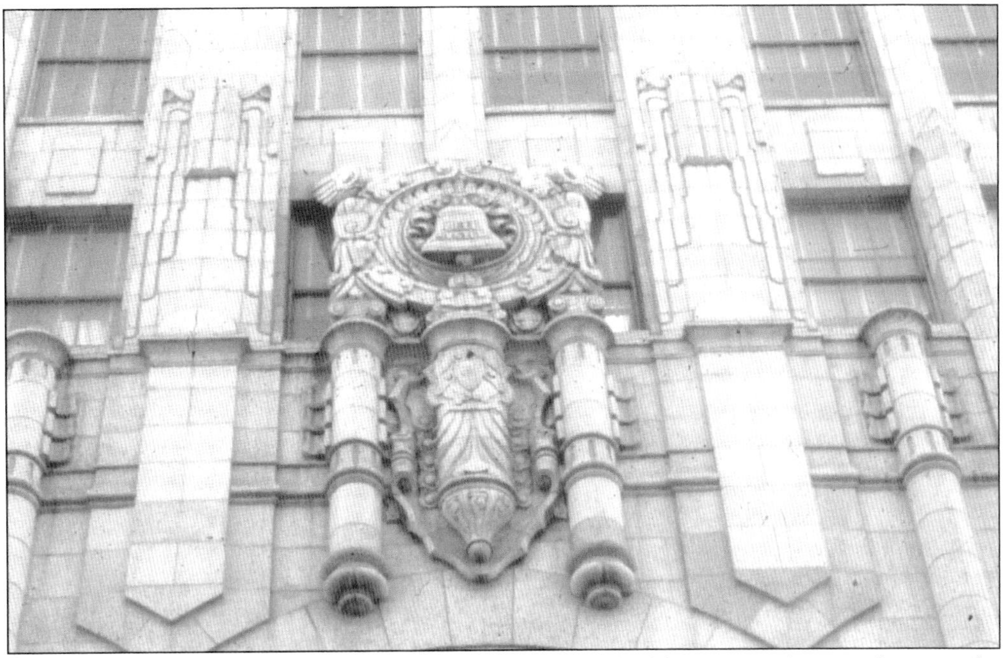

Pflueger always paid close attention to the details of his buildings. Here he complements the bluebells at the cornice, the flower symbol of the company, with phone books. The stylized wings add to their unique design, making them the only "flying phone books" on a telephone company building in the city.

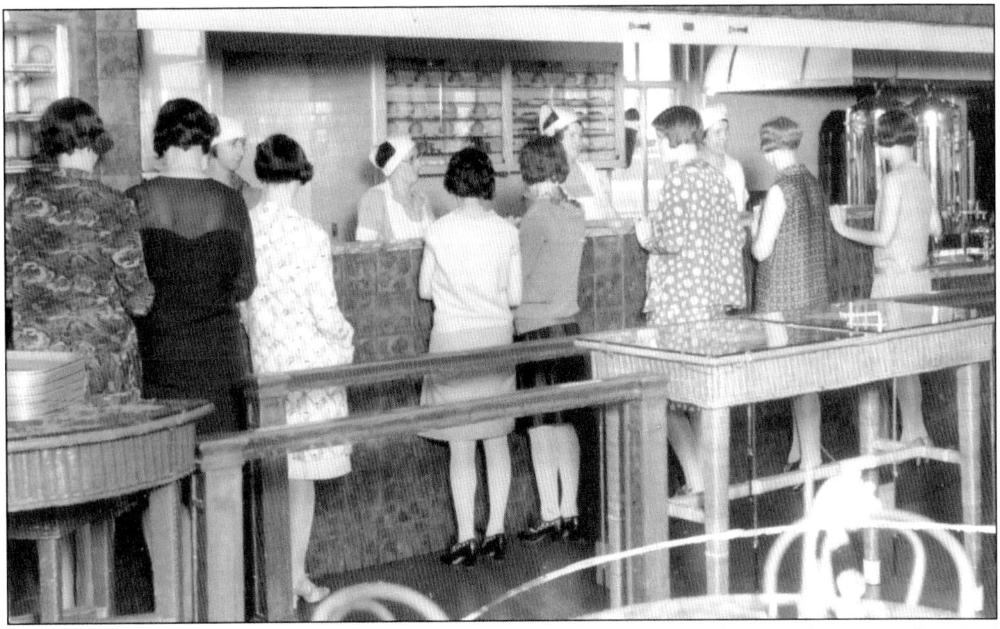

One innovative feature at 140 New Montgomery Street was the employee cafeteria on the 22nd floor. This was the era when women were entering the work force in earnest, and this dining facility was for ladies only. In a room that could accommodate 250 people, employees were able to purchase well-cooked meals at a nominal cost, dine on glass-topped tables, and enjoy a spectacular view. (Courtesy San Francisco History Center, San Francisco Public Library.)

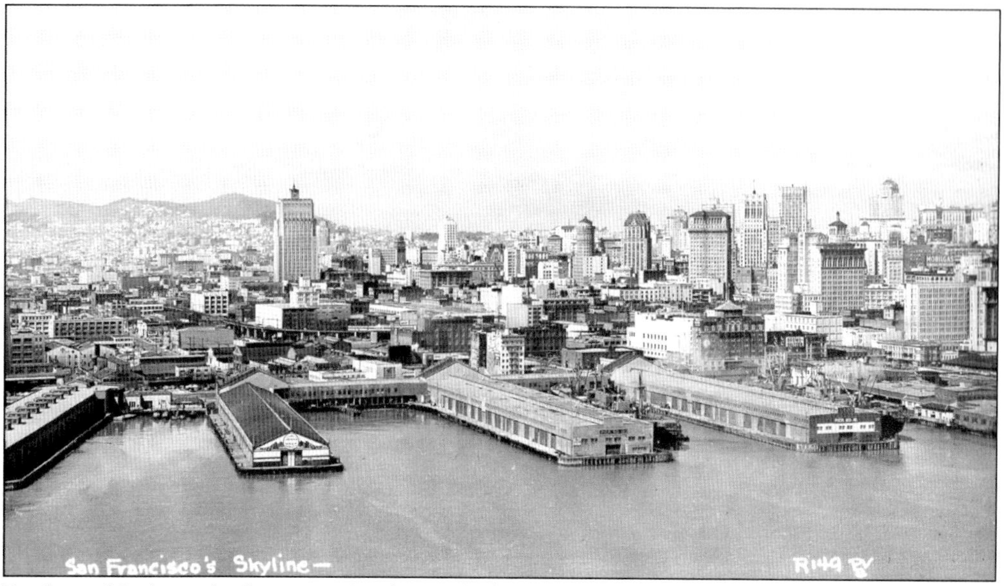

Easily visible from the bay, in 1934 the roof of 140 was chosen by the United States Weather Service for its storm-warning flags and beacons to alert boats about inclement weather: two red pennants, or a white light above a red one, meant gale warnings (39–54 miles per hour); and a red flag with a black center, or two red lights, meant storm warnings (55–73 miles per hour). By 1978, the building was obscured by newer high-rises, and the obsolete flags and lights were removed.

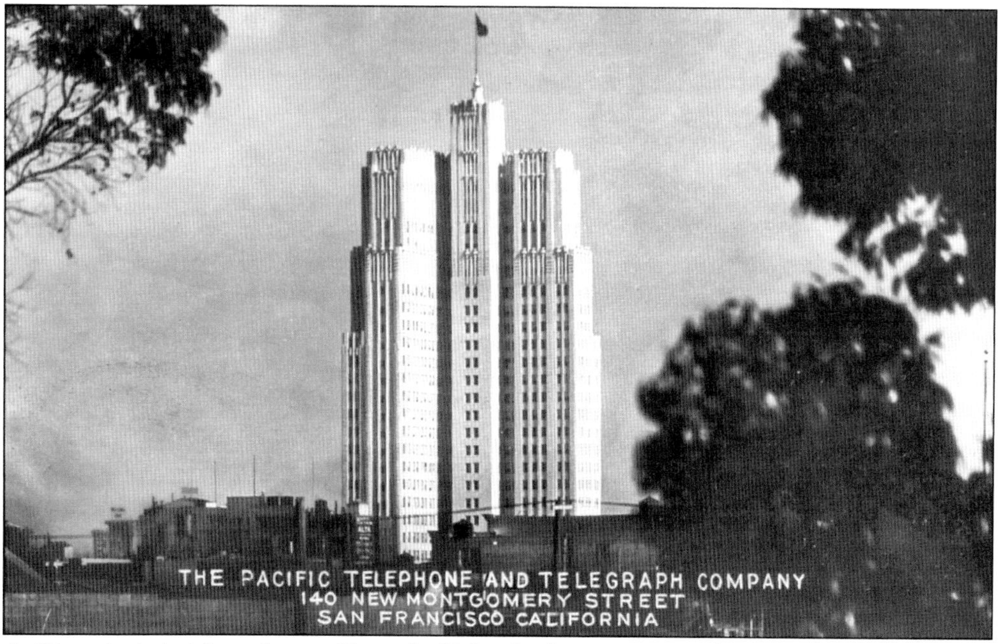

At 26 stories in height and topped by eight 12-foot-high terra cotta eagles, the telephone company skyscraper was a feat of cutting-edge design, as seen in this view showing the west or rear side of the building. Harris Allen, A.I.A., stated in the *Pacific Coast Architect* that 140 New Montgomery Street was "a combination of massive strength and airy grace." Poet Miles Overholt, in the *San Francisco Examiner*, wrote, "An architectural dream come true . . . a shimmering gleaming monument to TALK!"

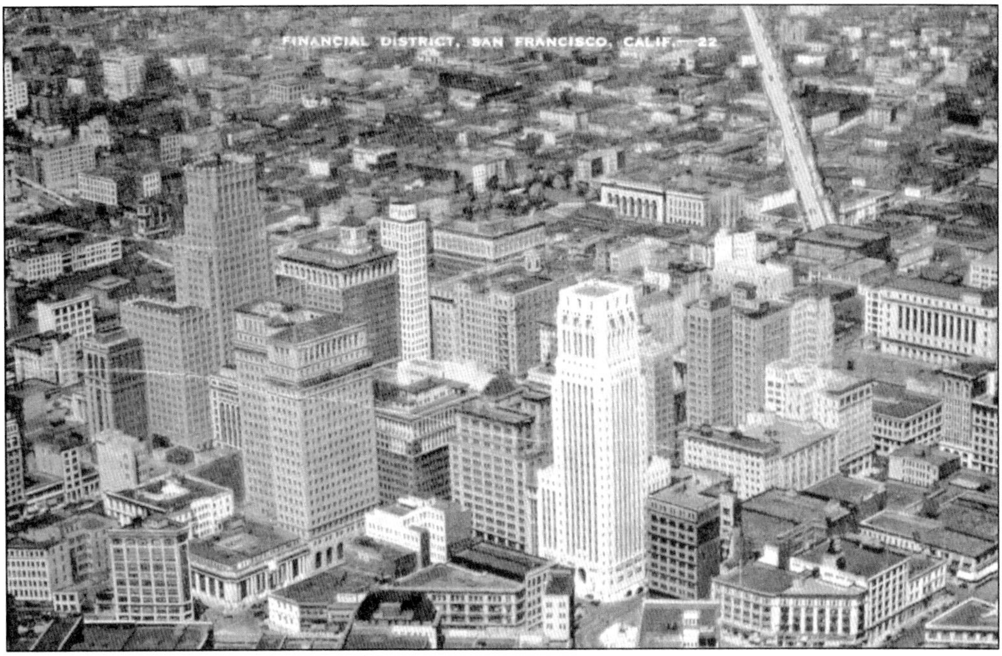

North of Market Street, this aerial from the 1930s shows the city's commercial district, when San Francisco was still considered the financial capital of the West. The building boom of the 1920s propelled many new high-rises skyward. Corporate headquarters like the moderne Shell Building, the Standard Oil Building, and the Russ Building, popular with the city's legal community, stand out beside the district's banks, insurance companies, and shipping concerns. All three skyscrapers were designed by architect George W. Kelham.

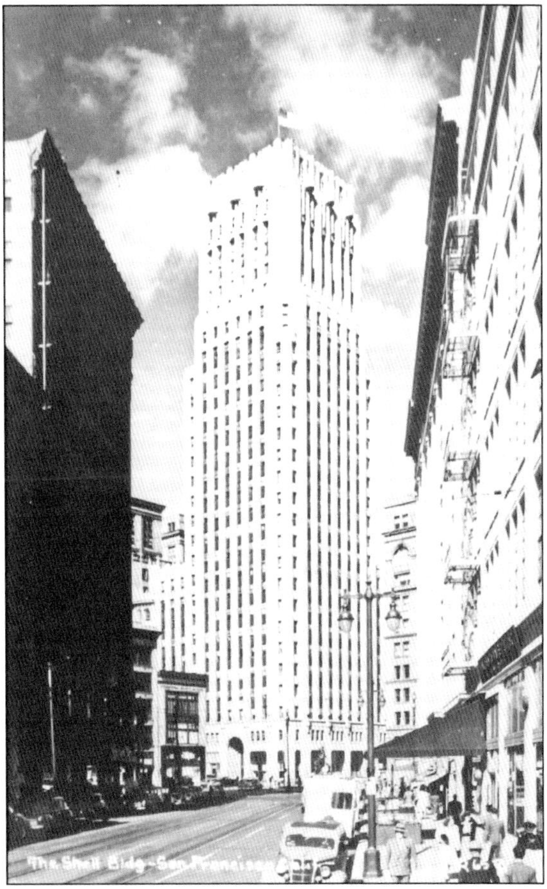

Located on what was once San Francisco's original shoreline, the 29-story Shell Building at 100 Bush Street was erected in 1929 as the western headquarters of the Shell Oil Company. L'École des Beaux Arts–trained architect George W. Kelham modeled the Shell Building after Saarinen's Chicago Tribune Tower and Pflueger's Pacific Telephone Building. To provide foundation support to resist wind and earthquake stress, the building was constructed on 66 concrete caissons extending to a depth of 80 feet.

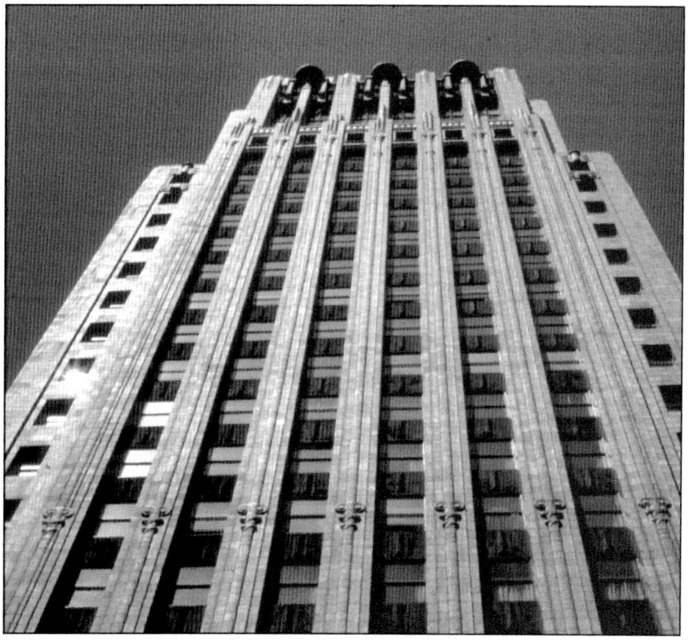

George Kelham abandoned the classical- and Gothic-style vocabulary of his earlier buildings to design the Shell Building in a distinctly modernistic mode in 1929. Kelham used the expected forms to create a signature building. The vertical piers terminate in stylized floral elements set back on the lower levels. The stepped profile at the upper level ends with light pods that flooded the building at night. The molded terra cotta cladding was often used during the period because of its adaptability to the design elements.

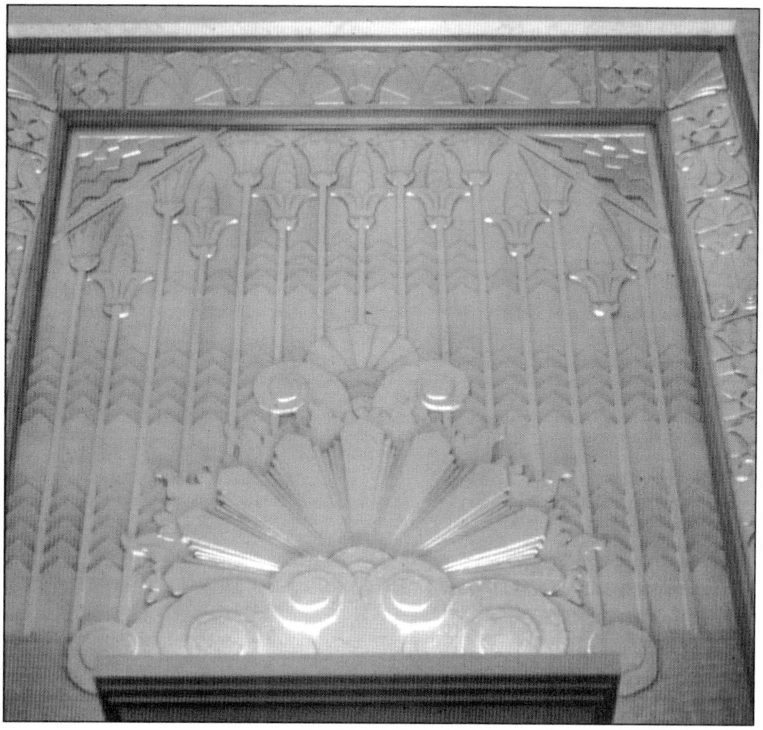

The rays, chevrons, and zigzags are classic design motifs of the Art Deco style. The lotus flowers are part of Egyptian exoticism that often appeared in designs during the period. The luminosity dramatically plays up the light and shadow affects of the designs. This use of indirect effect gained popularity with the advances in lighting technology.

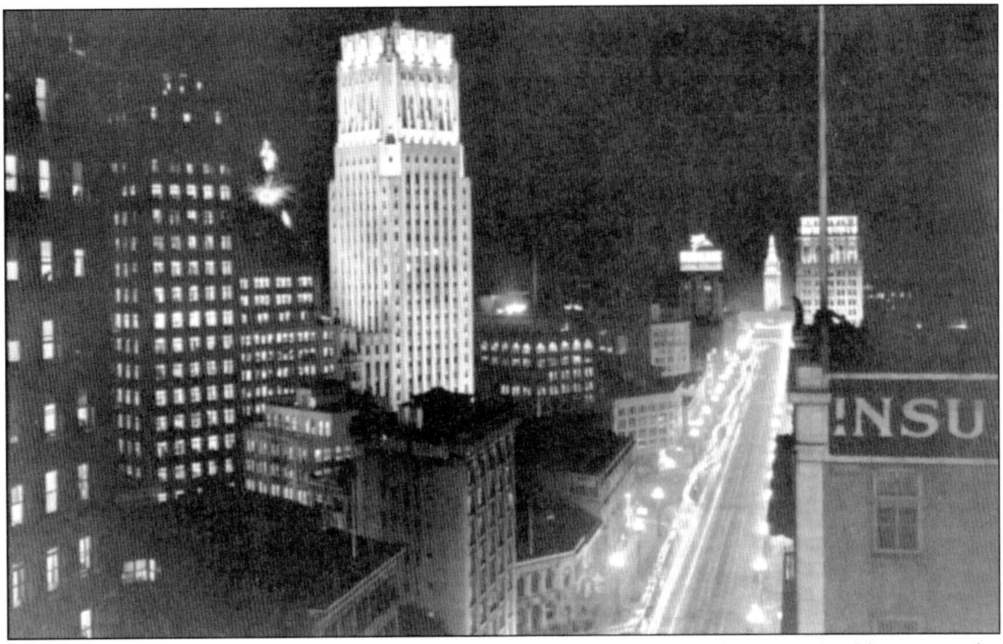

Along lower Market Street at night, glowing streetlamps lead to the Ferry Building past the dramatically floodlighted Shell Building. By day, it was a richly decorated sepia terra cotta office building with blue-green concrete spandrels, but after dark, the amber floodlights and built-in light pods gave the Shell tower the appearance of a mystical Babylonian temple.

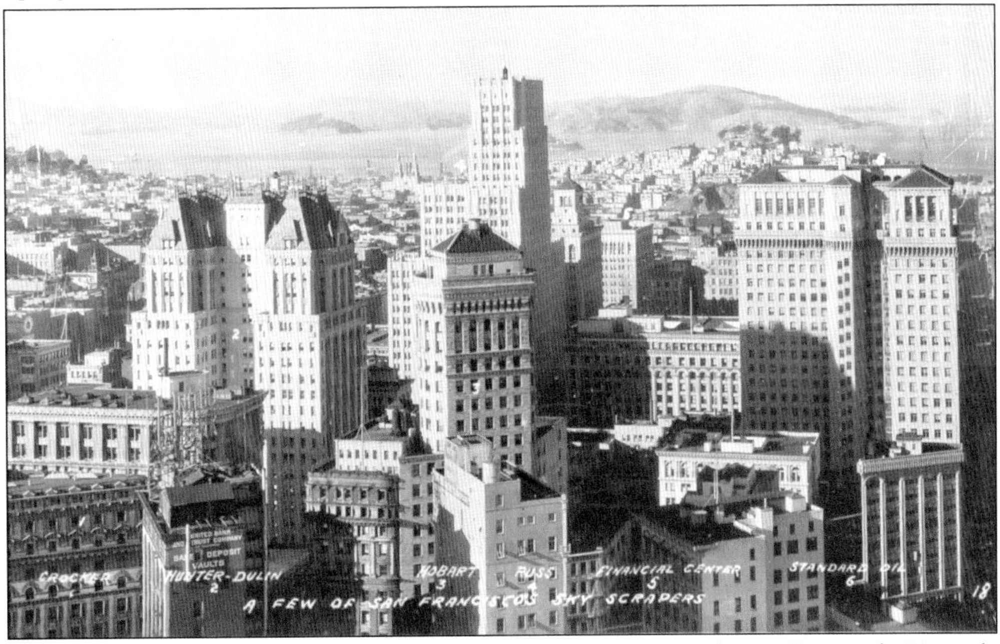

Where's the Deco? Not all buildings built during the period were in the Art Deco style. Versatile George W. Kelham's towering Russ Building at 235 Montgomery Street, in the center, had a Gothic motif. Architects Leonard Schultze and S. F. Weaver designed the Hunter-Dulin Building at 111 Sutter Street with a high mansard roof. Dashiell Hammett's detective Sam Spade had his office on the Hunter-Dulin's sixth floor.

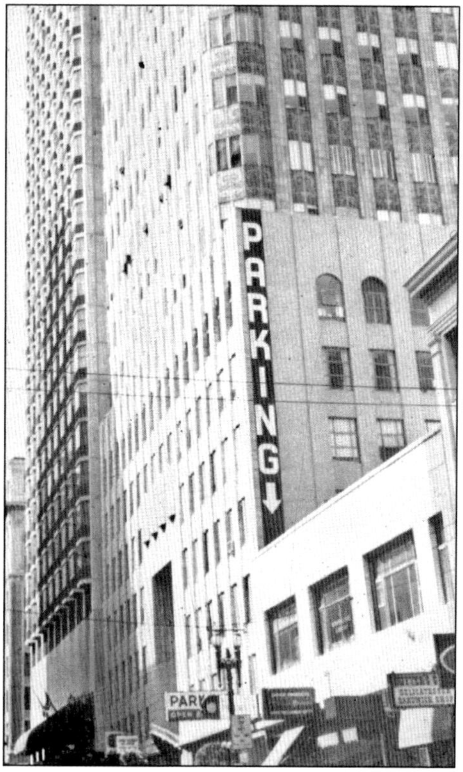

In 1929, thr building at 450 Sutter Street was another design triumph for Timothy Pflueger. It was innovative in the use of a new method of attaching the terra cotta cladding by wires to the steel superstructure. This technique allowed the walls to be thinner and thus increase the rentable square footage.

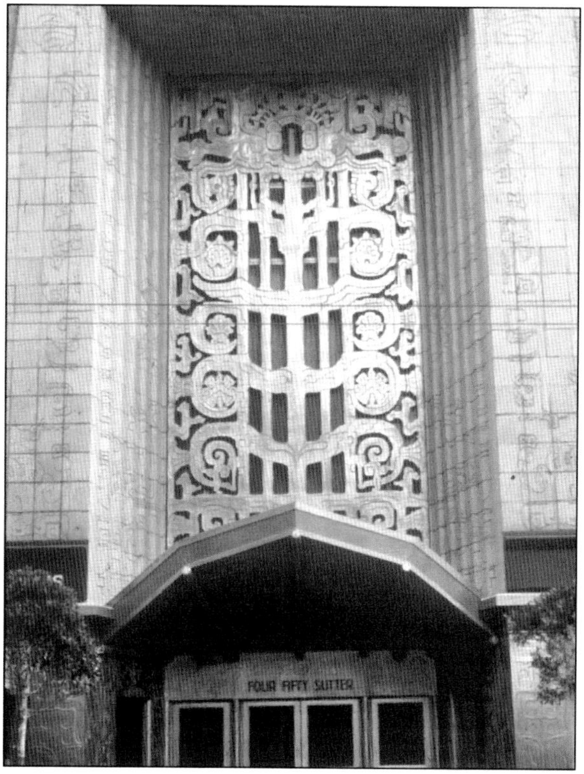

The entrance encapsulates the design motifs derived from Mayan architecture and design. The shaped marquee, the molded ornament on the entry transom, and the incised lines in the terra cotta are all examples of how the Mayan motifs were used on the building.

The simplicity of the building's design profile is a harbinger of the International style. The simple vertical piers, unadorned cornice, and undulating rhythm of piers and windows are a departure from what other Deco architects were producing during the period.

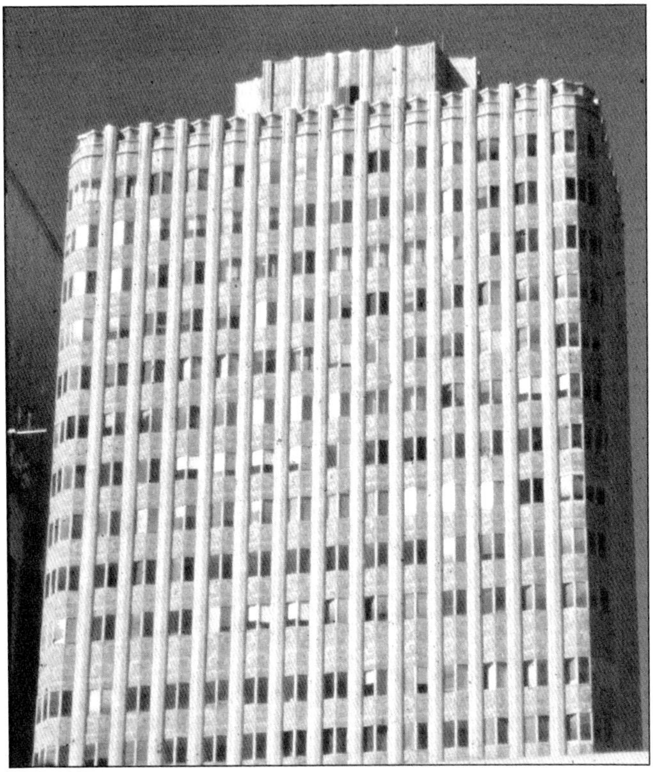

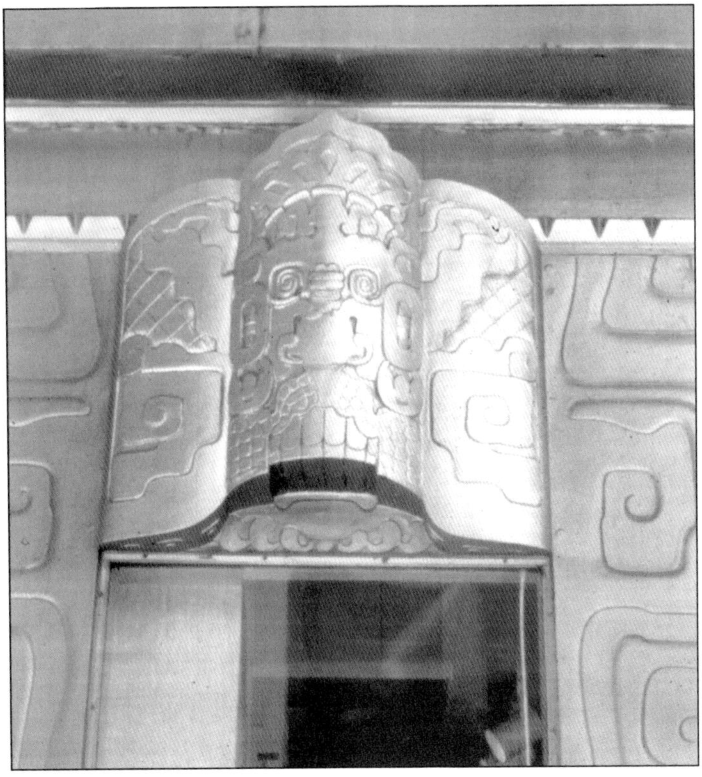

This simple detail is taken from the designs found on the Mayan architecture from Central America. The Mayan design source was championed by Robert Stacy Judd and was used for all kinds of buildings, including theaters, houses, churches, and hotels.

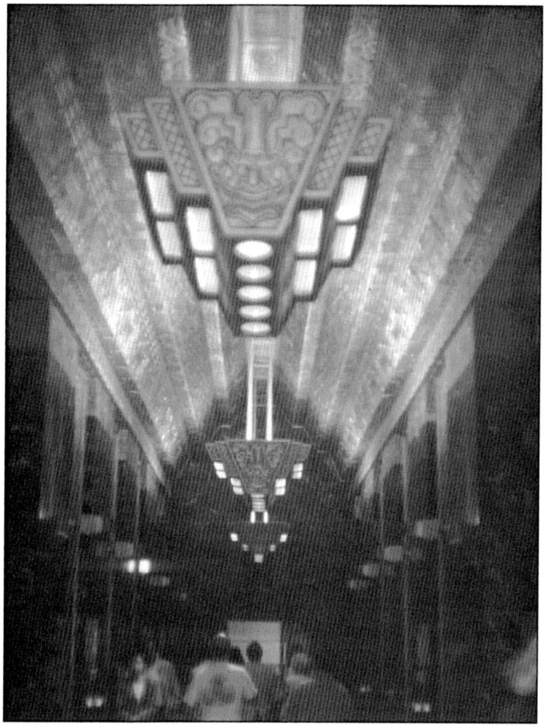

Timothy Pflueger used his formula for the spectacular lobbies of the Telephone Company Building and Stock Exchange Tower. The stepped, gilded plaster ceiling sets off the dark marble walls, intricate marble flooring, and elaborately etched elevator doors. As on the exterior, Mayan design sources were used to maximum effect. The light fixtures are later designs to play up the ceiling. The only thing missing is a Mayan princess in a feathered headdress.

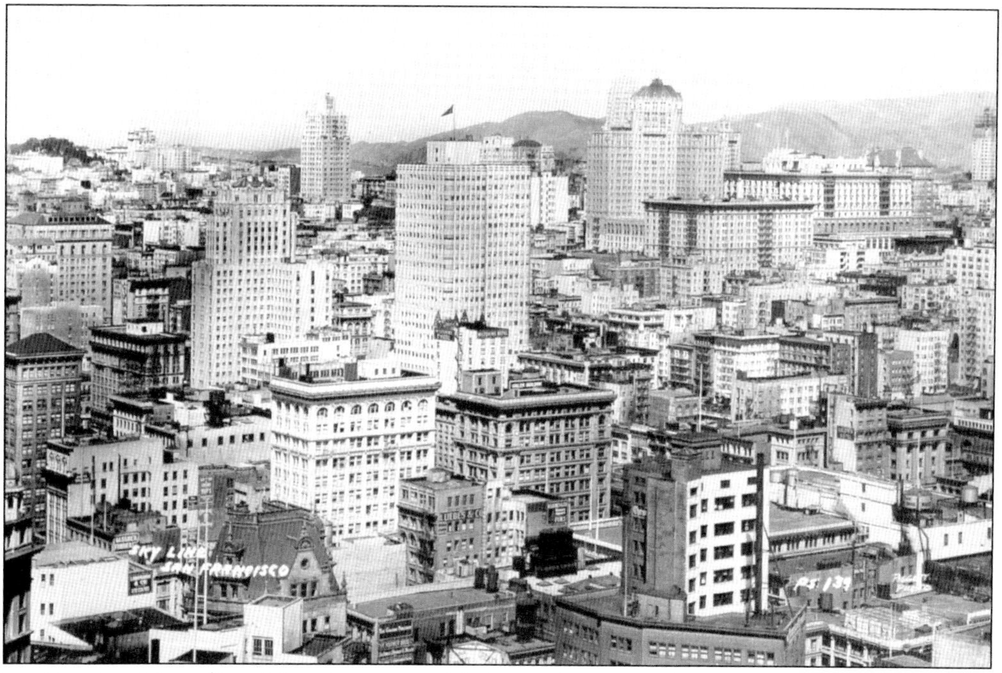

Looking just like a $5-million skyscraper, 450 Sutter Street, in the center, stands out among a variety of downtown buildings. Thirty stories high and topped off with a rooftop solarium, when built it was said to be the largest medical building in the world. Large windows flooded every office with natural light and provided great views. Extremely popular with physicians and dentists, 1930s tenants paid $75 to $85 a month in rent.

The neo-baroque building at 703 Market Street was constructed in 1898 for Claus Spreckels to house the *Call* newspaper. Architects James and Merritt Reid and structural engineer Charles Strobel designed a 315-foot-high building, steel-framed with Z-bar columns and capped by a large ornate dome. The Call Building remained standing in 1906 despite the earthquake and being engulfed in flames. A U.S. Geological survey stated, "Structurally, it is the best designed building in the United States."

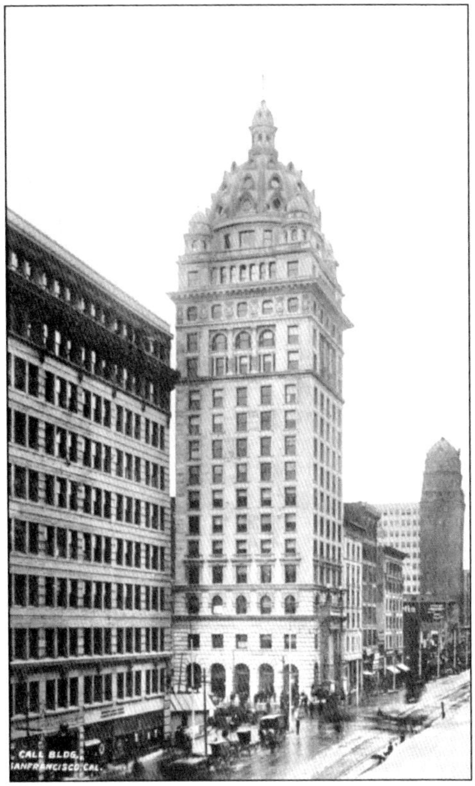

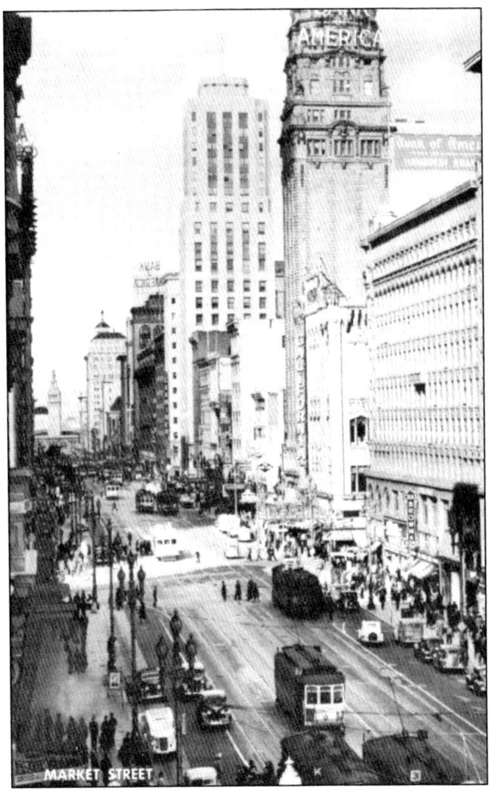

Thirty-two years after the 1906 earthquake, 703 Market Street needed additional space. Structurally the building was able to support additional floors and was "modernized" in a remodel design by Albert Roller. The dome was removed and six new floors were added to create a moderne tower set back at the upper levels. New smooth stucco replaced 19th-century ornamentation, and in the lobby, heat-tempered glass cladding (Vitrolite) covered the walls. The remodeled building can be seen in the rear center.

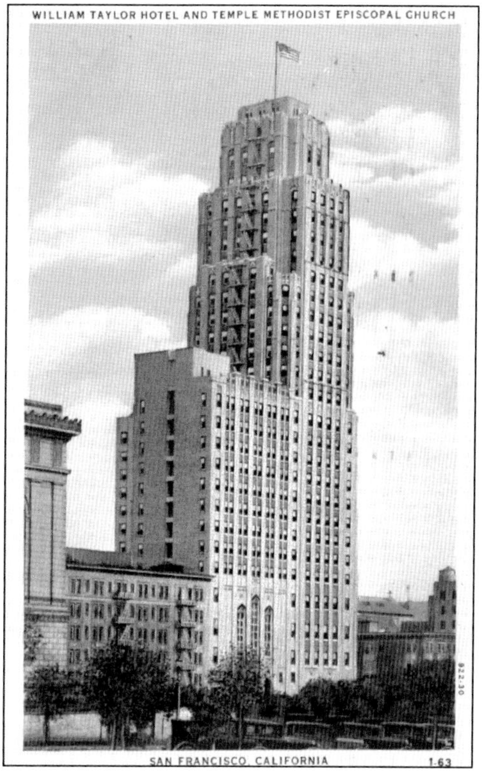

A 28-story set-back tower faced in buff terra cotta with green panels, 100 McAllister Street was designed in 1927 by James R. Miller and Timothy L. Pflueger and was completed in 1930 by Lewis P. Hobart. The Methodist Church had the building constructed to provide its members a "dry" hotel in "sinful" San Francisco. They named the building, in honor of a 19th-century street preacher, the William Taylor Hotel and Temple Methodist Church. In their design, the architects also provided tall church-like windows above the elaborate entry portal.

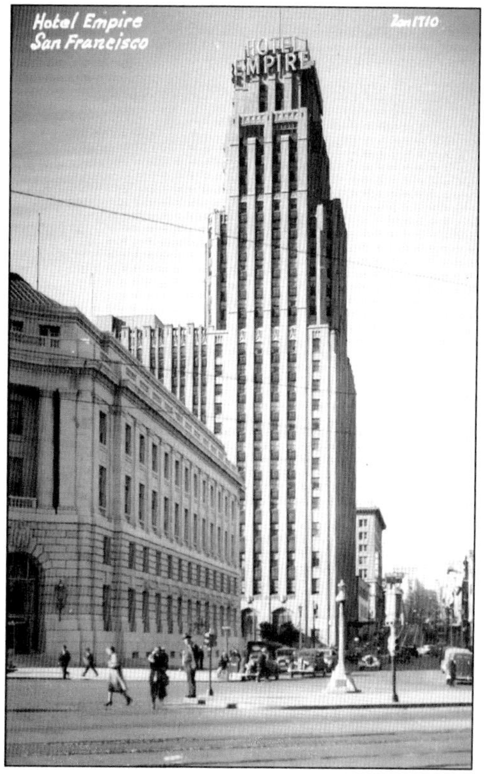

The attempt to combine religion and commerce was unsuccessful, and in 1937, the Methodists sold the building to secular entrepreneurs who renamed it the Hotel Empire. In World War II, the federal government acquired the location to use as offices for the Internal Revenue Service and Army Ordnance Procurement. For several years, 100 McAllister Street was notorious as the home of the local draft board.

Three

Cocktail Lounges and Art Deco Restaurants

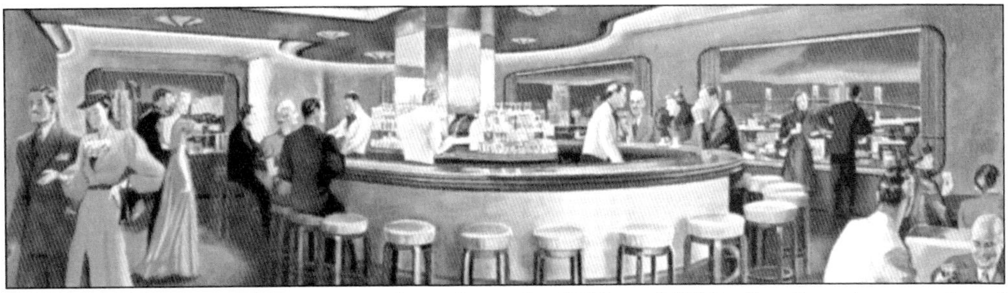

Despite Prohibition and Depression throughout the 1920s and 1930s, San Francisco continued its longtime traditions of fine dining and serious drinking. The proprietors of hotels, restaurants, and bars took advantage of the highly stylized decorative elements of Art Deco and the many new building materials to create streamlined and exotic environments for consuming food and drink. The cocktail lounge in restaurants and hotels was a new concept that allowed men and women to drink together in a socially acceptable location. In the 1930s, hotels in particular hired designers and decorators to create glamorous new drinking establishments that would hopefully bring in more guests and customers. Templeton Crocker, co-owner of the Saint Francis Hotel, brought in prestigious architect Timothy Pflueger to create a new cocktail lounge. Pflueger designed a sleek, swanky, ultramodern room with a metal-fin ceiling, walls covered with black patent leather, mirrored columns, and a 60-foot-long serpentine bar. Crocker called his new cocktail lounge the Patent Leather Bar. Near the civic center, at the Hotel Empire, the new owners opened a penthouse bar in the formerly alcohol-prohibited hotel. The Sky Room, pictured here, was a luxurious cocktail lounge with deep carpets, a large oval bar, and plate-glass windows that provided unparalleled views of the city.

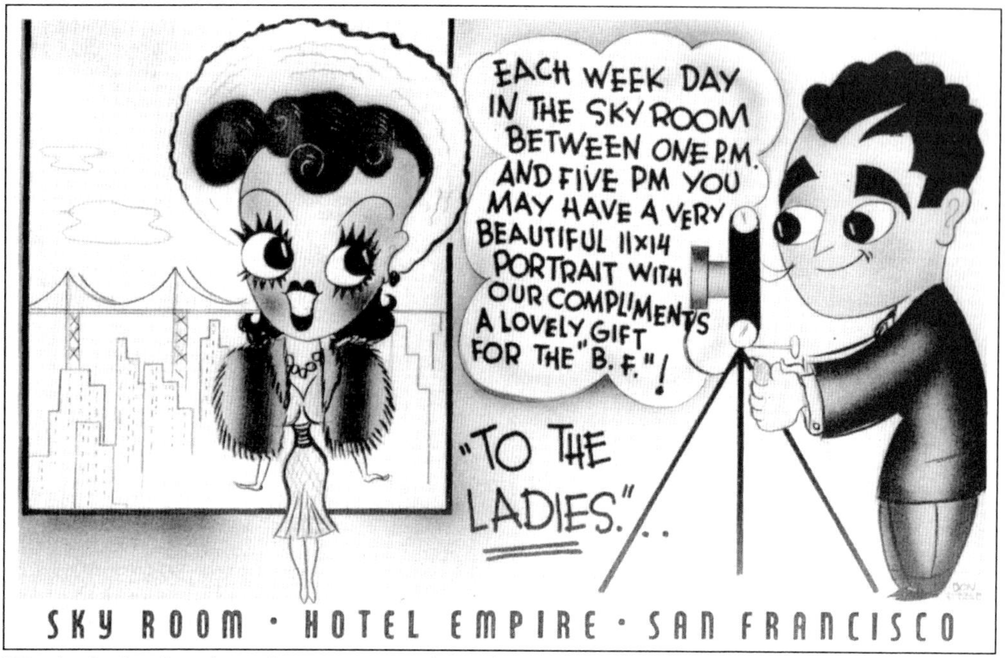

"To the Ladies," with its fantastic views from the Sky Room as background, the Hotel Empire provided complimentary 11- by 14-inch portraits, as seen in this promotional cartoon by Don Steele. Comic characters like this were popular in the 1930s and 1940s.

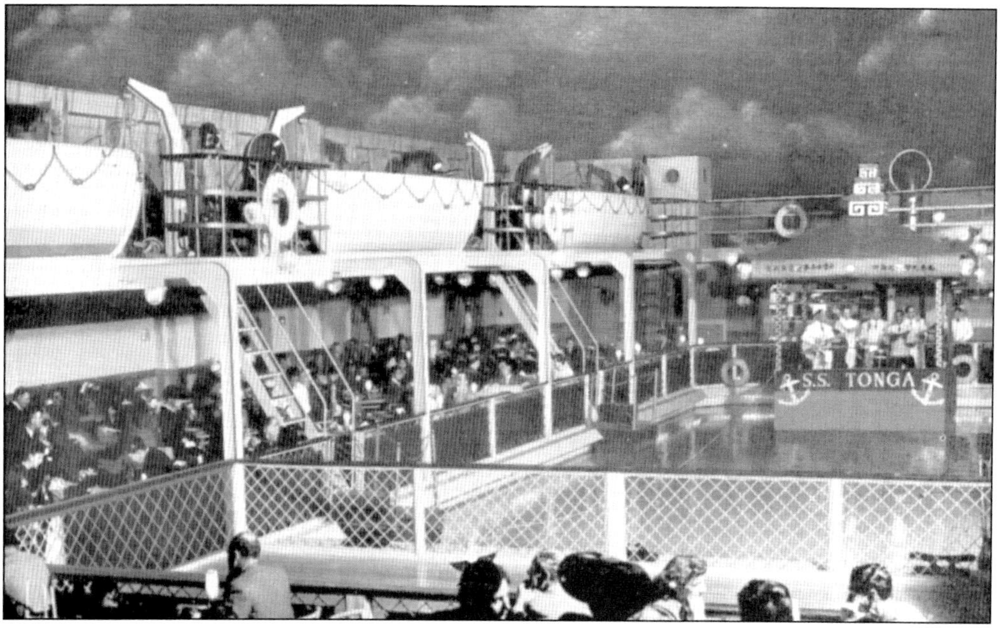

In 1929, Fairmount Hotel owner George D. Smith added an indoor swimming pool, the Fairmount Plunge. Ten years later, guests going for a dip in the plunge found themselves aboard the SS *Tonga*, a cocktail lounge and restaurant with a nautical, South Seas decor. Only in San Francisco, the room featured a dance floor made from the deck of an old sailing ship, a floating bandstand, and every half hour an indoor tropical rainstorm. The room is still going strong as the Tonga Room today.

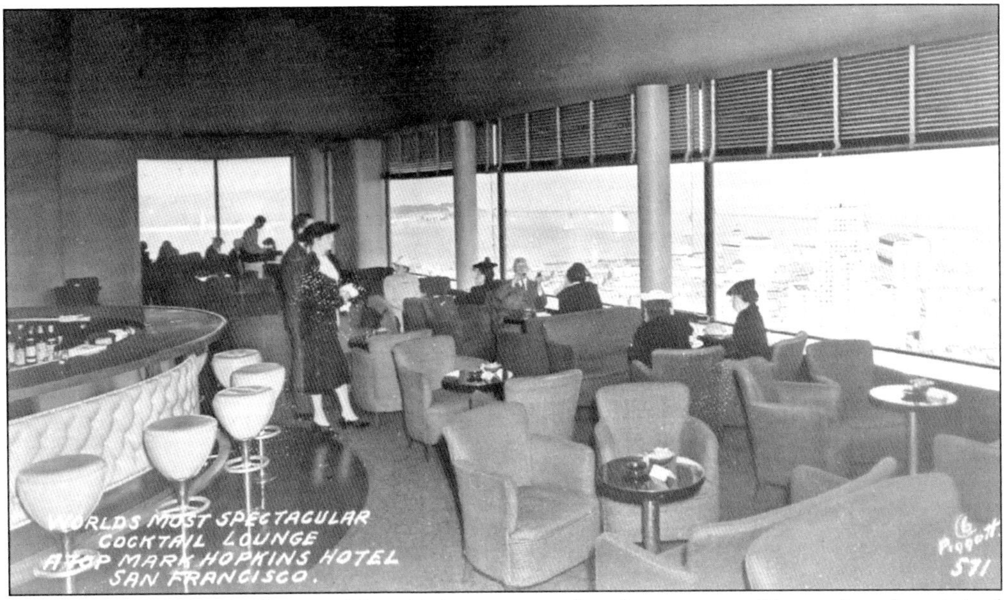

The Mark Hopkins Hotel, named for a 19th-century railroad magnate and located on the original site of his Nob Hill mansion, opened its doors in 1926. In the 1930s, owner George D. Smith hired Timothy Pflueger to transform the 19th-floor penthouse into a glass-walled cocktail lounge with a classic central bar. Located 537 feet above the bay, with panoramic views and a 100-martini menu, visitors considered the "Top of the Mark" to be quite a spot, as seen in this 1939 photograph postcard by J. K. Piggott. Over the years, most of Pflueger's original design has been altered.

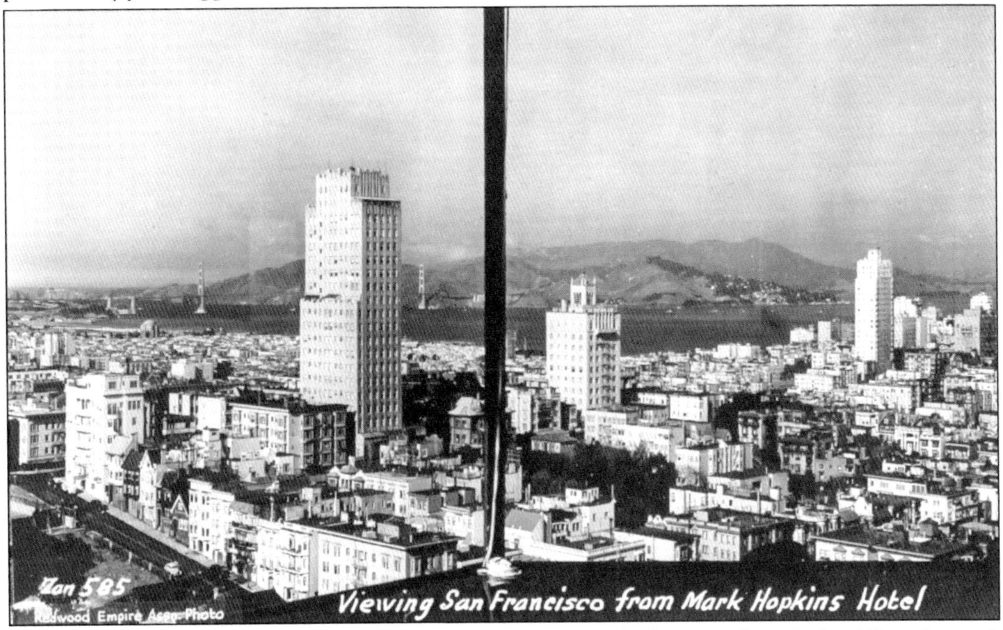

The must-see view from the Top of the Mark in this Zan Stark photograph includes Albert Larsen's Art Deco–style Clay-Jones Apartments and Herman C. Baumann's masterpiece at 1101 Green Street. The Mark's northwest corner in World War II earned the nickname "Weepers Corner" for the wives and sweethearts who gathered there to watch their servicemen sail under the Golden Gate Bridge on their way off to war.

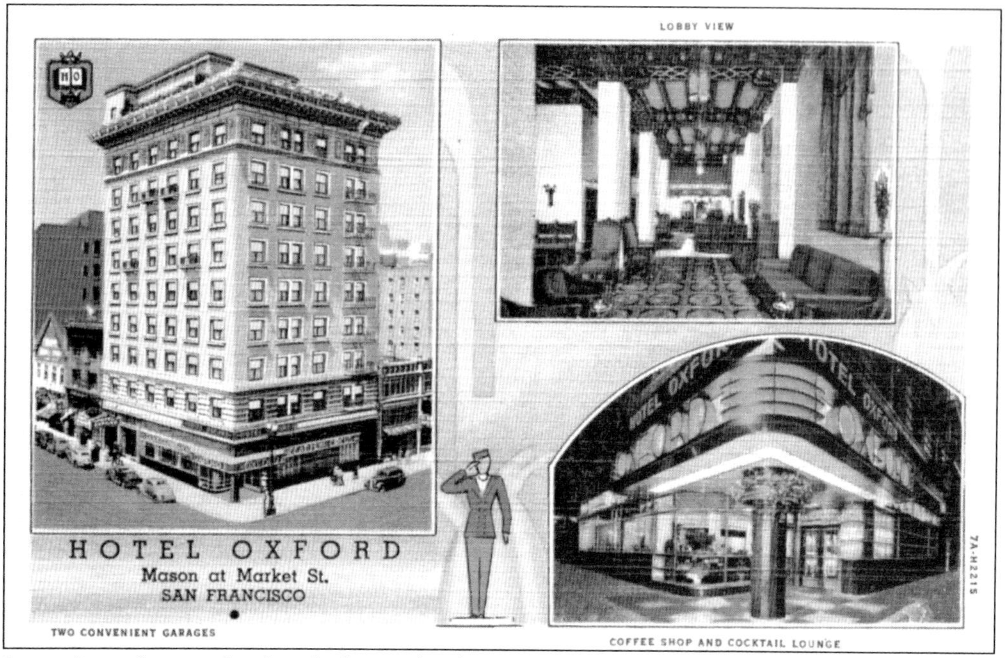

It wasn't just luxury-class hotels that took advantage of remodeling in the moderne style. In the post-earthquake era, Hotel Oxford, the coffee shop, and the cocktail lounge, at diagonal angles on the corner of Market and Mason Streets, were upgraded with neon, mirrors, and Vitrolite.

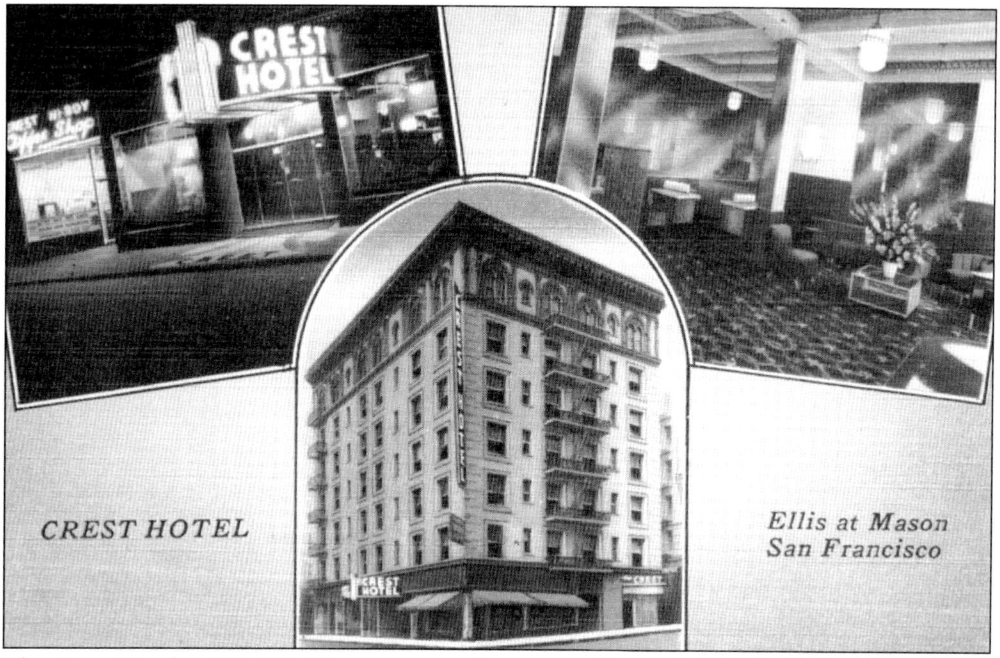

The Crest Hotel at 210 Ellis Street was another venerable post–1906 Earthquake hotel that modernized and Art Deco-ized its coffee shop, cocktail lounge, and hotel entry. The hotel's large new neon sign was prominently featured on the corner of Mason and Ellis Streets.

Located near Union Square, none of the Hotel Crane's 1910 Renaissance/baroque ornamentation is visible on this linen postcard that seems to be celebrating an Art Deco look with a background illuminated by searchlights.

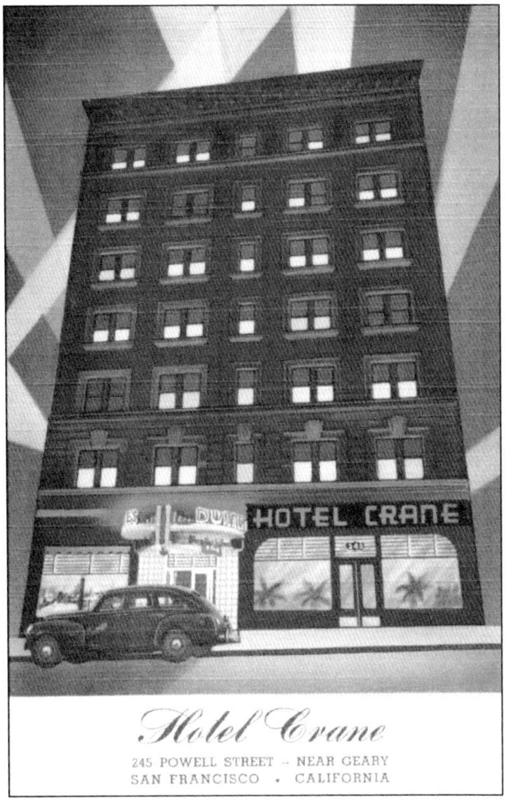

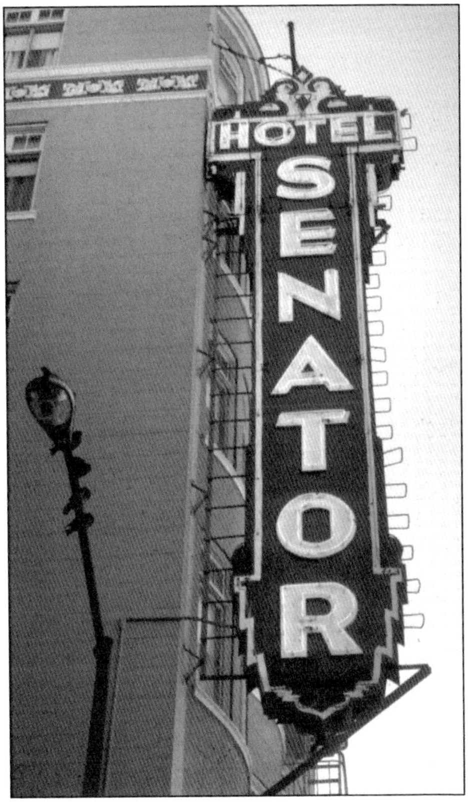

Neon signage, a French invention, was introduced to the United States in 1924. The first sign was installed on a Packard car dealership in Los Angeles. The phenomenon of this kind of sign lighting rapidly spread across the country. The Hotel Senator sign, dated about 1928, was installed on a building constructed earlier. It was a way of giving a building a more updated or modern look.

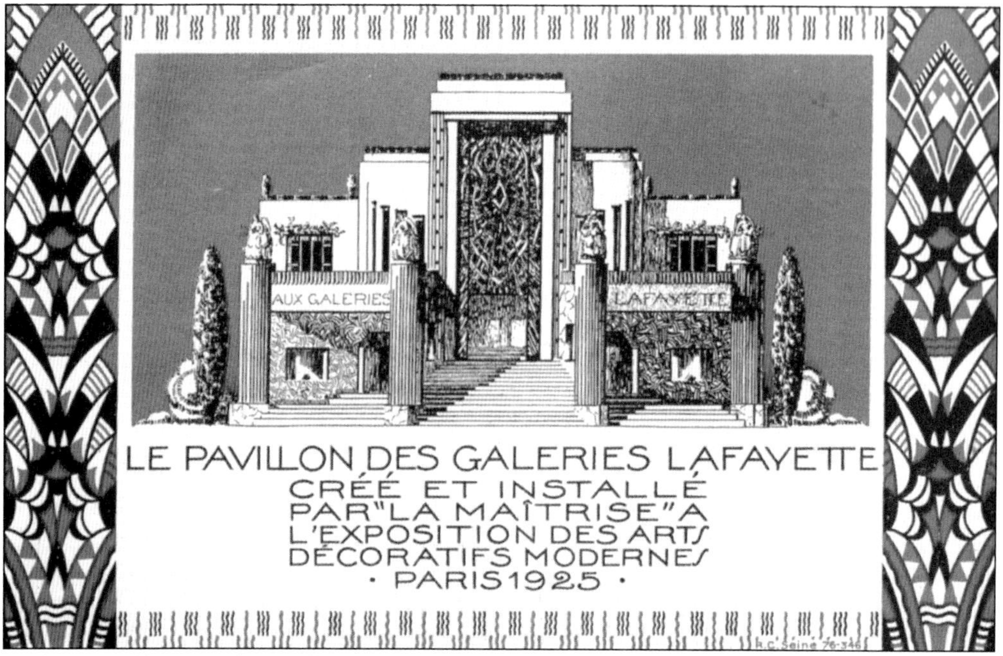

Architects Ellison and Russell were hired by Safeway Grocery Stores in the 1930s to create a standardized moderne look for their chain of neighborhood stores. The architects based their design on the Galeries Lafayette's La Maitrise Pavilion from the 1925 Paris Exposition Internationale des Arts Décoratifs et Industriels Modernes, seen here in a vintage French postcard.

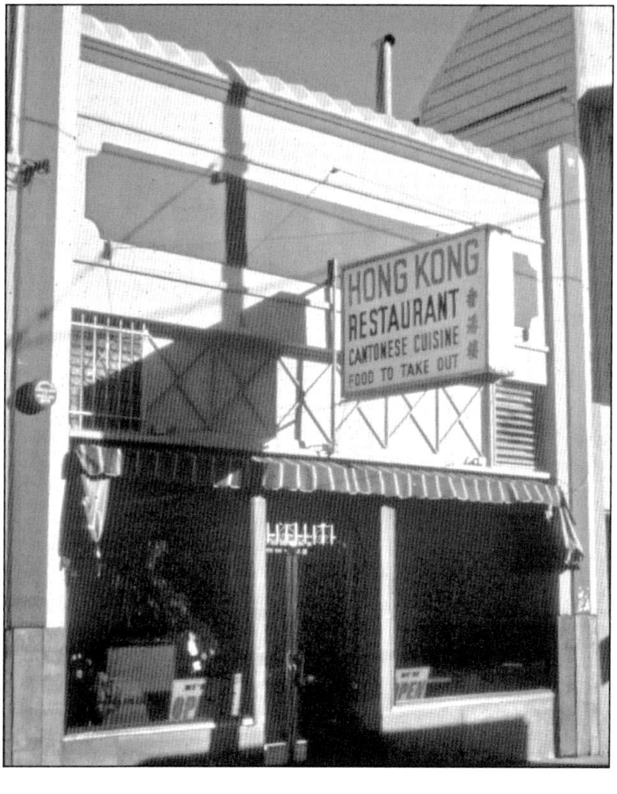

This building is a former Safeway that was designed for the company by a company engineer. The decorative elements—the stepped end piers and zigzag lines at the cornice—are motifs first used at the 1925 Paris Exhibition on the Galeries Lafayette Department Store Building.

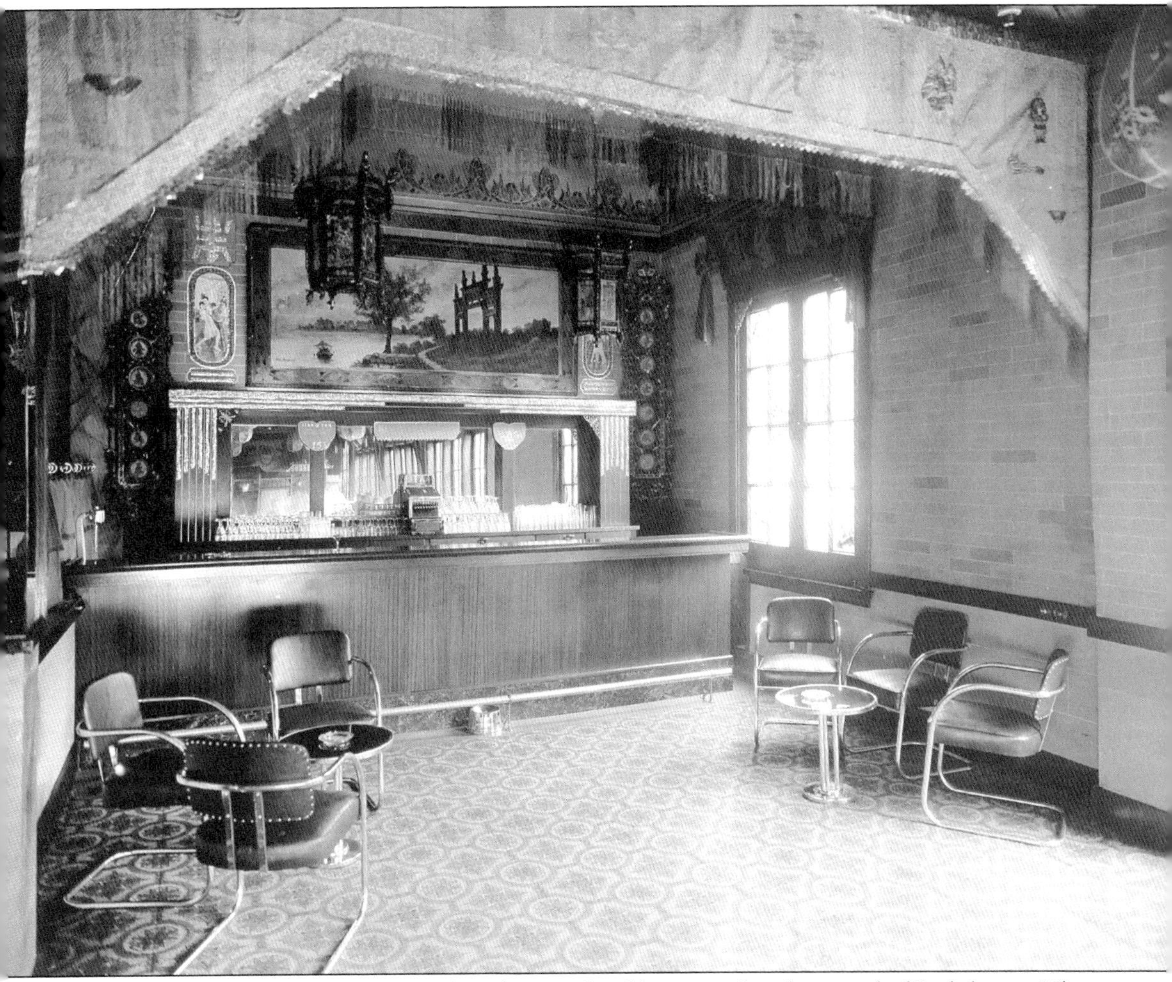

Many restaurants and hotels added modern cocktail lounges after the repeal of Prohibition. The Shanghai Low Restaurant settled for minimalism with an Art Deco–appearing back bar and the addition of chrome-plated tubular steel chairs. The Irish-born Parisian designer Eileen Gray was the first to design this type of chair in 1926. She was a pioneer in introducing lacquerware tables, screens, and modular metal furniture in a modernist mode.

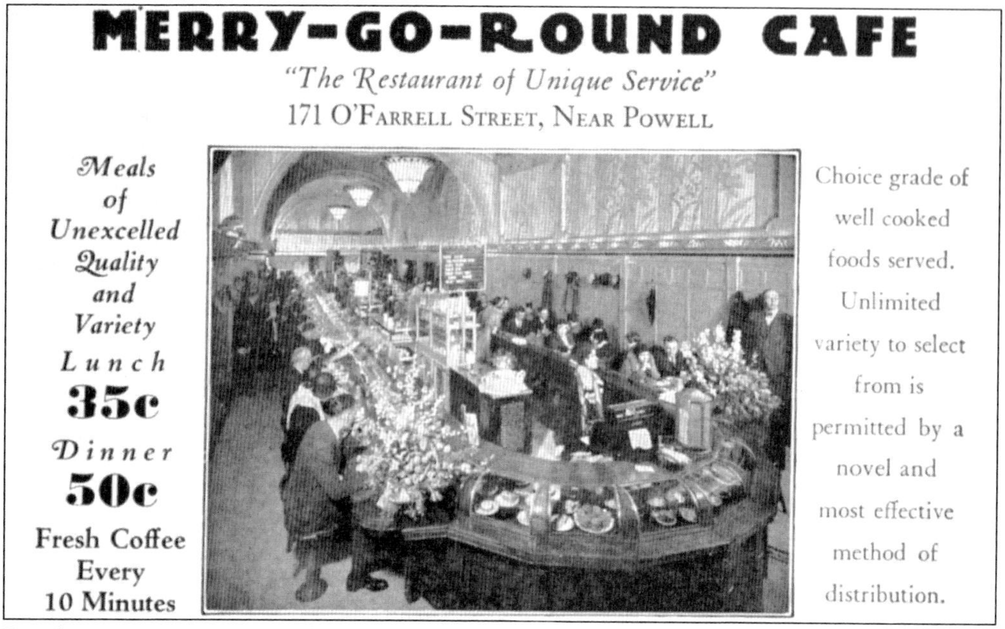

Fun dining in San Francisco during the 1930s was an inexpensive meal at the Merry-Go-Round Café. Entrees and drinks were served, but the salads, pies, and cakes appeared on the "merry-go-round." Diners selected their food from a 275-foot-long conveyor belt revolving around a U-shaped counter by raising a glass door and snatching their salad or desert as it came by.

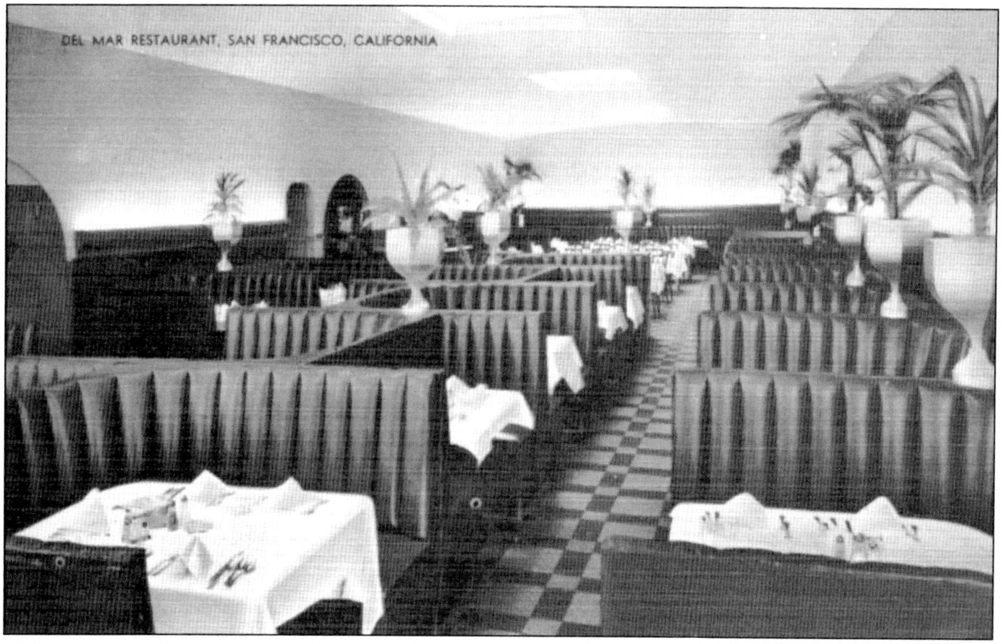

If diners wanted a more traditional ambience, they could enjoy seafood and continental cuisine seated in tufted upholstery booths within the quiet atmosphere of the Del Mar Restaurant and Cocktail Lounge at 3721 Buchanan Street.

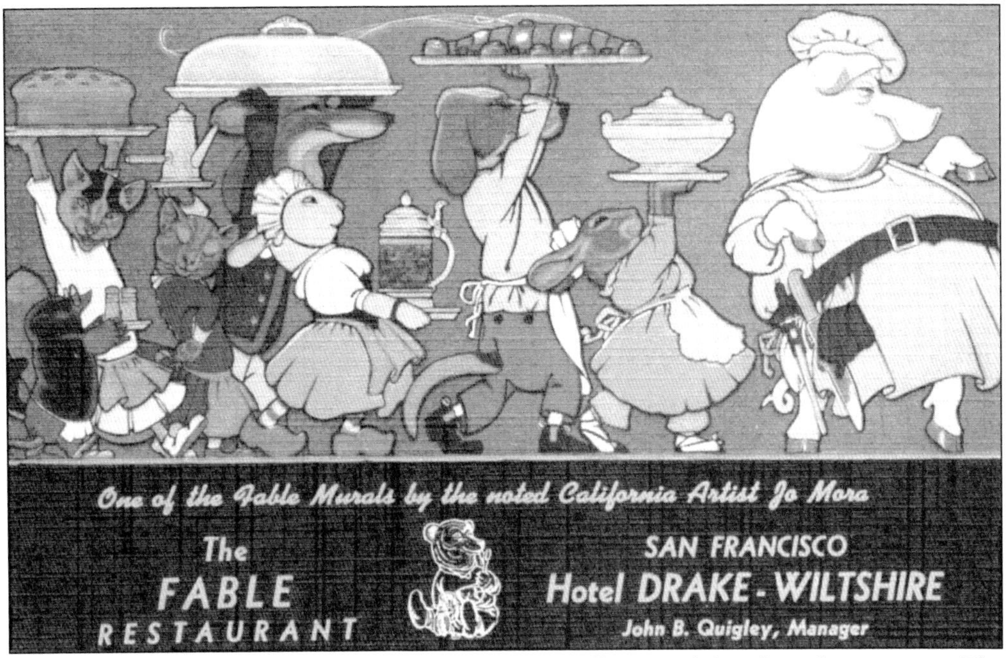

Decorative wall paintings had a long tradition in San Francisco's hotels and restaurants. The tradition continued in the 1930s with the newfound popularity of murals. The Drake-Wilshire Hotel at 340 Stockton Street hired California artist Jo Mora to create a series of murals for the hotel's Fable Restaurant and Cameo Lounge. Mora's creatures performed a variety of human activities in illustrations lacking the political dogma found in most of the city's public murals.

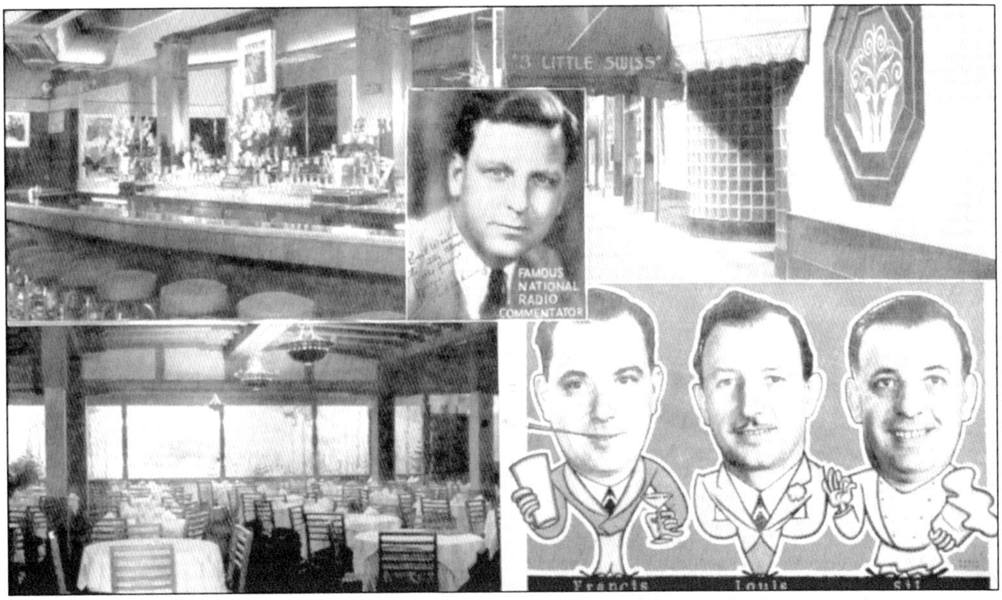

Italian-Swiss immigrants Louis Margnetti, Silvio Antognoli, and Francis Rodoni were the proprietors of the St. Moritz Restaurant, also known as the "Three Little Swiss," located at 530 Broadway. Radio commentator Fulton Lewis Jr. was acknowledged by the Three Little Swiss in this World War II–era postcard for the help he gave them overcoming the government bureaucracy of the Office of Price Administration.

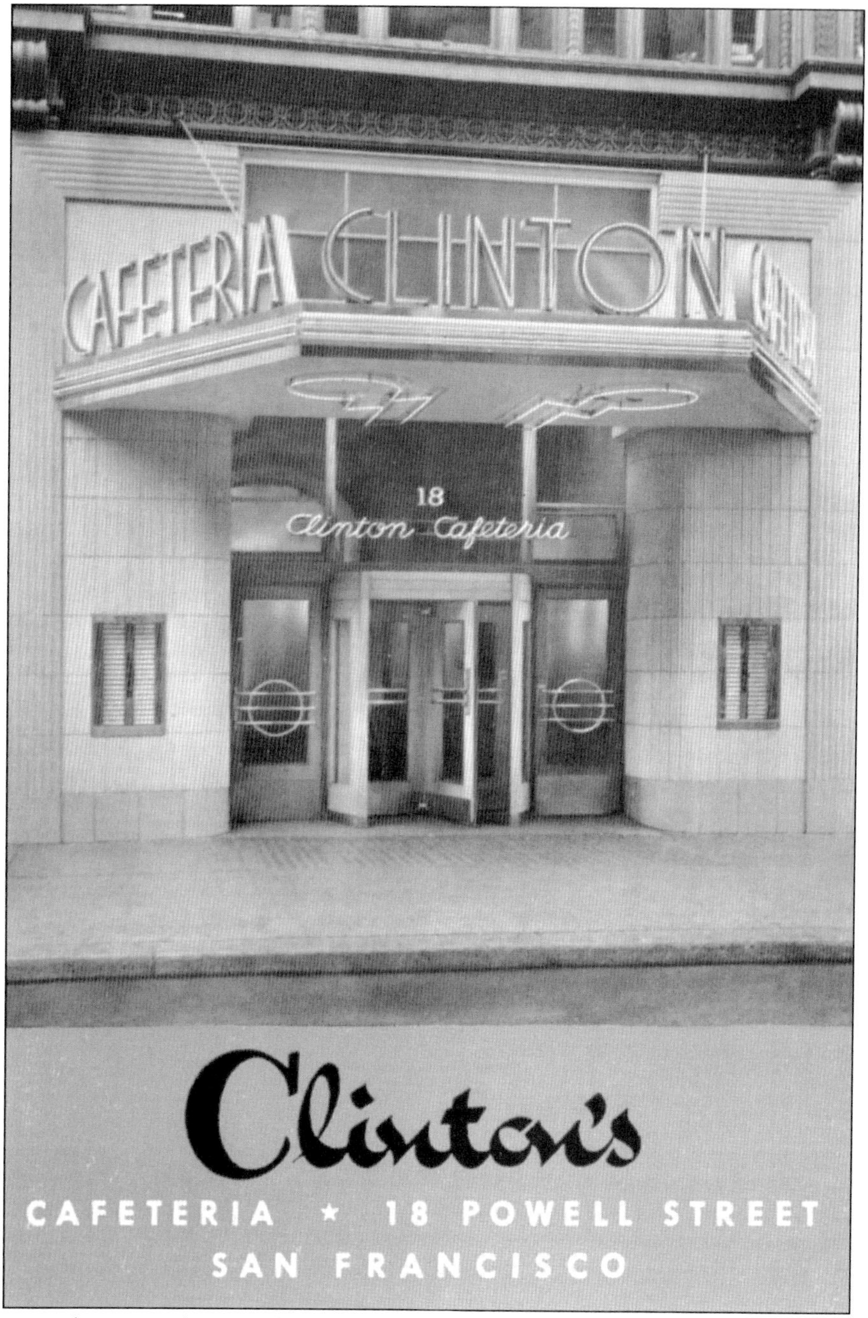

Art Deco ambience and casual dining was epitomized by the Clinton Cafeteria at 18 Powell Street, seen in this 1937 postcard. Neon-enhanced, Bauhaus-styled decorative letters announce the name "Clinton Cafeteria," attracting customers through a stylized entrance of brass, glass, and fluted terra cotta lines. Customers descended a wide staircase into a huge basement dining room with marble floors and potted plants. From 6:00 p.m. to 8:00 p.m., the self-served diners could enjoy their meals while listening to dinner music played by a string orchestra. The wide variety of food, elegant decor, and pleasant atmosphere guaranteed that the Clinton Cafeteria was one of *the* places to dine in San Francisco.

Four

NIGHTLIFE
HIGH JINKS AND HIGHBALLS

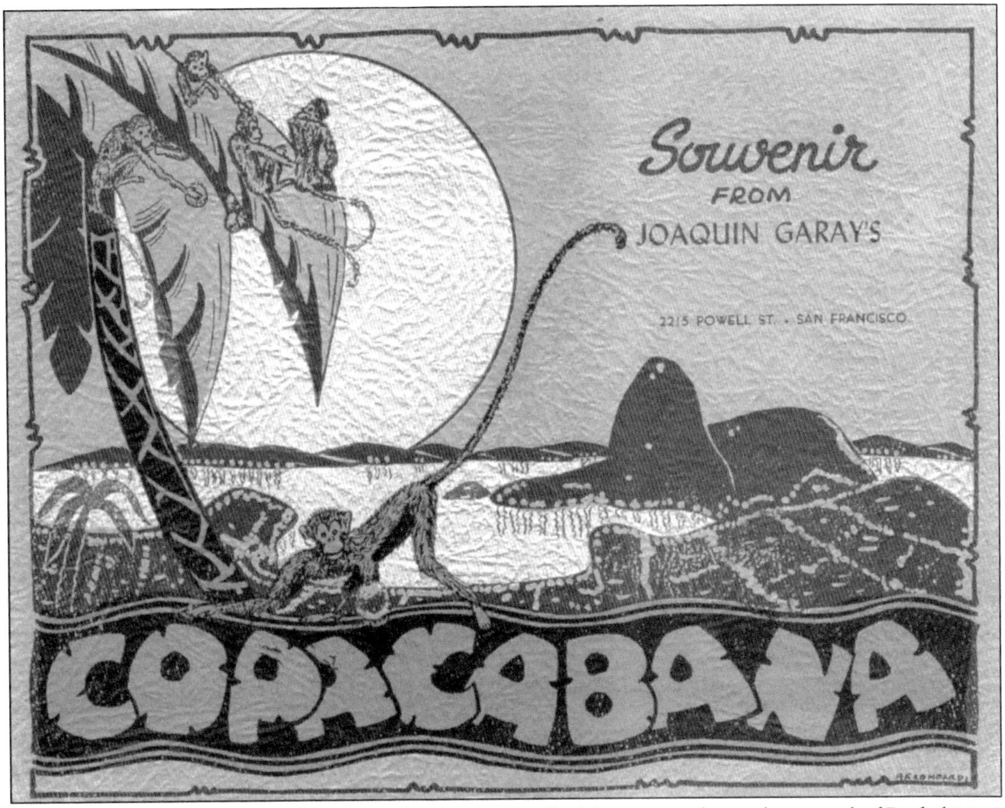

On December 5, 1933, the 21st Amendment was ratified, bringing about the repeal of Prohibition and at the same time unofficially ushering in the age of the great nightclubs. San Franciscans were no longer forced to tote a hip flask or drink bootleg wine from a coffee cup. In the Jazz Era of the late 1920s and early 1930s, speakeasies were hidden in the back rooms behind locked doors, but with repeal, the city's drinking establishments could move to the front room. Despite the Depression, labor strife, and eventually a world war, the next 20 years became the golden age of nightclubs. Local residents and visitors could drink, dine, dance, and take in a floor show. San Francisco clubs included the Copacabana at 2215 Powell Street, John's Rendezvous on Osgood Place, and the Moderne at 555 Sutter Street. A person could find Latin entertainers at Sinaloa and LaFiesta and Chinese performers at the Forbidden City, Club Shanghai, and Kubla Khan. Finnochio's on Broadway was the place to see female impersonators. Jack's Tavern and the California Club were "Negro" clubs featuring nationally known African American entertainers. Art Deco decor enhanced the glamour of these clubs, where every night couples could imagine they were Ginger Rogers and Fred Astaire while dancing the night away.

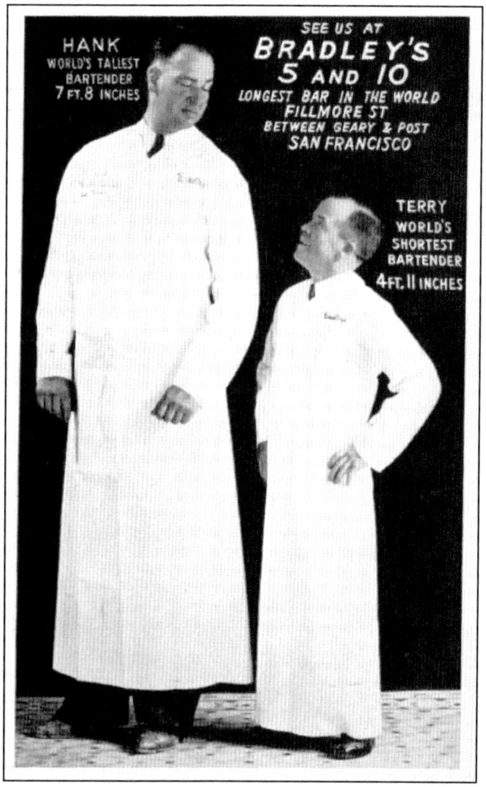

While barrooms may not have had floor shows and snazzy decor, they reflected the Art Deco spirit with promotions of their best assets. Bartenders Hank and Terry were the featured attractions at Bradley's 5 and 10, along with what the proprietors claimed was the longest bar in the world.

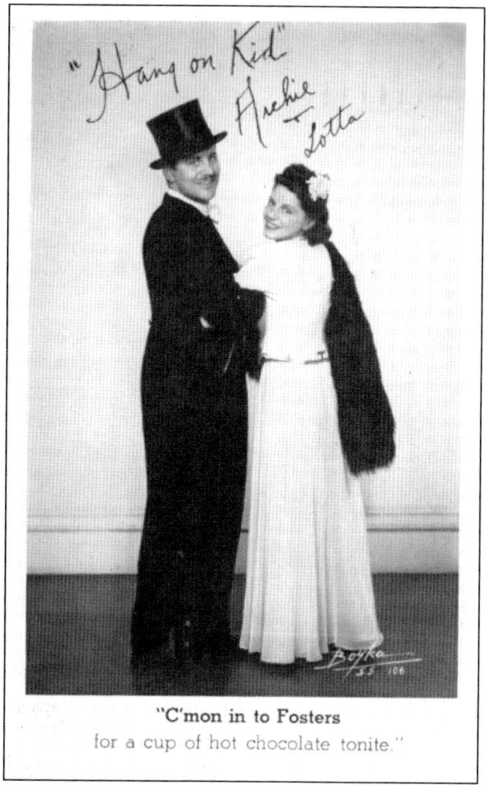

Restaurateurs Archie and Lotta Foster show suave style and elegance as they step out for a night on the town while encouraging other nightclubbers to finish off their evening with a cup of hot chocolate at Fosters. If not wearing a top hat and tails, a San Francisco gentleman always dressed in his best suit and tie. The ladies always wore their finest apparel and accessories for their night out.

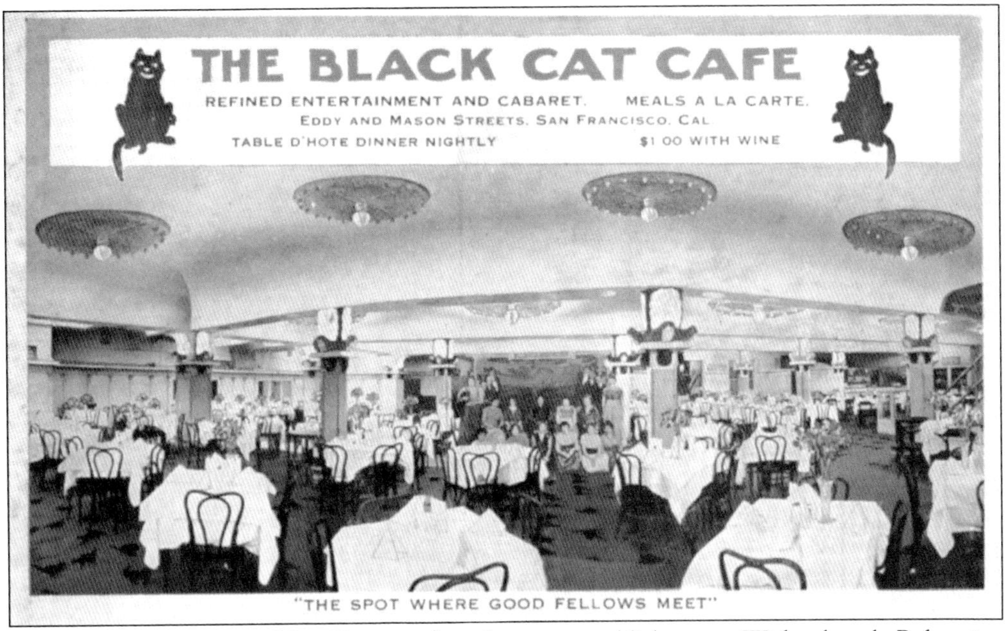

The Black Cat was one of San Francisco's earliest gay establishments. With a largely Bohemian clientele, the club featured a café and cabaret entertainment. With the repeal of Prohibition, the club moved to 710 Montgomery Street. The State Alcoholic Beverage Control Board closed the Black Cat on Halloween in 1963. Whether located downtown at Eddy and Mason Streets or in North Beach, all through the Art Deco period the Black Cat remained "the spot where good fellows meet."

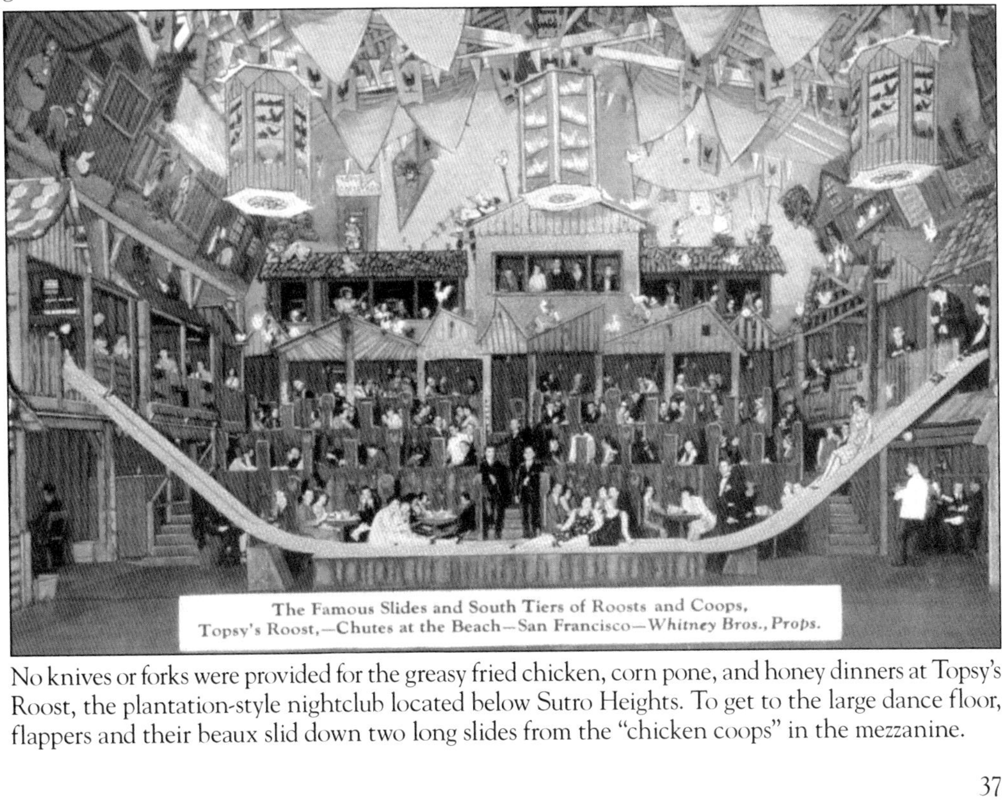

No knives or forks were provided for the greasy fried chicken, corn pone, and honey dinners at Topsy's Roost, the plantation-style nightclub located below Sutro Heights. To get to the large dance floor, flappers and their beaux slid down two long slides from the "chicken coops" in the mezzanine.

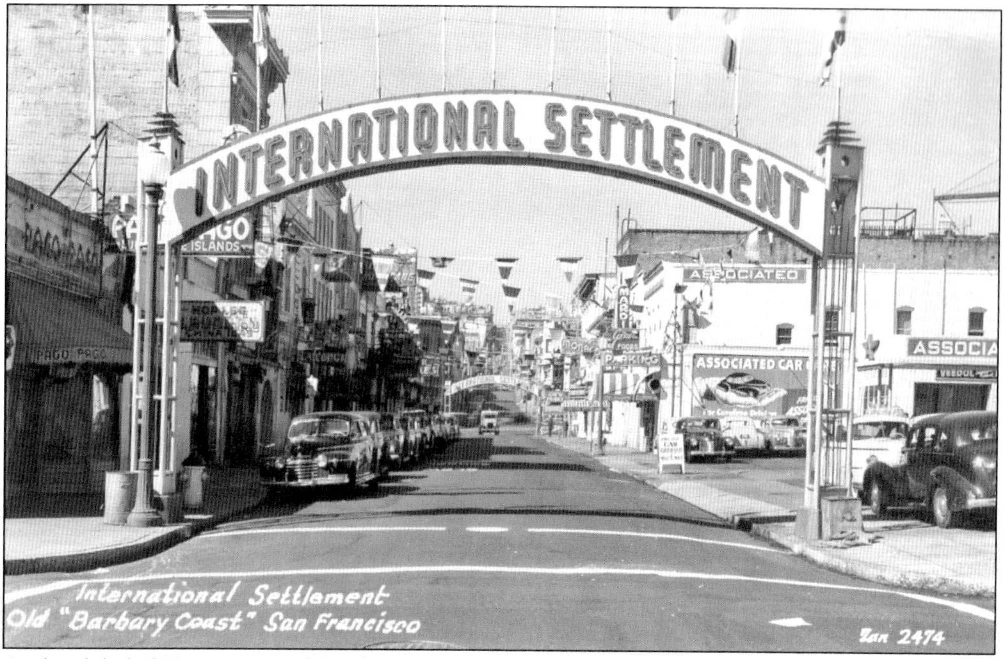

Arches labeled "International Settlement" set off the intersection of Pacific Avenue, Columbus Avenue, and Kearney Street. On what was once the site of the infamous Barbary Coast, in 1939 restaurateur Pierino Gavello developed a new version of the "Terrific Street" with streamlined nightclubs and cocktail bars.

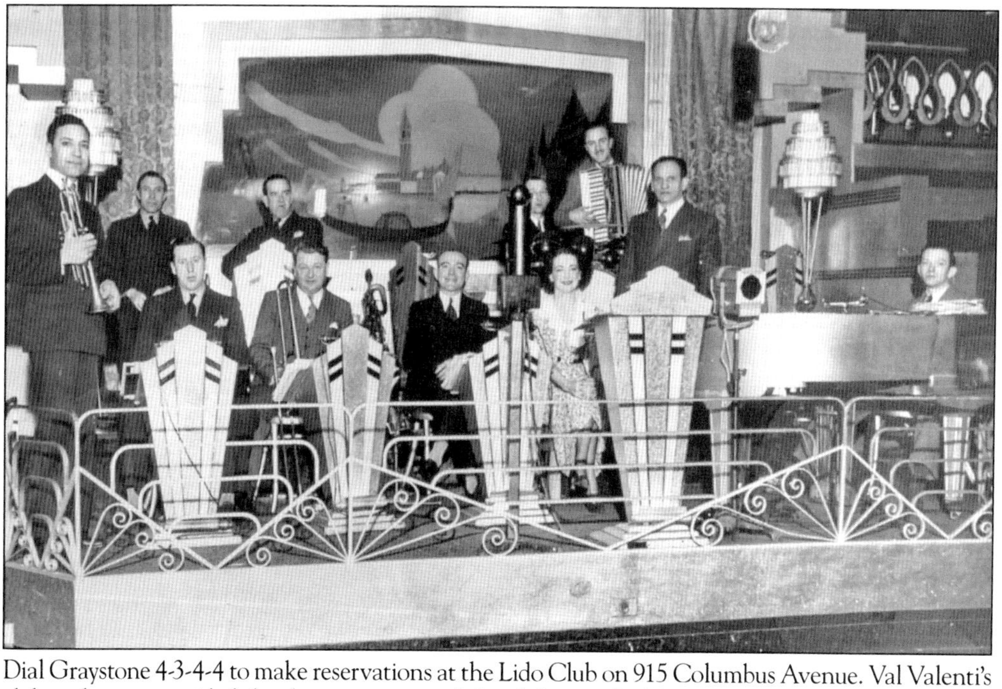

Dial Graystone 4-3-4-4 to make reservations at the Lido Club on 915 Columbus Avenue. Val Valenti's club orchestra provided the dance music, and the club seated 400 on its main floor and basement rooms. On Thursday and Sunday afternoon, the Lido hired an extra band, one for each floor, for its popular matinee dances. (Courtesy San Francisco History Center, San Francisco Public Library.)

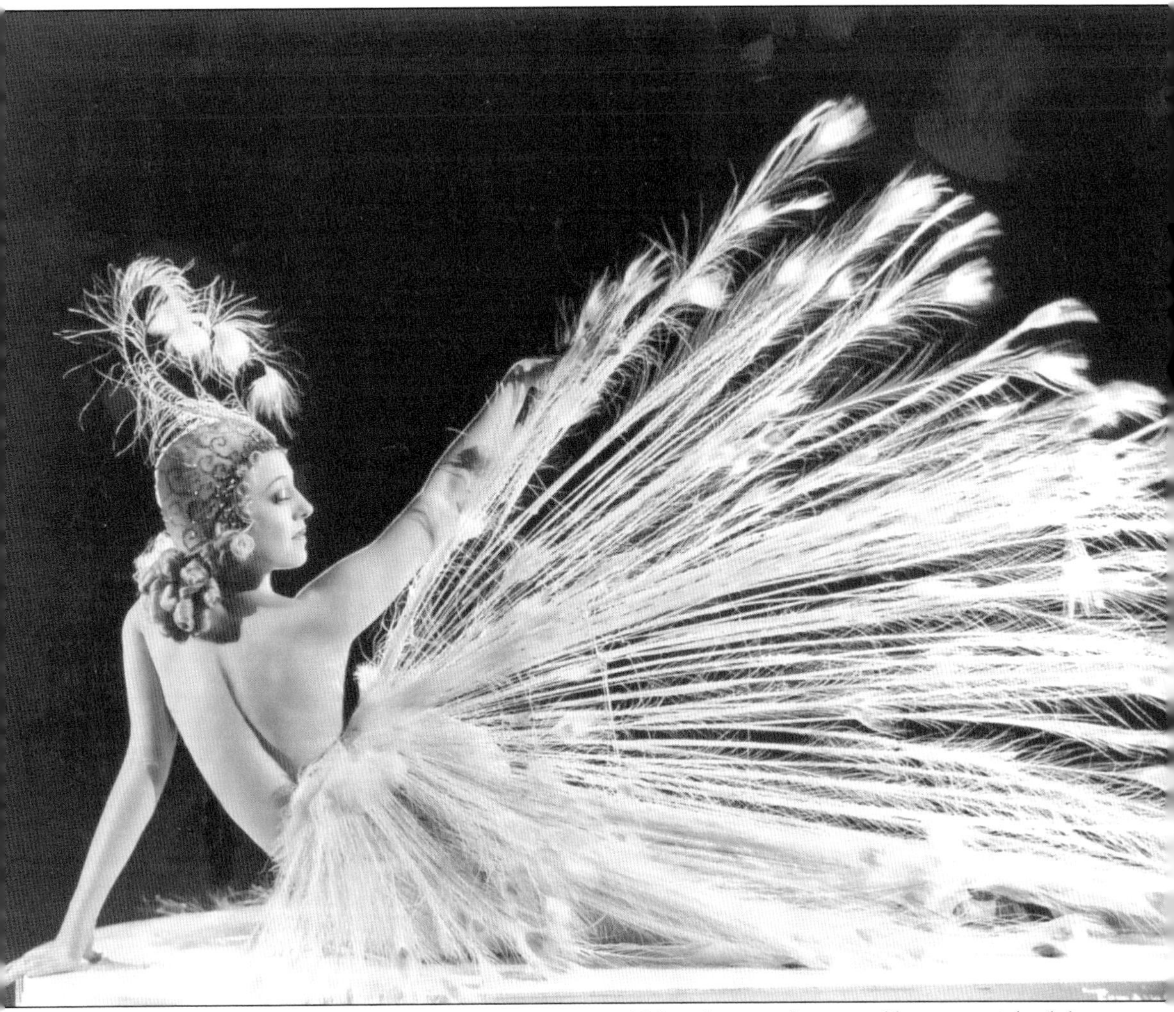

Fan dancer Sally Rand arrived in San Francisco in 1936 and promptly opened her own nightclub, the Music Box, at 859 O'Farrell Street. With her famous ostrich-feather fans, Rand's look in this publicity photograph by Romaine Photography Studio epitomizes Art Deco attitude and style. Like Sally's act, this image seems to reveal a lot while not really revealing anything. As a little lady from Hickory County, Missouri, Harriet Helen Gould Beck appeared in silent films as Billy Beck; director Cecil B. DeMille is credited with giving her the name "Sally Rand." In 1933, Rand joined the chorus line at the Century of Progress world's fair in Chicago. Having to perform outdoors, she conceived and developed a bubble dance to cope with the wind. Rand catapulted to fame and fortune when Chicago police arrested her for indecent exposure. Along with a chorus line of the "world's most beautiful glamour girls," the notorious Miss Rand brought her risqué act to "Frisco," performing three shows nightly. A good businesswoman as well as the star attraction, Sally Rand made the Music Box one of San Francisco's most popular nightclubs in the 1930s. (Courtesy San Francisco History Center, San Francisco Public Library.)

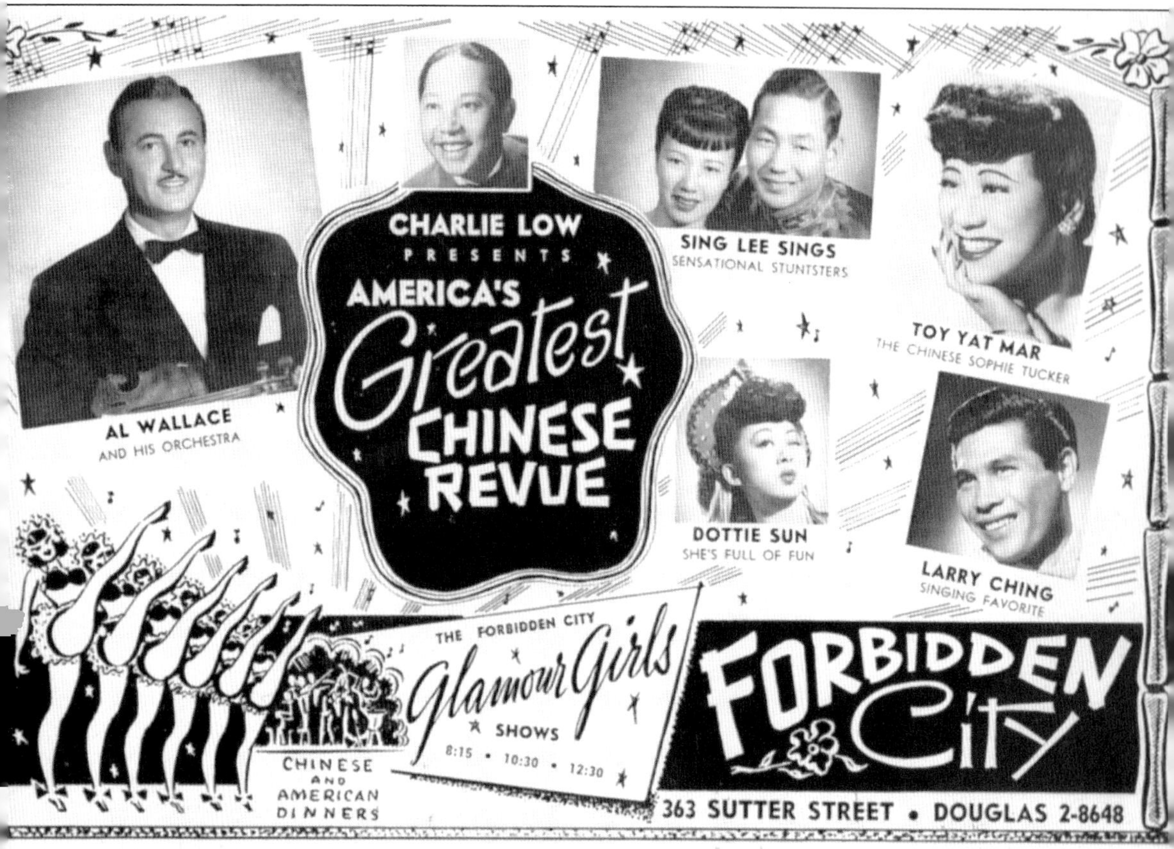

East met West in nightly all-Asian revues at Charlie Low's Forbidden City Supper Club. Located upstairs at 363 Sutter Street, the Forbidden City was large enough to seat 300 patrons in a restaurant with a dance floor and luxurious Sino-deco decor. Every evening, the performers put on three one-hour shows featuring seven acts of dancing, singing, magic, acrobats, and slapstick comedy. Performers sang and danced like the actors in Hollywood musicals of the time. Featured tenor Larry Ching was acclaimed as the "Chinese Frank Sinatra." Female vocalists included Charlie Low's wife, Li Tei Ming, Frances Chun, and Toy Yat Mar, "the Chinese Sophie Tucker." For the chorus line, Low hired veteran choreographer Walton Biggerstaff to create the dance routines and train the chorines, who were usually hired more for their fetching good looks then their dancing ability. Featured dance acts ranged from bubble dancers to technically skilled dancers Toy and Wing, the Tai Sings, and Jack Mei Ling performing everything from ballroom in long coattails and silk gowns to exotic slave dances. Opened just 14 years after the exclusionary Immigration Act of 1924, for most of its existence the Forbidden City counted many celebrities among its guests, but few inhabitants of Chinatown patronized the well-known nightspot.

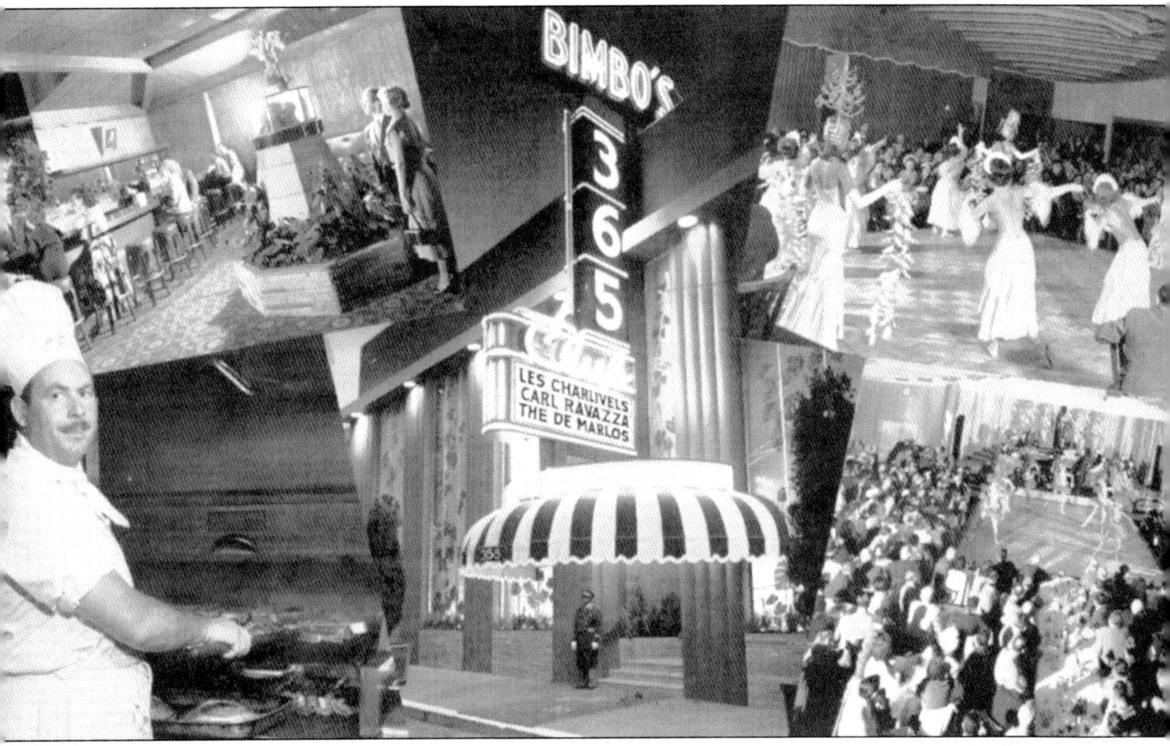

Two nightclubs first opened their doors in the early 1930s: one in North Beach, the Bal Tabarin at 1025 Columbus Avenue, and the other, Bimbo's 365 Club, located downtown at 365 Market Street. Partners Monk Young and Agostino Giuntoli named their downtown club after the building's street number and Guintoli's nickname, the Italian word for boy. Bimbo's featured dinners, gin in coffee cups, and floor shows. One early club dancer, Margarita Cansino, later gained greater fame as actress Rita Hayworth. The club's most popular attraction was always Dolfina, the nude girl in the fish tank, an optical illusion created with mirrors. In North Beach, Bal Tabarin partners Frank Martinelli and Tom Gerunovich went all out to create an elegant supper club by hiring architect and designer Timothy Pflueger. The club's exterior featured a facade with fluted pilaster columns. Inside Pflueger created a metal-fin ceiling, an original concept of indirect lighting in the space above the fins providing colors in all ranges and hues. The stage backdrop also featured indirect light reflecting from curved metal strips. Within this grand ambience, the Bal Tabarin seated 600 guests, provided chicken or steak dinners for $1.50, a floor show of three or four acts, and a line of eight dancing showgirls. Dance music was provided by maestro Tom Gerunovich's famous 16-piece Brunswick Recording Band. In 1951, the Bal Tabarin closed its doors at 1025 Columbus Avenue, and Bimbo's 365 reopened in its place, where it still remains—the last of the old great nightclubs.

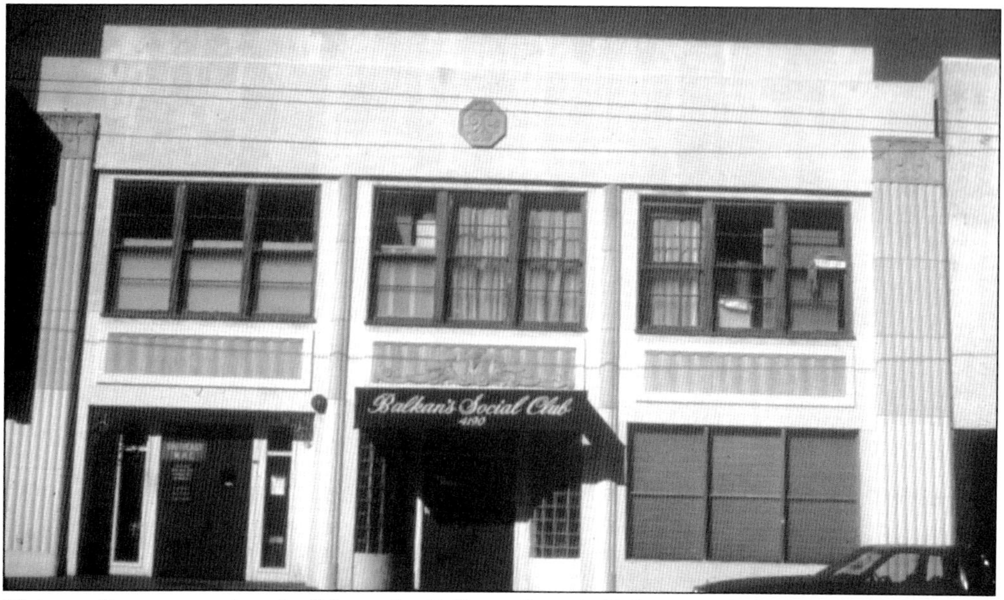

This small, unpretentious building, the Balkans Social Club, is a condensation of decorative elements that still gives a sense of style to the building. The architect is unknown, but the stepped cornice line, octagonal plaque, and simple flanking end piers with stylized capitals show that the designer had mastered the style. There are numerous examples of these kinds of fraternal social clubs around the city.

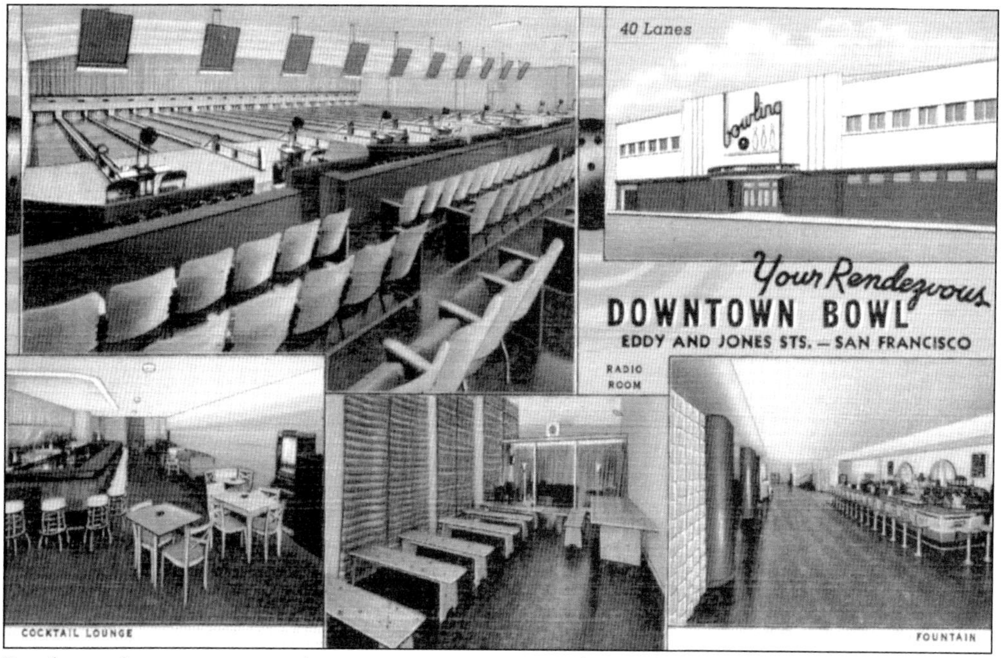

For those who were interested in sports recreation, a night on the town and a chance to pick up a few spares might include a visit to the Downtown Bowl at Eddy and Jones Streets. As seen in this linen advertising postcard, the modern building featured 40 bowling lanes, a radio room, a fountain, and a cocktail lounge.

Five

Commerce, Industry, Theaters

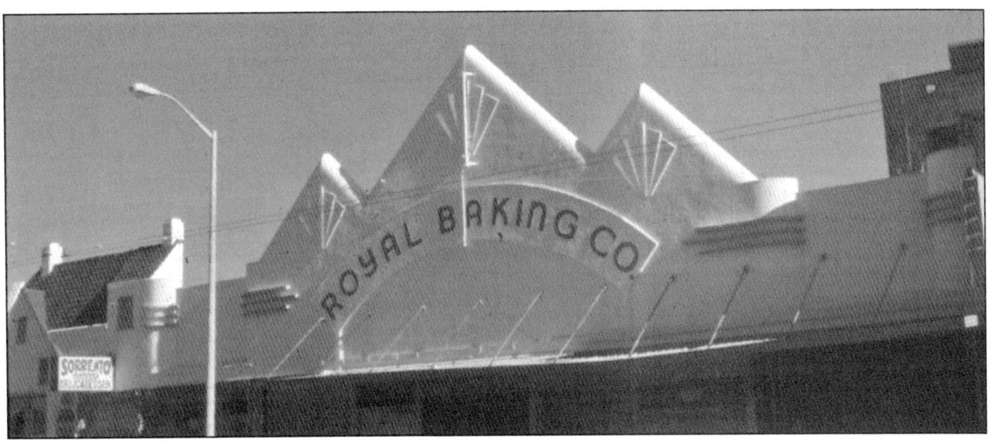

Although the architect is presently unknown, the Royal Baking Company at 4769–73 Mission Street was built in 1935. The three peaks are enhanced by rayed plaques and pulvinated (curving outward) speed lines at the rounded ends of the center section. The lettering on the company name reflects the sans serif (no embellishments) look of lettering that characterized the graphics of the time.

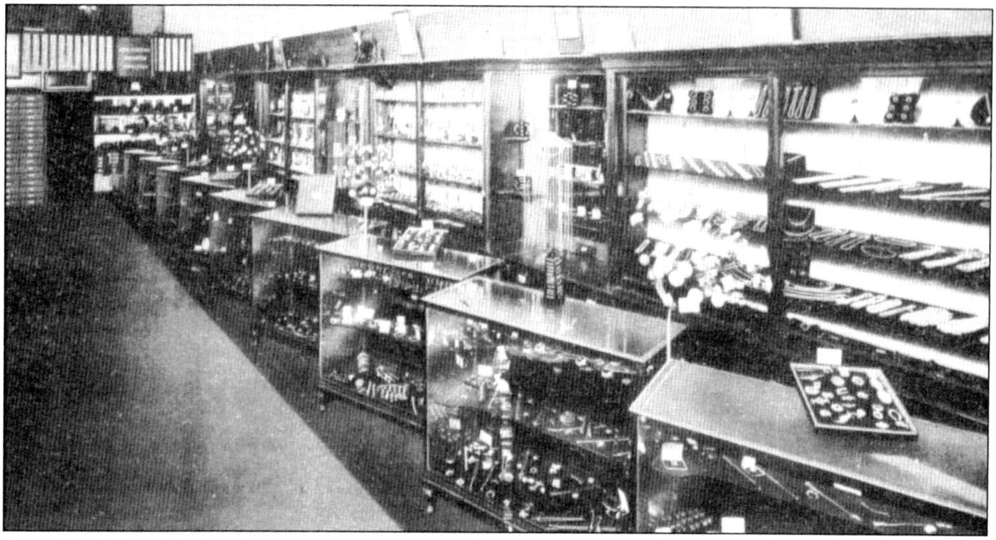

European jewelry was showcased in glass display cabinets arrayed in a cascading geometric pattern in John Robbins's Geary Street store. In the prosperous 1920s, more women were able to afford jewelry and accessories to go with their shorter dresses and bobbed hair. Designers used imported gemstones in a range of geometric designs as well as Egyptian and Oriental motifs. By the 1930s, synthetic substances such as Bakelite and galalite put the price of costume jewelry within the reach of average buyers.

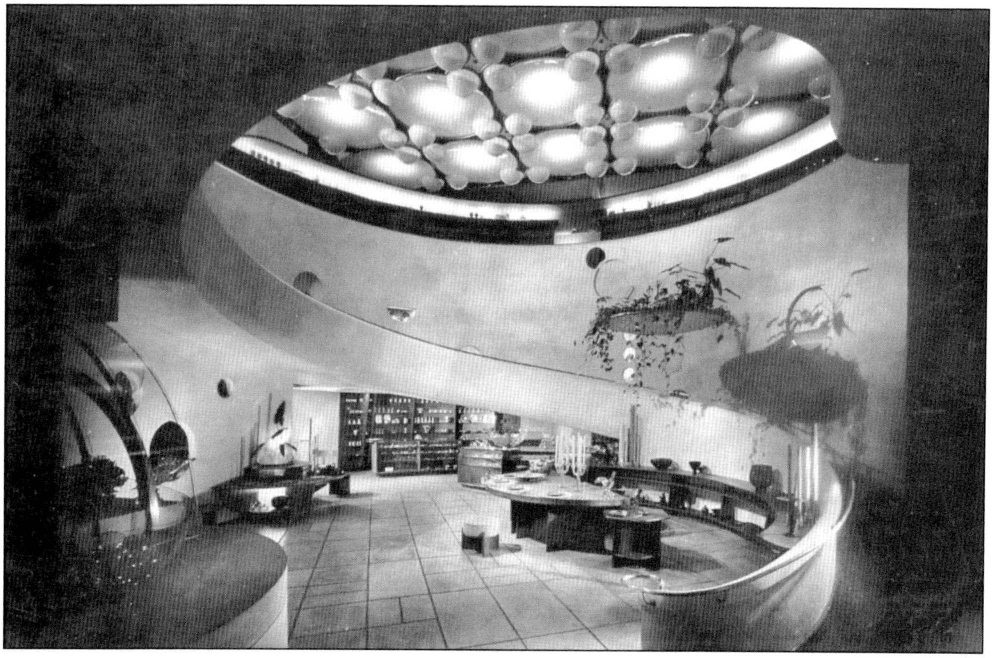

A photograph shows the futuristic interior of the V. C. Morris store, purveyors of fine china, silver, glass, and linens. Located at 140 Maiden Lane, it is the only building in San Francisco designed by Frank Lloyd Wright. Although it was constructed nine years after the conclusion of the Art Deco era, Wright's use of building materials and refined design, particularly the open showroom and undulating ramp going up to the mezzanine, show a relationship to Art Deco architectural design.

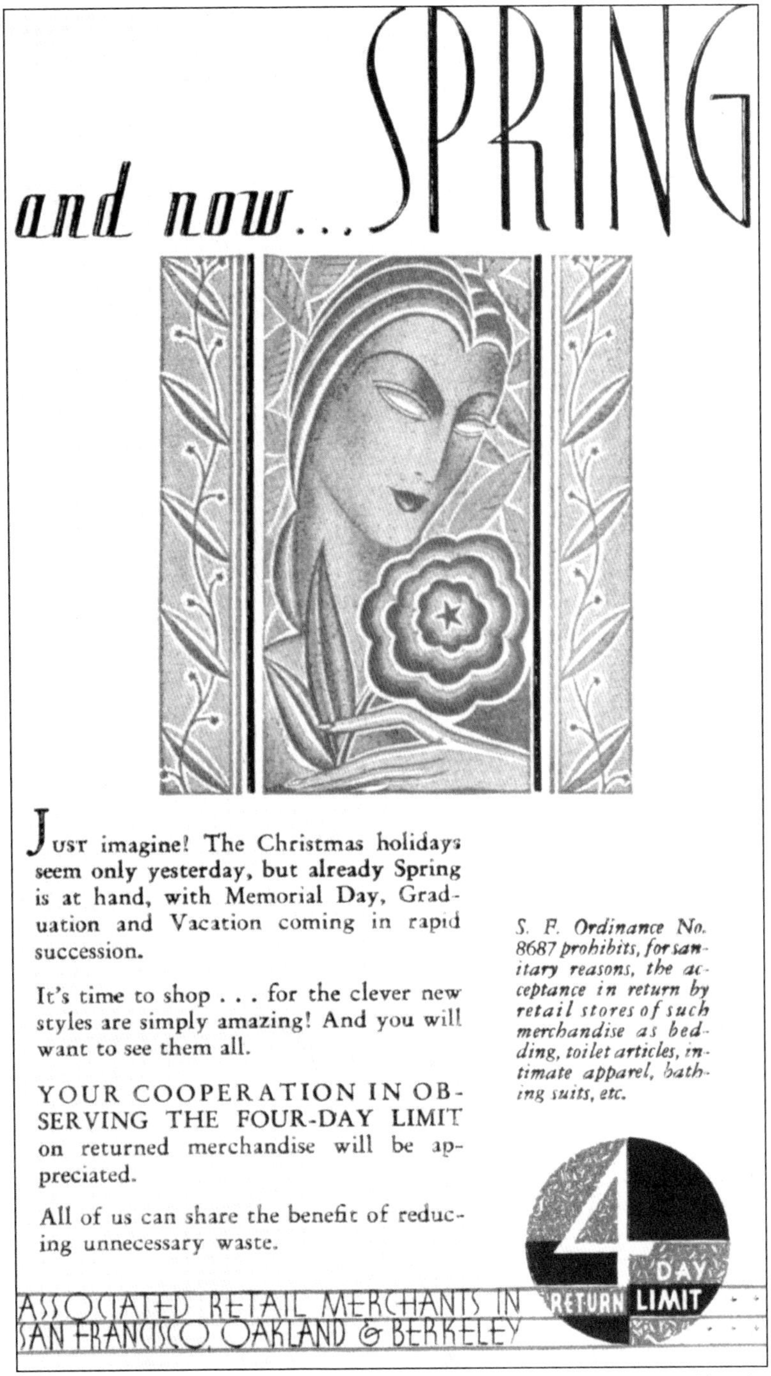

An unknown commercial artist's romantic modern graphic design was utilized by the Associated Retail Merchants in San Francisco, Oakland, and Berkeley to promote their spring sales. This advertising flyer from the late 1920s features a lime-green French-style illustration to evoke a sense of springtime. A mix of black-colored letter types present the retailers message in a simple and straightforward style. Note the merchants' request that buyers observe a four-day return limit and the reminder "all of us can share the benefit of reducing unnecessary waste."

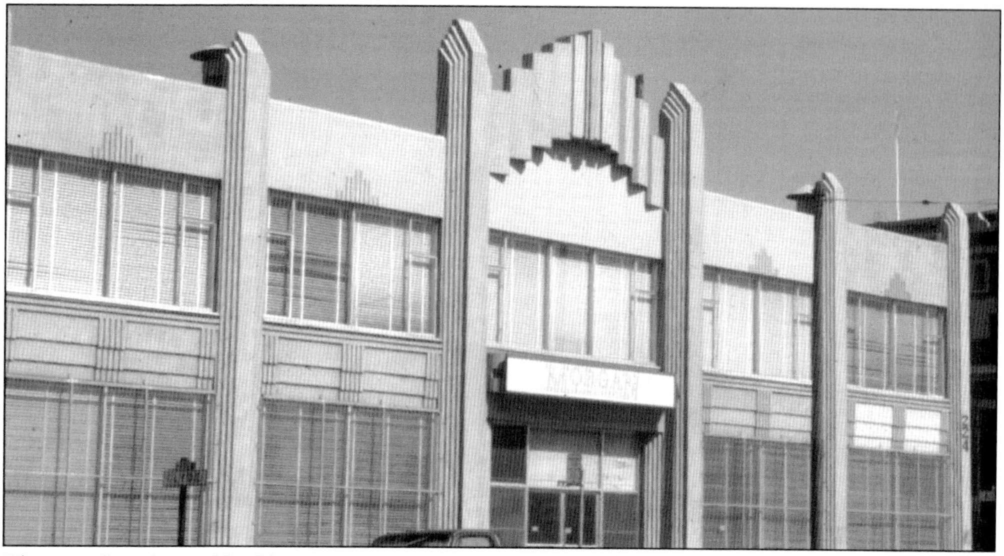

This simple industrial building at 224 Townsend Street is a good example of how molded plaster can be used to great decorative effect. The stepped piers and the stepped arch over the entry are classics of the Art Deco style. Simple stepped-back window spandrels further enhance the decorative scheme. Many of these types of buildings in the South of Market area were constructed in the 1930s.

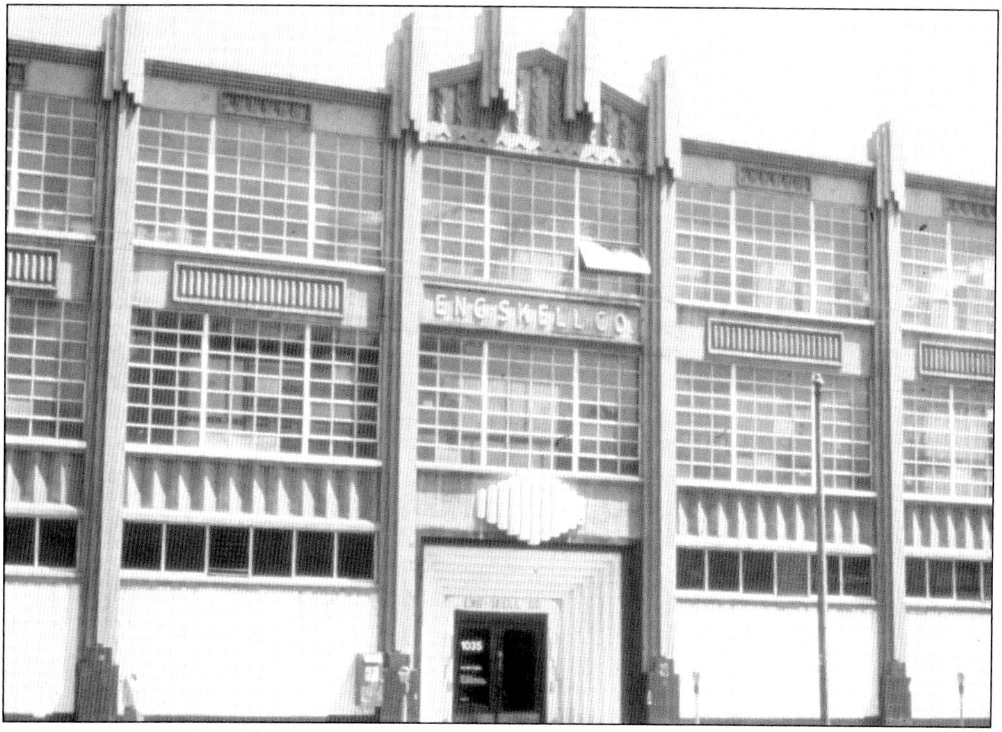

The former Engskell Building shows that industrial structures were not immune from Art Deco–style treatment. The stepped arches seen at the top of the piers and over the entry are simple but effective in announcing the style. The large industrial windows have prism-like spandrel panels above the first-floor windows. This motif was first used on the Polish Pavilion at the 1925 Paris Exhibition. The recessed stepped entry, with the stepped motif above, completes the composition.

Wilbur Peugh designed this building at 125 Hyde Street in 1930. The central stepped arch at the cornice line is derived from Mayan architecture that was gaining in popularity due to the writings of Robert Stacy Judd, a proponent of the style. Here Peugh uses it to great advantage and complements it with incised floral plaques. The curling out–leaf motifs are classic examples that clearly mark this as an Art Deco design.

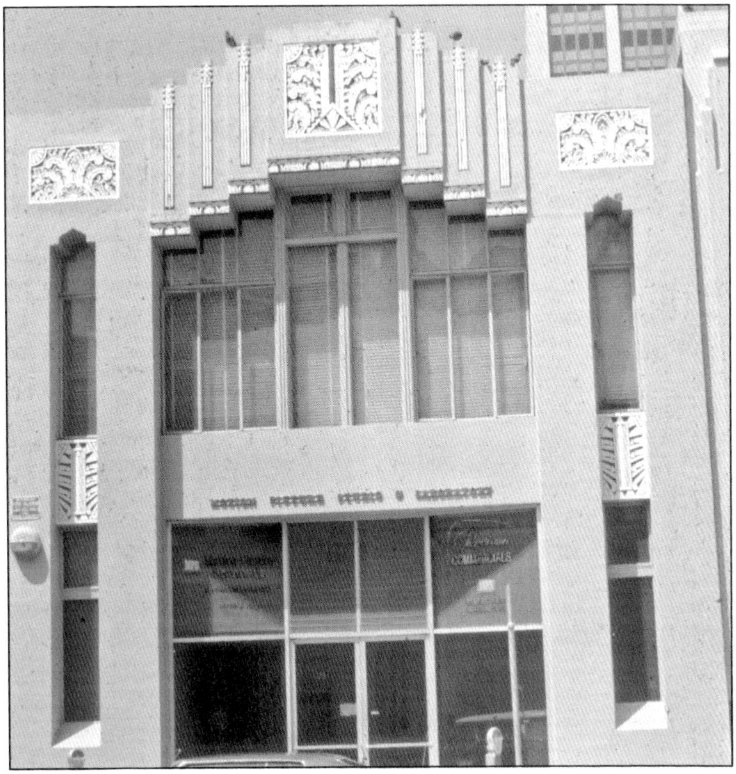

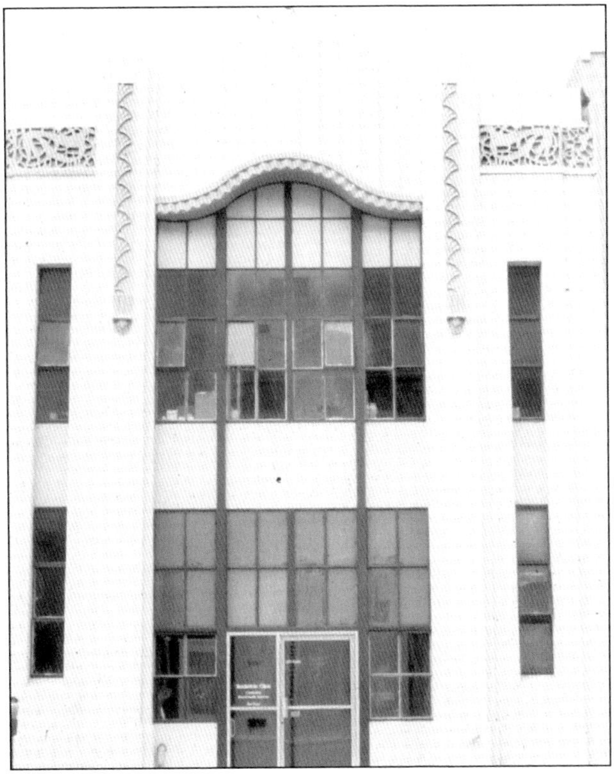

This building at 251 Hyde Street shares some common design motifs with the structure at 125 Hyde Street. The O'Brien Brothers were architects for building, constructed about 1930. Here the central stepped arch is fluted and flanked by incised plaques with forms that can be traced to the influence of German expressionist graphics. Similar designs can be found in plasterwork on the exterior of industrial buildings South of Market and in apartment lobby ceilings in the Marina.

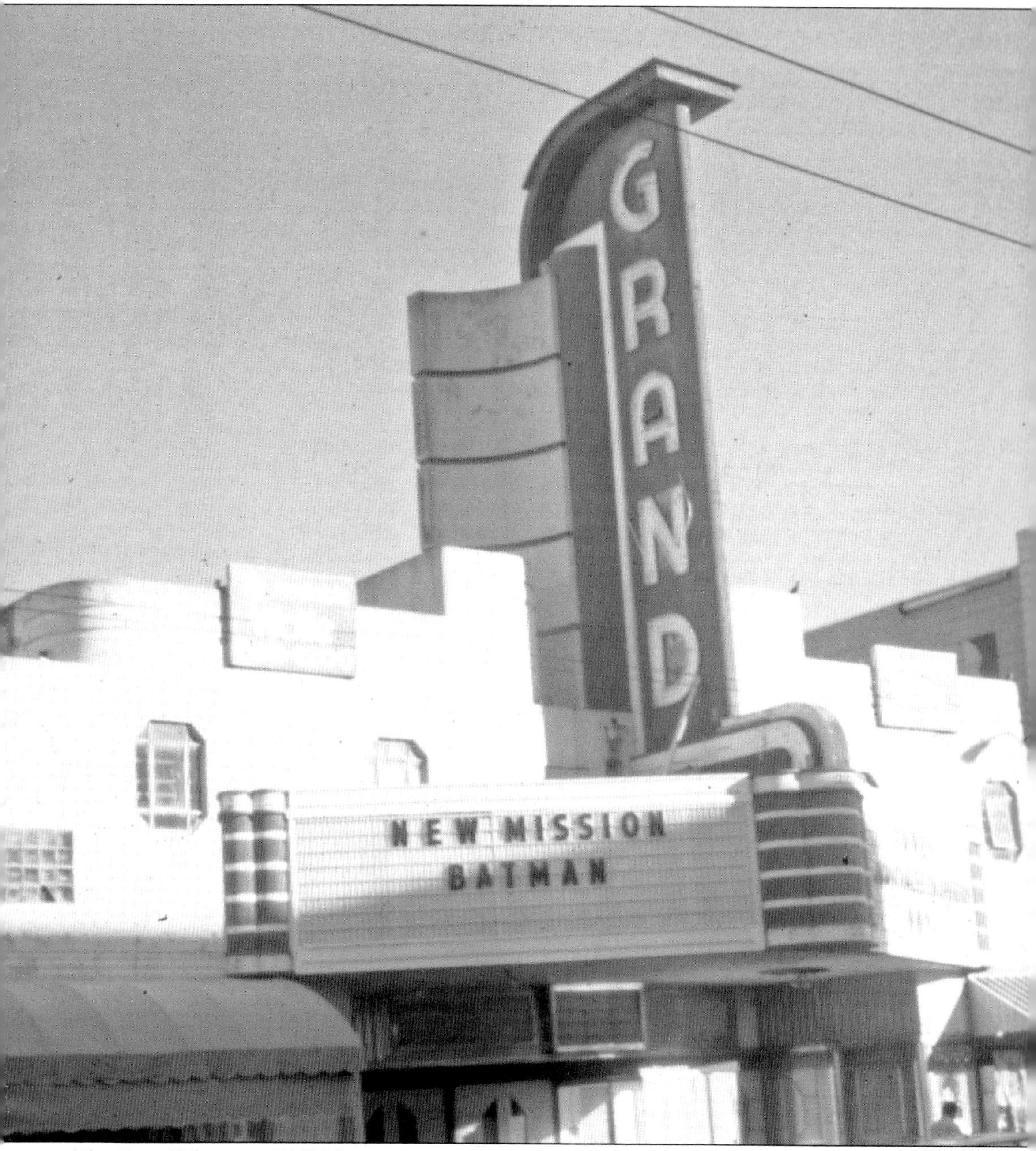

The Grand Theater at 2665 Mission Street in the theater district that runs for several blocks along Mission Street is a superb example of the streamlined Art Deco style. The vertical neon sign is integrated into the facade, a later development in period theater design when neon technology was in full swing. The sweeping curves, speed lines, octagonal windows, and rectangles of glass block all marked it as good a place to see the latest Buck Rogers movie.

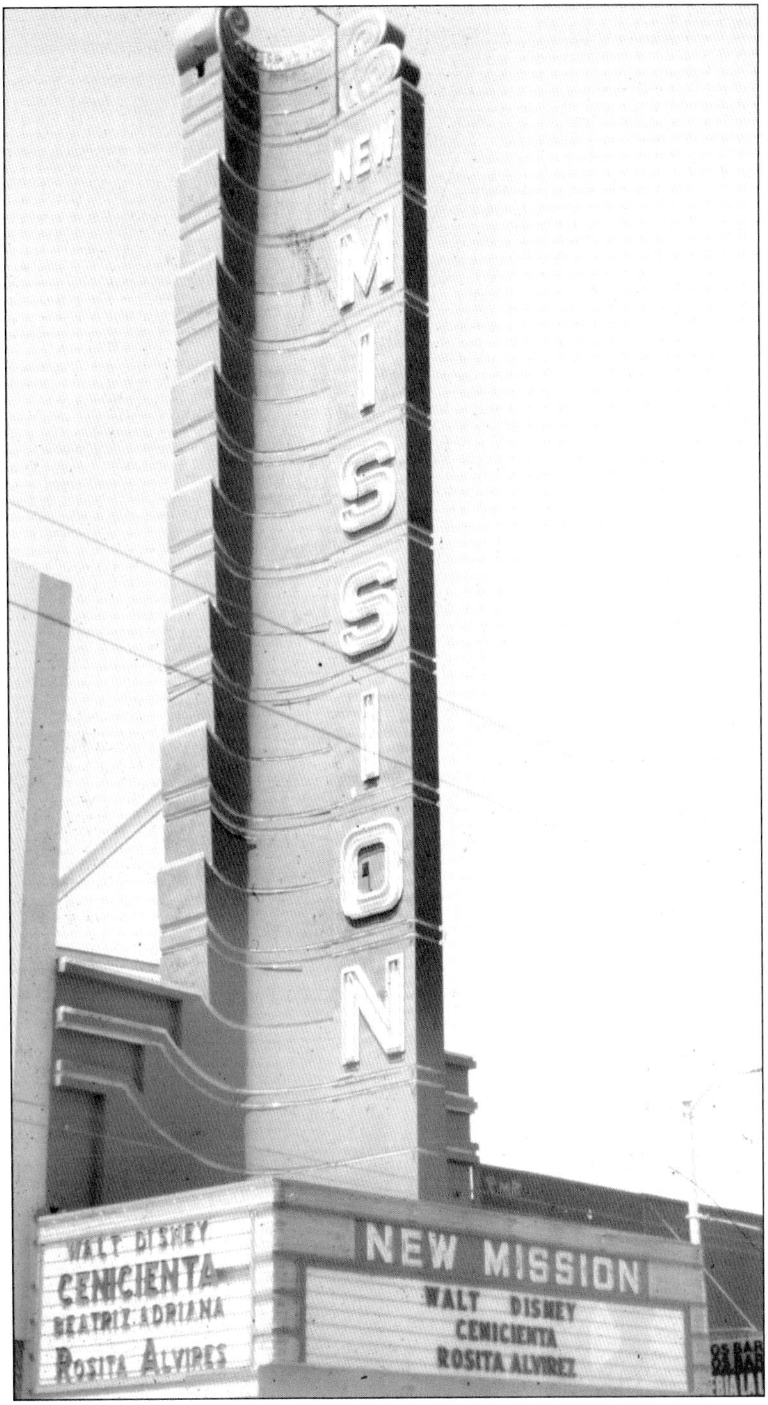

Behind the streamlined-style vertical sign is a classical theater at 2550 Mission Street designed by the Reid Brothers that dates from the early years of the 20th century's second decade. It was one of the largest theaters on Mission Street. In the mid-1930s, Timothy Pflueger was commissioned to give it an updated look. He added the vertical sign and reworked the entry lobby with more streamlined forms and new light fixtures; however, the auditorium portion was left intact.

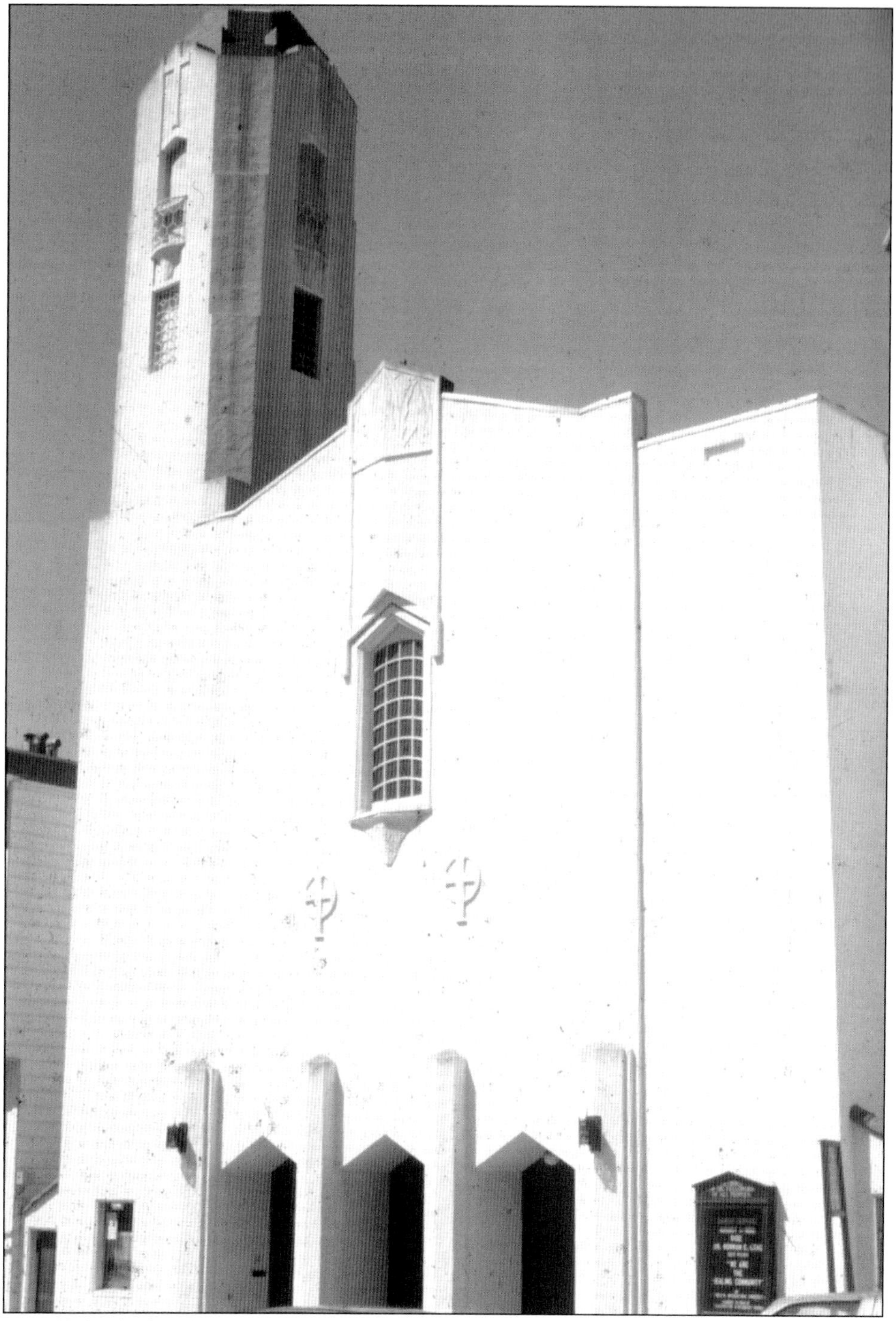

Originally built shortly after the 1906 earthquake and fire, the Church of All People at 2050 Larkin Street received a new look around 1930. This involved changing the facade with the addition of stepped piers flanking the entries and a decorative plaque centered above the entries at the roofline. The flanking tower also reflects this modern change with stepped elements at the top.

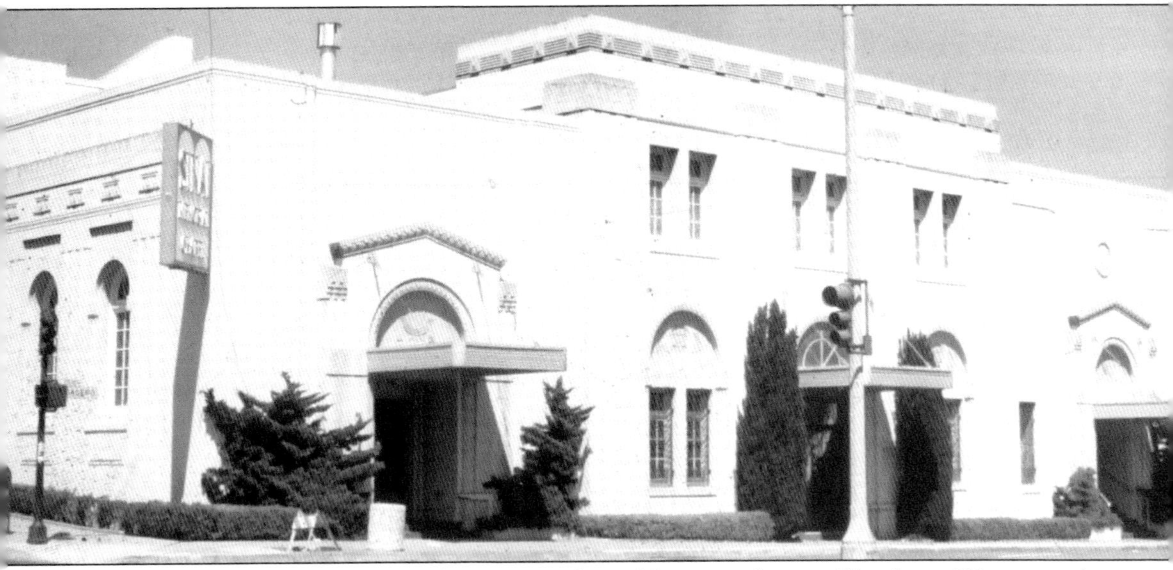

Sinai Memorial Chapel is the only Art Deco funeral home in the city. The firm of Hyman and Appleton designed the building at Divisadero Street and Geary Boulevard, constructing it in 1938. At first glance, the round arches suggest a Romanesque-style building, but a closer inspection shows the Art Deco style in the details at the metal entry gates, marquees, cornice-line details, and pier capitals. The interior has two chapels with molded plaster ornaments, decorated pews, and other details that carry out the same designs found on the exterior.

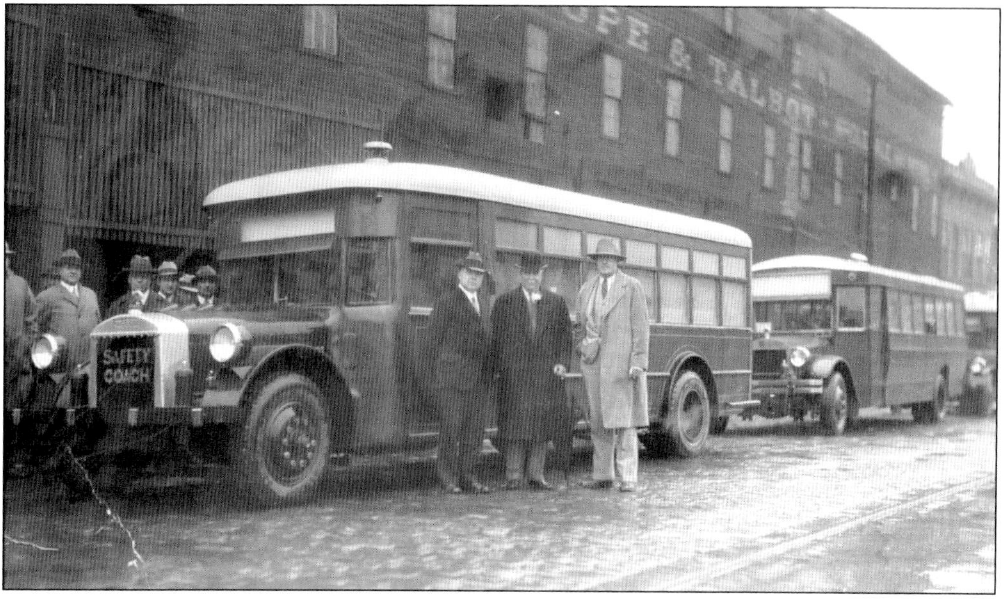

Speedy public transportation was an important symbol of modernity in the Art Deco era. Municipal Railway's first motor coaches went into operation in 1918 and increasingly gained approval with the general public. In 1927, Mayor Rolph, with the derby and dark overcoat, appears in front of the city's new Fageol Safety Coaches for the opening of the No. 4 Embarcadero Line. The Fageols had a composite wood and metal body, a "conventional" engine out front, and featured sharp-looking rattan seats.

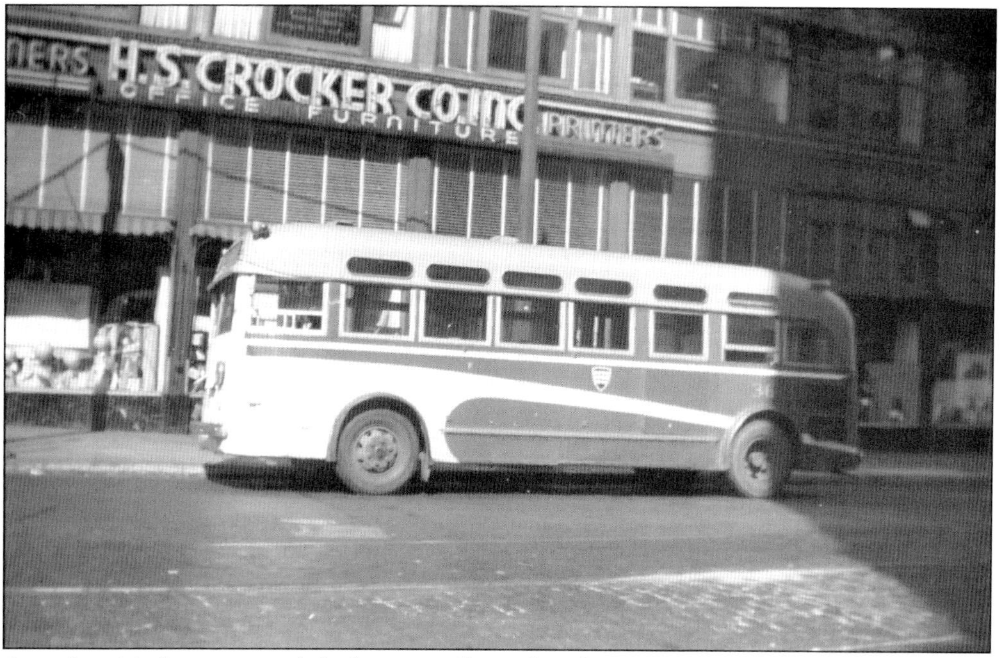

A modern Mack motor coach looks especially swift with its sensuous curving speed lines as it cruises past the H. S. Crocker Company at 599 Market Street. As the Market Street Railway continued to abandon streetcar lines in the 1940s, the privately owned corporation purchased buses as replacement vehicles.

Six

Moderne Houses, Flats, and Apartment Art Deco

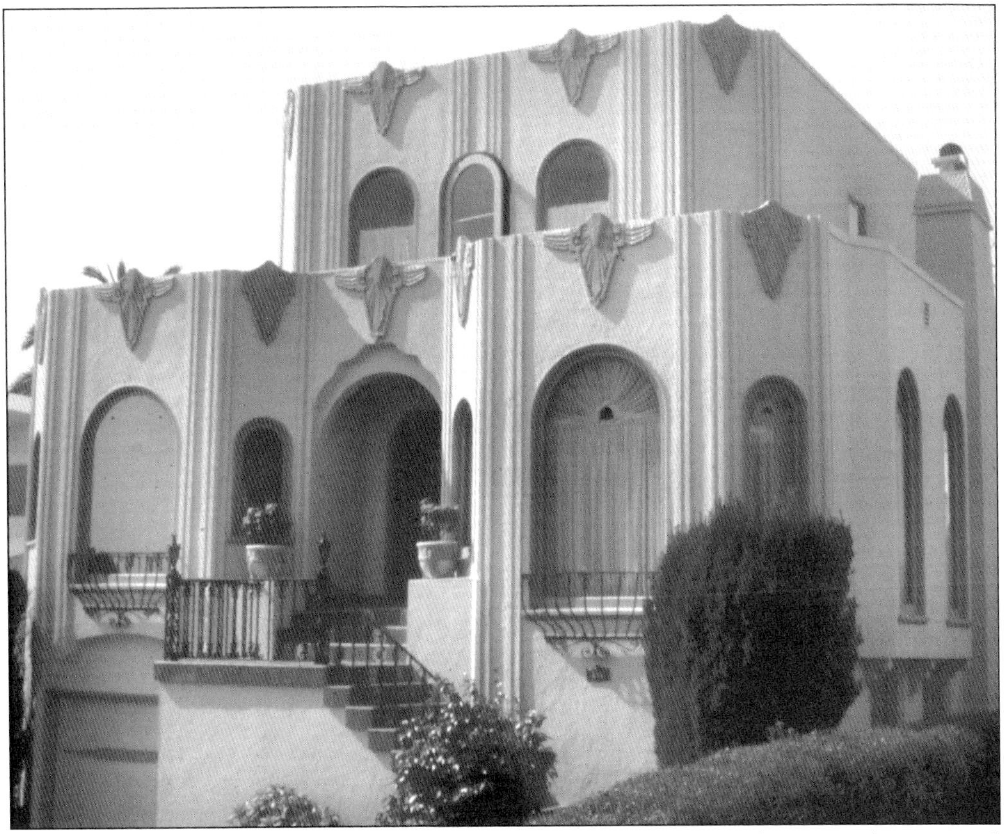

If one's home is one's castle, then in this case it must be a skyscraper. This unique house at 815 Miramar Avenue stands out among the bungalows and Craftsman-style houses in the Ingleside District. It fulfills all of the design elements that began to characterize skyscrapers during the period: stepped profile, overall verticality, and unique ornamentation. This house has it all. The two sections of different sizes give the small building the impression of being larger. The vertical channels and winged cartouches with rays all mark it with modernity.

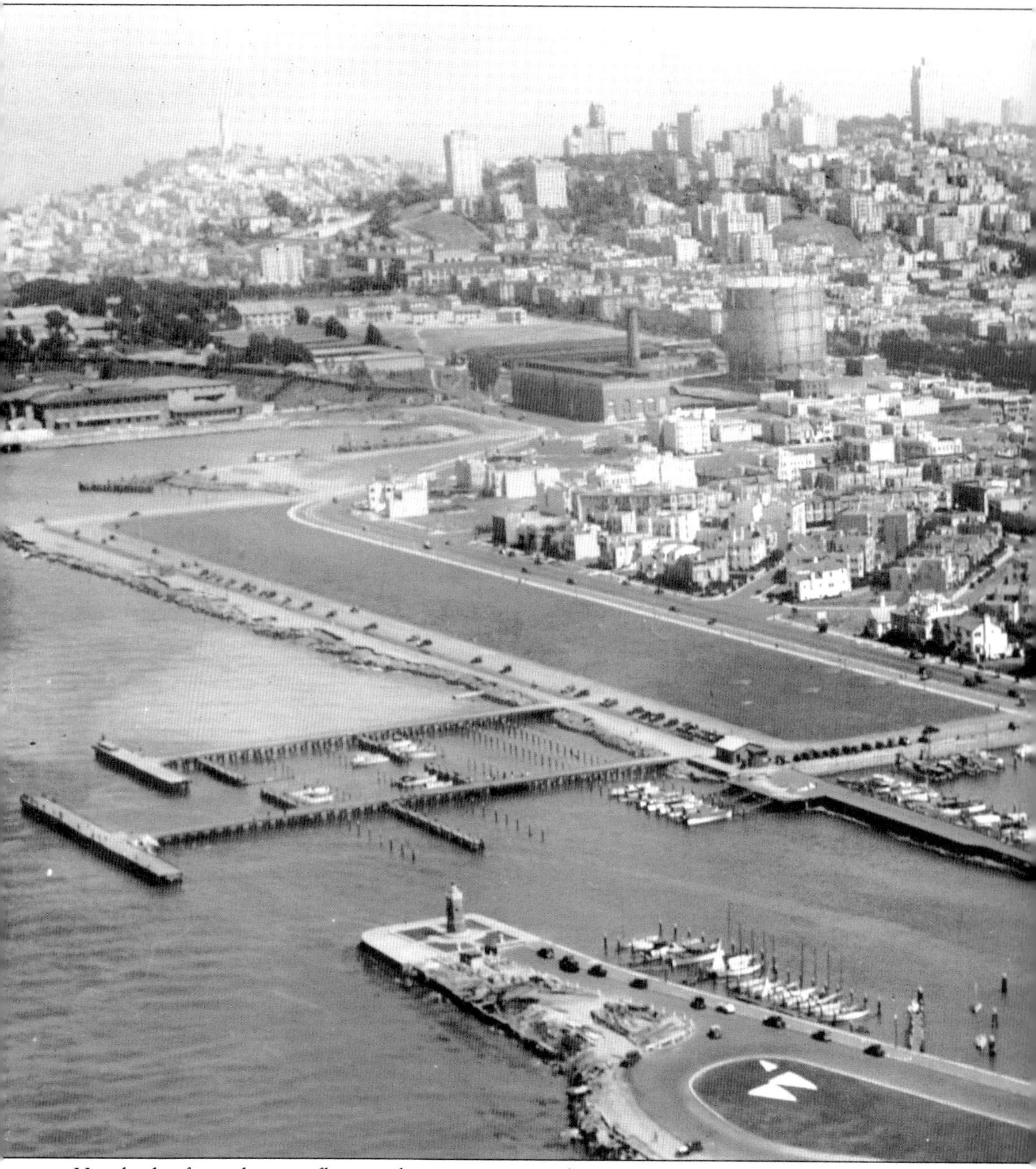

Hundreds of new houses, flats, and apartments can be seen in this Fred Mae aerial showing the Marina District in October 1933. The area, originally consisting of sloughs, wetlands, and dairy farms, became prominent as the site of the 1915 Panama Pacific International Exposition. Development, delayed by World War I, took off with the building boom of the mid-1920s. Developers originally called the district the Marina Vanderbilt Tract after Virginia Fair Vanderbilt, a major property owner. Architects who designed residences in the Marina included Herman C. Baumann, R. R. Irvine, Mark Jorgensen, Oliver Rousseau, Julia Morgan, and Richard Neutra. Building in the new neighborhood coincided with the growing interest in Art Deco style and architecture,

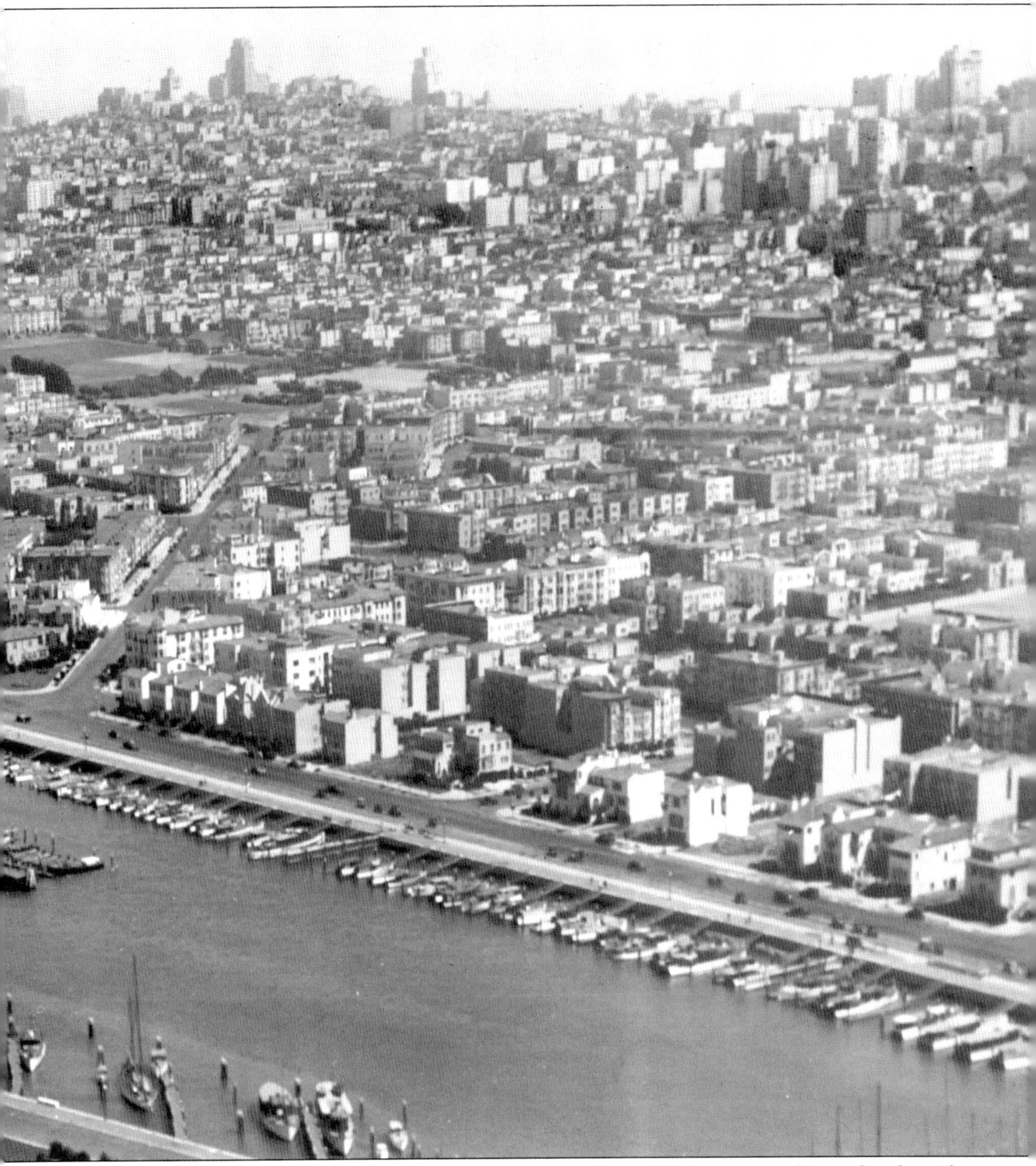

although most of the houses and flats were constructed in a Mediterranean Revival style with flat roofs, tile accents, and stucco. Apartment exteriors featured a variety of decorative elements from Mayan influences to a more streamlined look. All apartments had Art Deco entries and lobbies with terrazzo, tiles, stenciling, and elaborate mirrors and light fixtures. It was the era of the automobile, and residences in the Marina were among the first to be built with garages on the ground floor. Unfortunately, during the 1989 Loma Prieta earthquake, large open-bay garages were a factor in those apartments that collapsed.

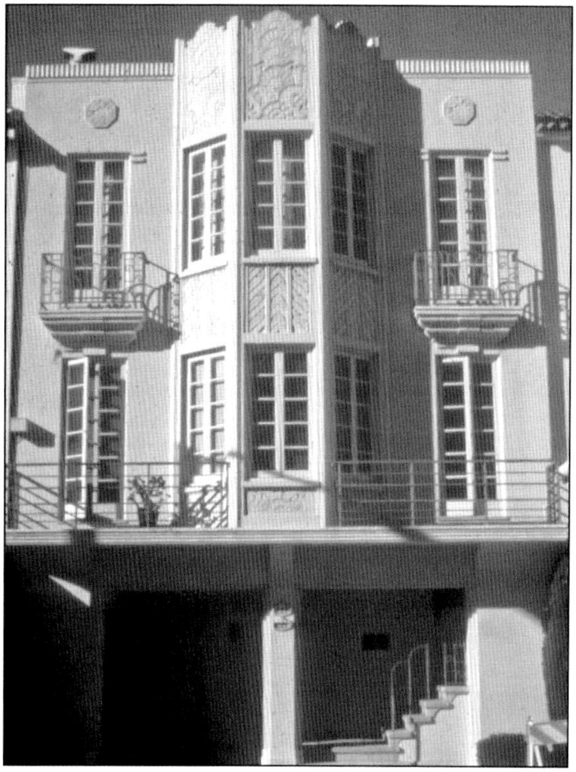

The two-flat building at 3639–41 Webster Street, constructed in 1932 in the Marina District, shows how the style was adapted to this building form. The more traditional Art Deco forms are used to great advantage. The central bay is capped by an uneven profile that reflects the shape of the ornamentation below with rays, stepped vertical channels, and chevrons in the window spandrels. The ironwork on the balconies also carries the same decorative elements.

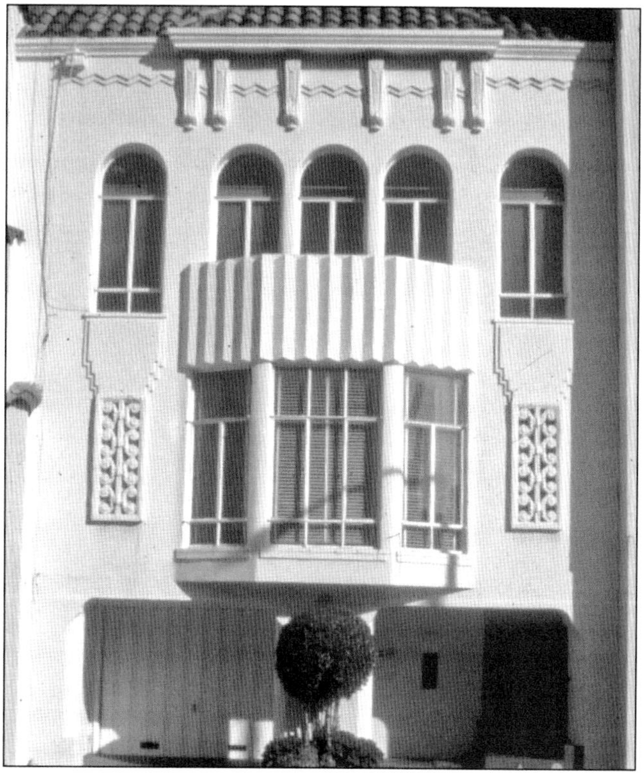

This house, built at 3760 Fillmore Street in 1932, is simpler in ornamentation than the flats building on Webster Street but is no less of the period. The red-tile roof is a bow to the then-popular Spanish Colonial Revival style. The use of zigzags at the cornice line, prisms on the front of the bay, and Mayan-derived grille work all show the variety that could be achieved within the design elements of the Art Deco style.

This two-flat building, created in 1941, shows how the style was beginning to change from the ornamented examples from the Marina District. Here the bay window carries most of the streamlined ornamentation: three parallel speed lines at the base and simple prisms at the base and top of the bay. The corner windows and horizontal orientation of the windowpanes are all characteristic of this later phase of the style. It points the way to and shows the influence of the International style, which would fully emerge after World War II.

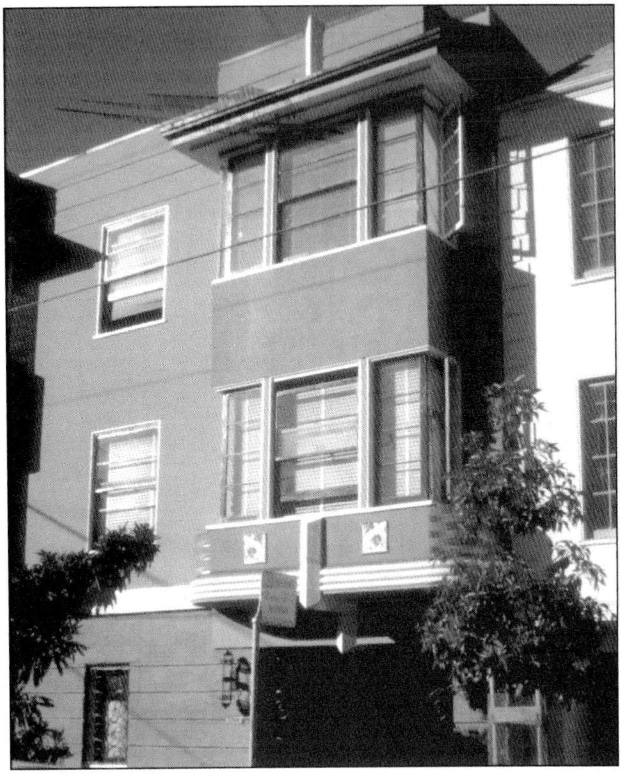

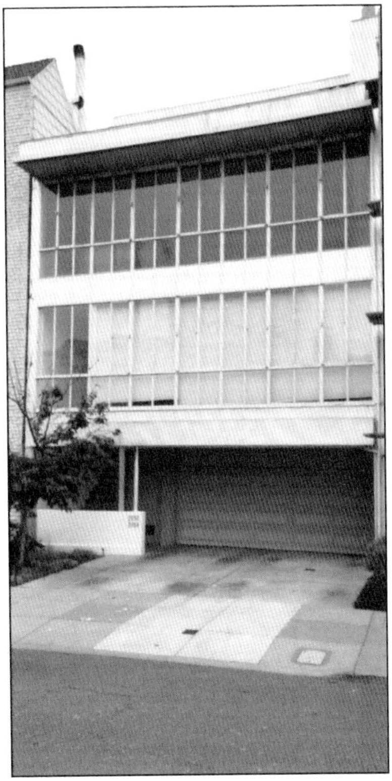

This distinctly modern house on Jefferson Street in the Marina District was designed in the late 1930s. It was built for Dr. and Mrs. William Schiff, a German refugee couple, to show their collection of modern art in a modern setting. The house is a rare example of the pre-war International style by one of the premier champions of the style, Richard Neutra. He was a German-born and -trained Southern California architect who designed a number of modernist houses in Los Angeles and La Jolla for sophisticated clients. The style was introduced at the 1925 Paris Exhibition by the architect Le Corbusier but was not fully appreciated by the public until after World War II.

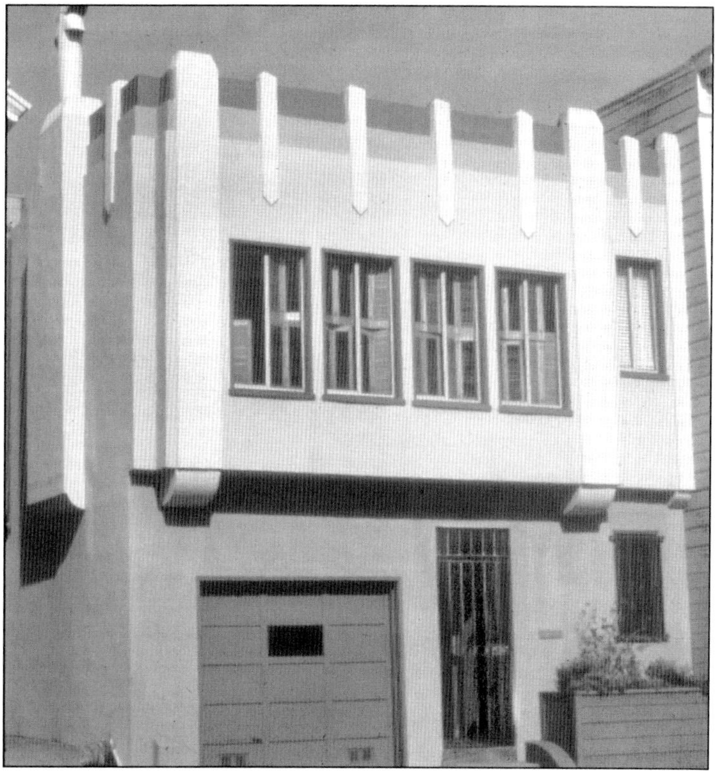

This house, built around 1940, shows how simple forms can convey the elements of the Art Deco style. It has a simple stepped-back cornice with pointed-end vertical elements. The bay is framed by larger vertical elements that have simple curved undersides. It's remarkable how simple plasterwork can be used so stylistically.

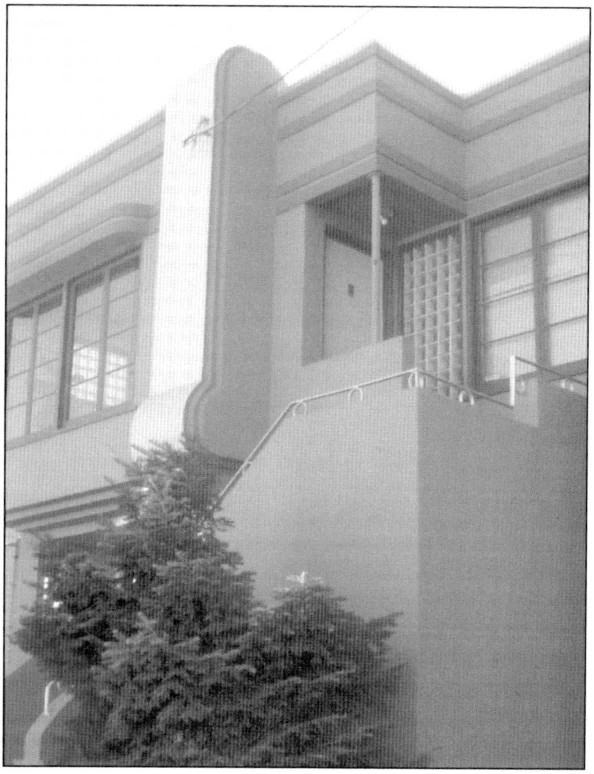

This house on De Montfort Street near City College, built about 1940, has many of the classic design elements of the streamlined phase of the Art Deco style. Often derived from sleek nautical forms, the simple curved shapes were combined with circular windows, rounded corners, and bays. Here there is a glass-block window, a large curved decorative "nose," and a simple entry railing with circular inserts. The original wood windows, with a horizontal pane configuration, are an important design element.

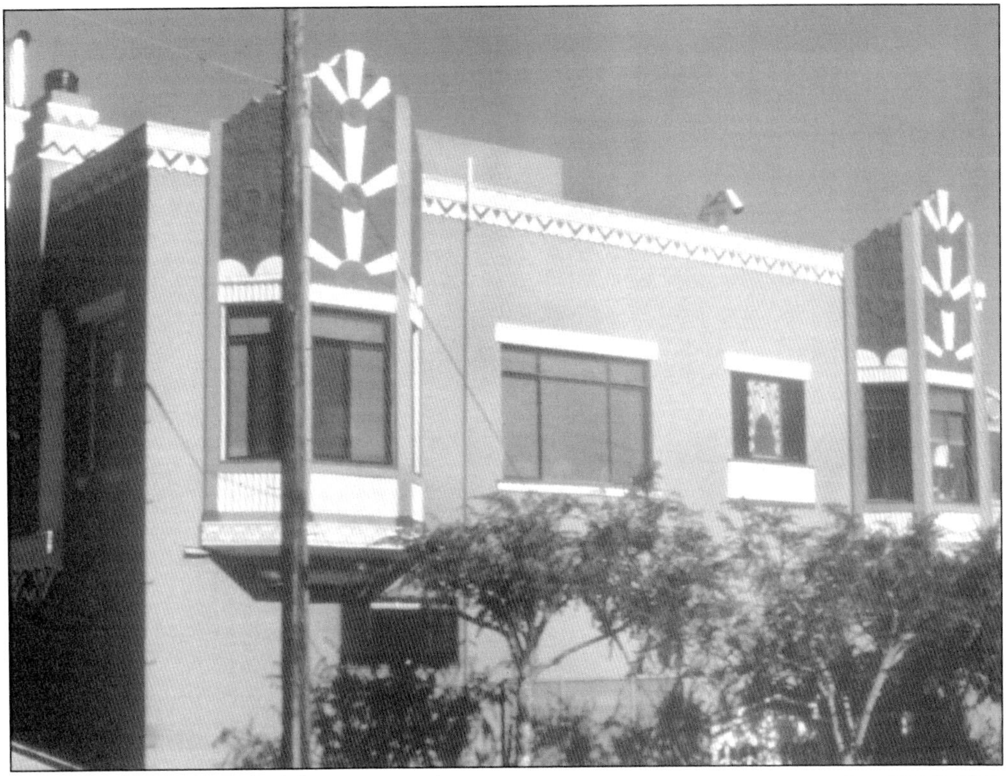

This 1932 house at 99 Ord Street is another example of the early phase of the Art Deco style. The combination of rays and zigzags at the cornice and the two bay windows with rays and other molded decorative elements give a stunning presence to the house in a Victorian neighborhood.

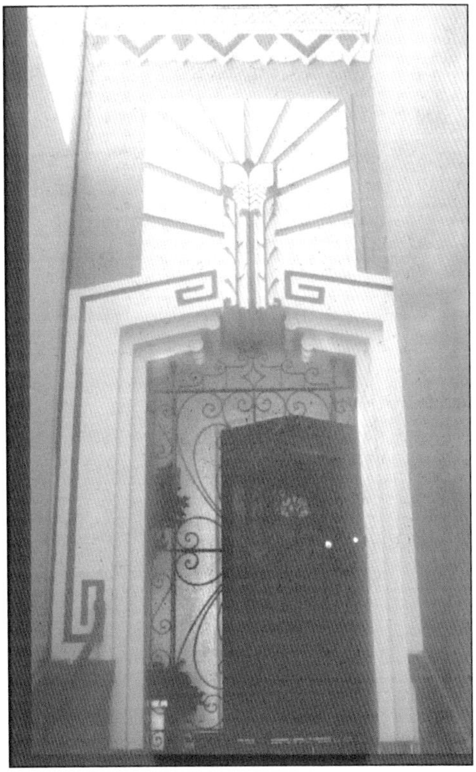

The entry of the house at 99 Ord Street is no less interesting. The entry has rays, a stepped arch, and a Mayan-inspired decorative element over the door that marks the exuberance of the style. The colorful painting scheme enhances all of the architectural elements.

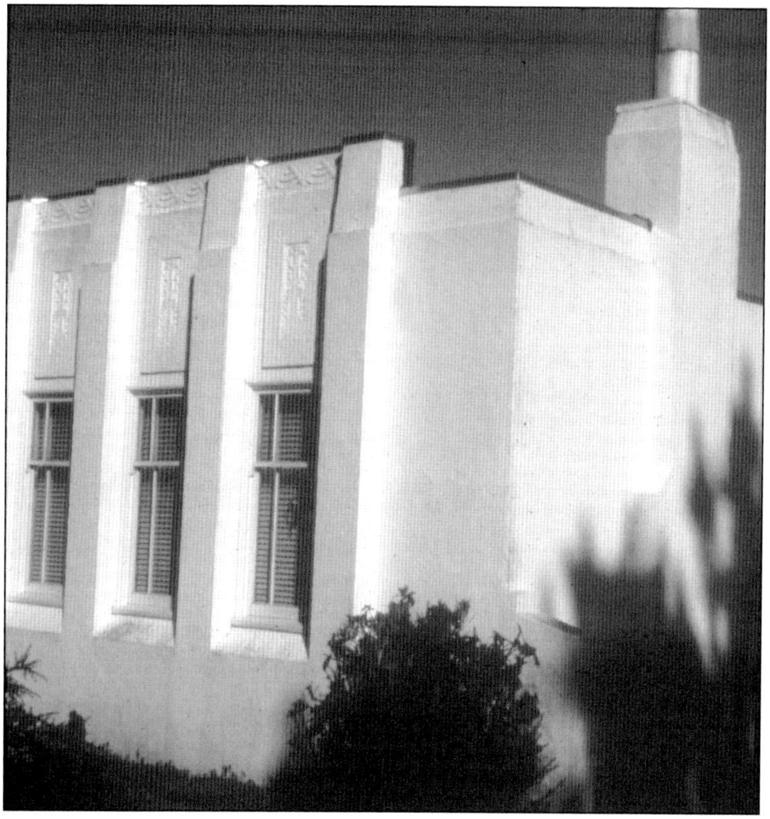

This house on Idora Street, near Mount Davidson, achieves its style in the economic use of simple details. Large stepped piers separate the three front windows. There are molded decorative panels above the windows, and above the panel is a zigzag cornice. With few details on the sides of the house, it is not unlike the attached houses found in the Richmond District.

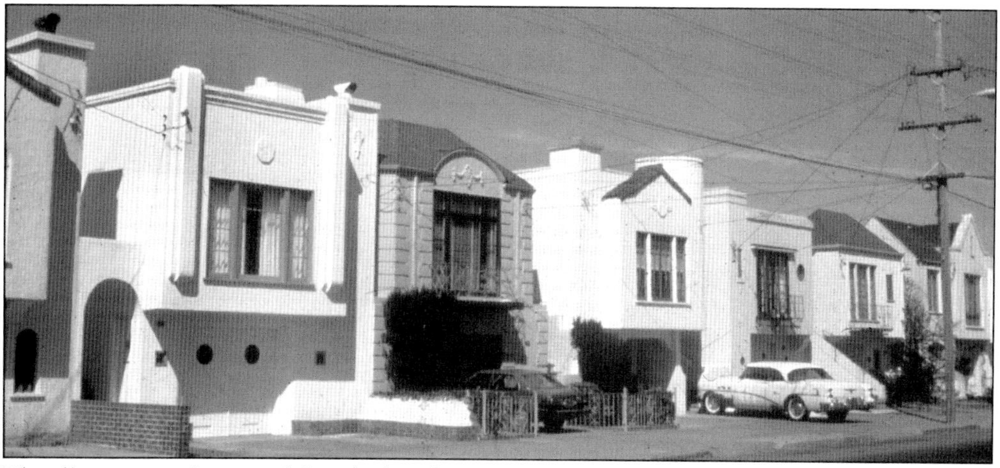

The illustration of a row of detached and semi-attached houses in the Richmond District is a good example of the range of the styles popular during the period besides Art Deco. The floor plans are virtually identical, but the fronts offer a variety of styles to please any taste, including Art Deco and streamlined Deco. There are numerous examples of these kinds of rows throughout the Richmond and Sunset Districts.

This building at 1000 Green Street, designed by Herman C. Baumann, was constructed about 1930. It clearly shows the stylistic influence of the 1925 Telephone Company Building designed by Timothy Pflueger. The stepped profile, unusual ornamentation at the cornice lines, and overall verticality are the classic style elements found on both buildings.

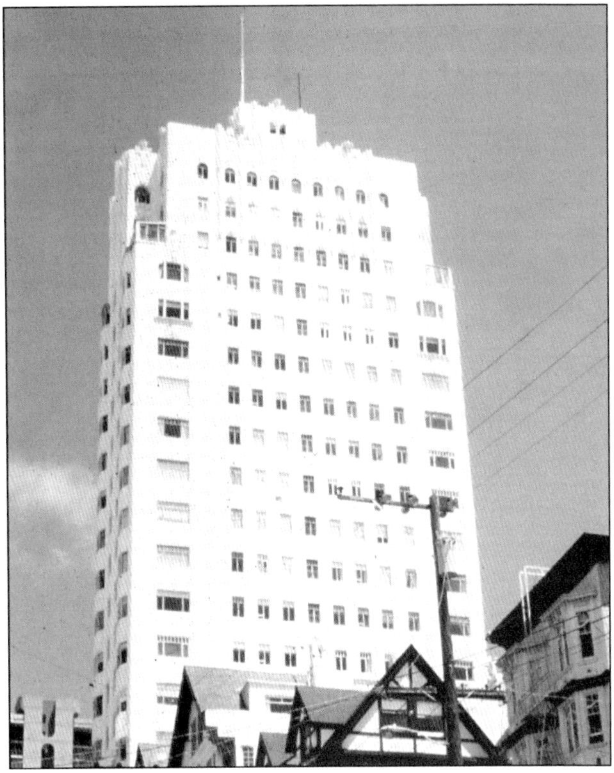

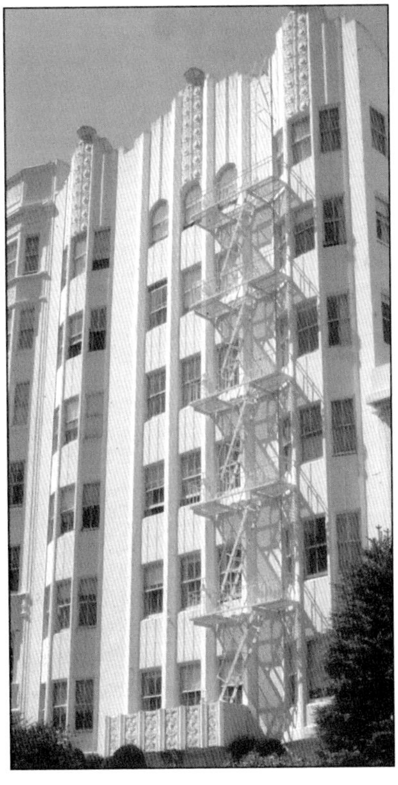

Herman C. Baumann designed this building on a smaller scale than the Green Street building. This structure has the same design elements on a much-reduced scale but is no less interesting. Here the stepped cornice is enhanced with decorative pots, since removed, with raised floral panels below. Simple incised lines in the window spandrels emphasize the verticality. Note how the termination of the fire escape is integrated into the entry canopy with raised floral panels.

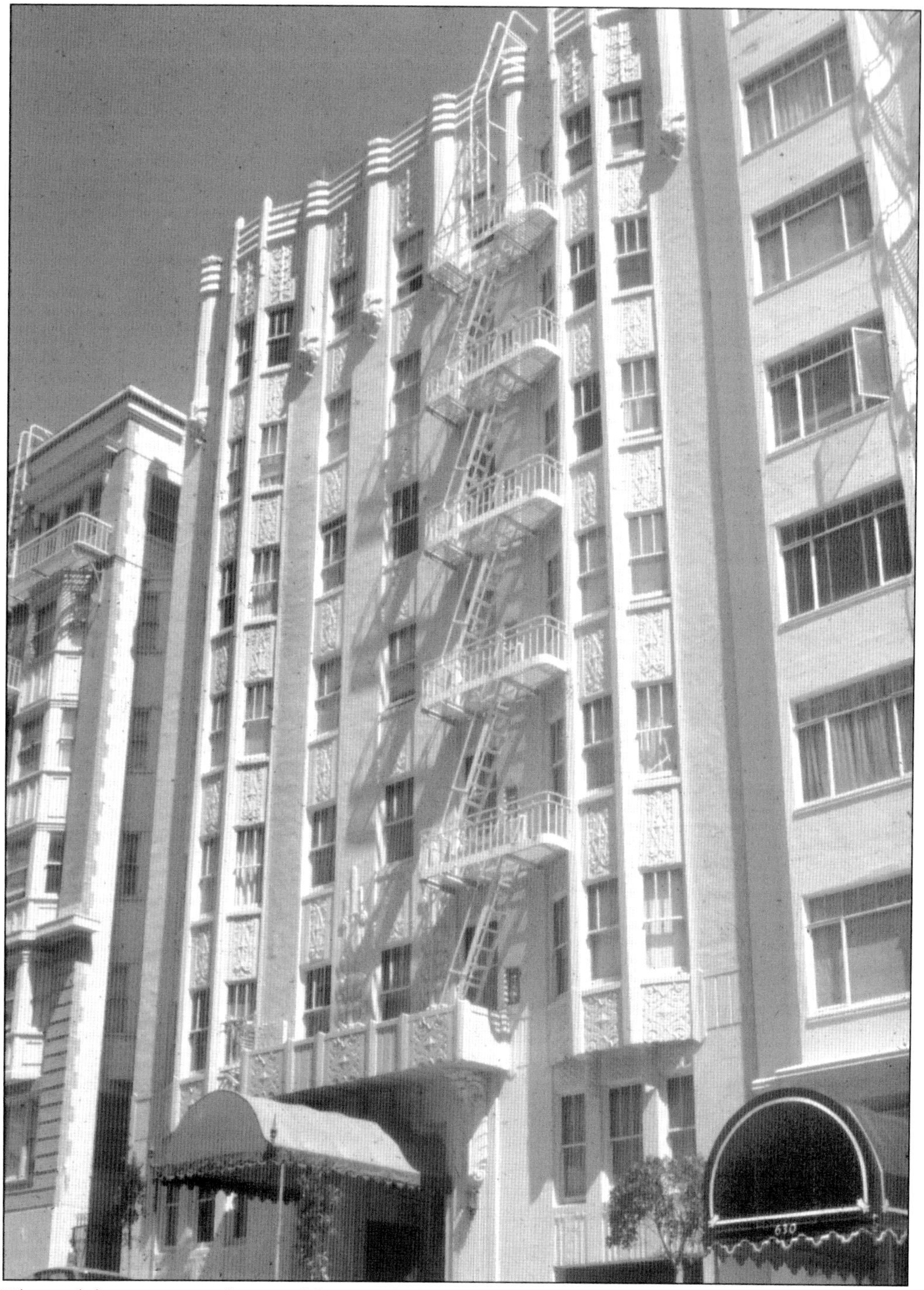

The prolific apartment designer Herman C. Baumann worked with this constricted Nob Hill site at 640 Mason Street and came up with a classic 1932 version of the Art Deco style. The vertical emphasis is carried out by the facade colonettes and even the windowpane configuration. The molded ornament in the window spandrels (below the window panels) is derived from German expressionist forms. The cornice is also enlivened with unique ornaments.

The entry door and sidelights' grille-work design can be traced to French sources, notably master ironwork designer Edgar Brandt. This kind of grille work can be found throughout the city on both large- and small-scale apartment buildings and brings a decorative touch to the entries.

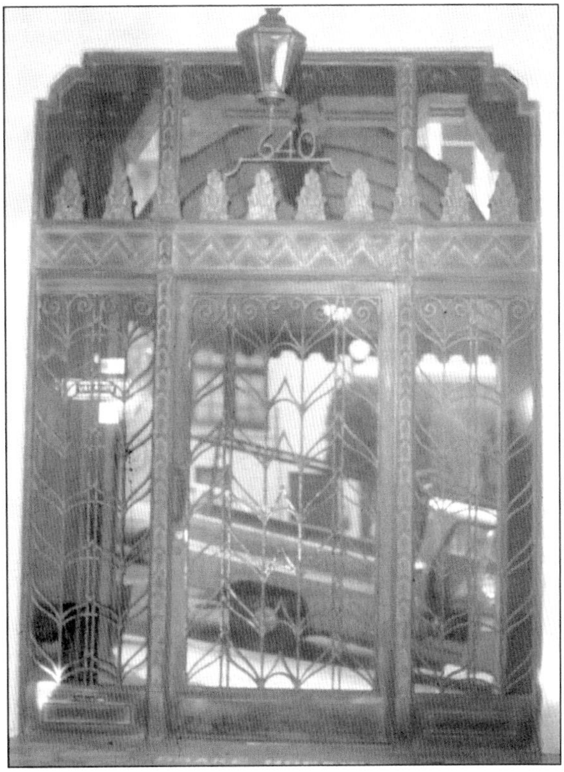

The entry lobby ceiling, looking like a gilded waffle iron, is a bow to the design influence of Timothy Pflueger and his Stock Exchange Tower lobby ceiling. Simple molded plaster with gold paint brings style to a small lobby entrance.

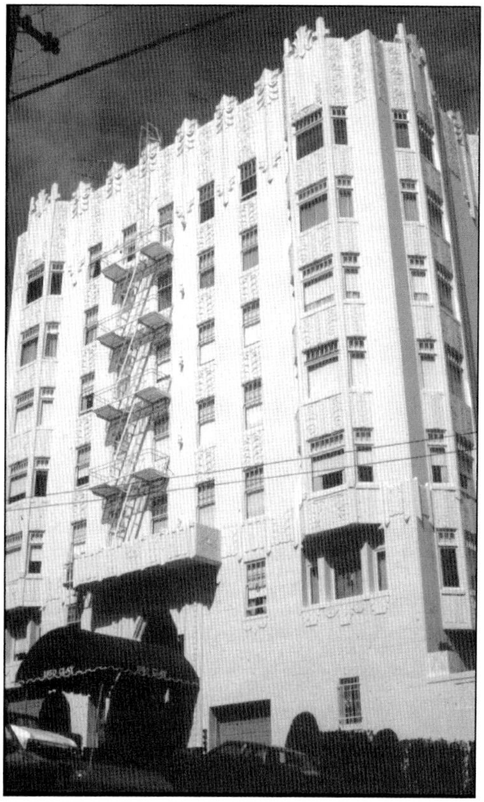

Once again at 1950 Clay Street, Herman C. Baumann uses his talented formula to great success: vertical colonettes, window spandrel ornamentation, and unusual cornice line detail are used. The spandrels' floral forms are classic stylized floral shapes, which probably were derived from Egyptian sources, a popular period source. Baumann again uses the entry canopy to act as the terminus of the fire escape, which frames the Mayan-style entry arch.

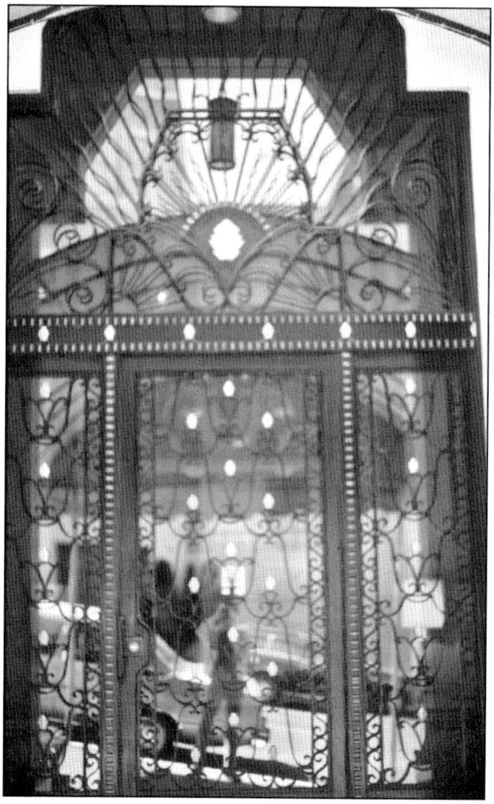

The entry door grille-work is derived from the work of the Frenchman Edgar Brandt, a notable and influential ironwork designer. Brandt showed his skills by designing some of the entry gates at the 1925 Paris Exhibition. He also designed lamps, vases, room screens, and other decorative items.

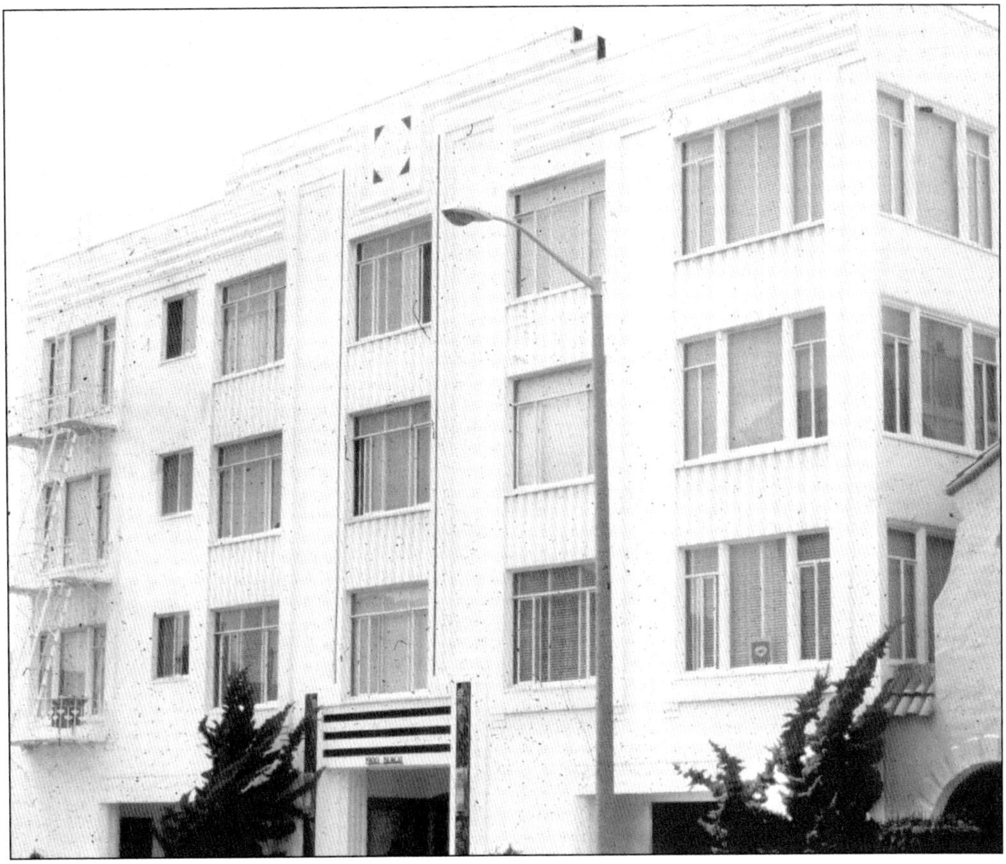

This apartment building at 1690 Beach is an example of how the Art Deco style changed in the later 1930s. Herman C. Baumann was the designer and shows his skill in stripping down the early floral manifestations of the style. Here he uses simple vertical fluting and a stepped cornice detail highlighted with black Vitrolux (structural glass) panel inserts. The Vitrolux panels around the entry are embellished with an incised floral design.

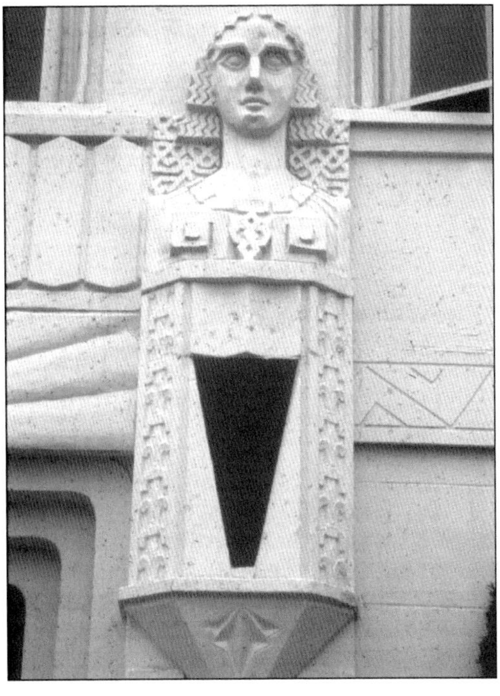

The amazing decorative detail of the stylized female form on this Marina District apartment is at 3665 Scott Street. The zigzag hairline is complemented by the equally unusual "cubist" breasts and the Vitrolux panel below. There are two other apartment buildings with this same ornament in other parts of the city.

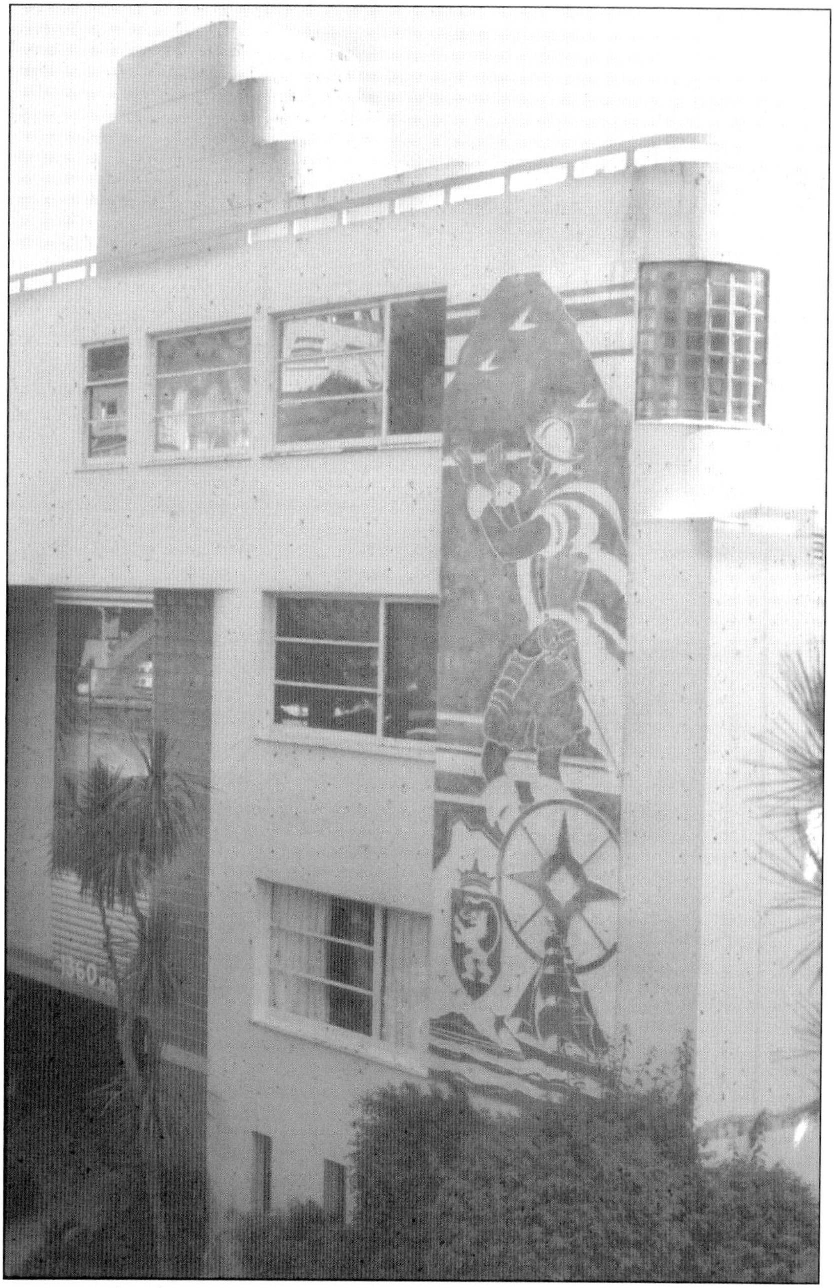

This iconic example of an apartment building at 1360 Montgomery Street on Telegraph Hill has a film history. It was the fictive site of Lauren Bacall's apartment in the movie *Dark Passage*. Humphrey Bogart, her love interest, recovered from plastic surgery in the bedroom and must have enjoyed spectacular views of the bay from her balcony. S. W. Goldstein designed the building in 1936 using the streamlined nautical forms, glass block, and polished metal that were part of the later development of the Art Deco style. The *sgrafitto* ornamentation, depicting a conquistador, was carried out by the artist Alfred DuPont. The *sgrafitto* (Italian for scratching) technique was developed first by the Romans and is a simple way of incising lines into two different colored coats of plaster to develop the decorative forms.

Seven

Public Buildings, Public Art

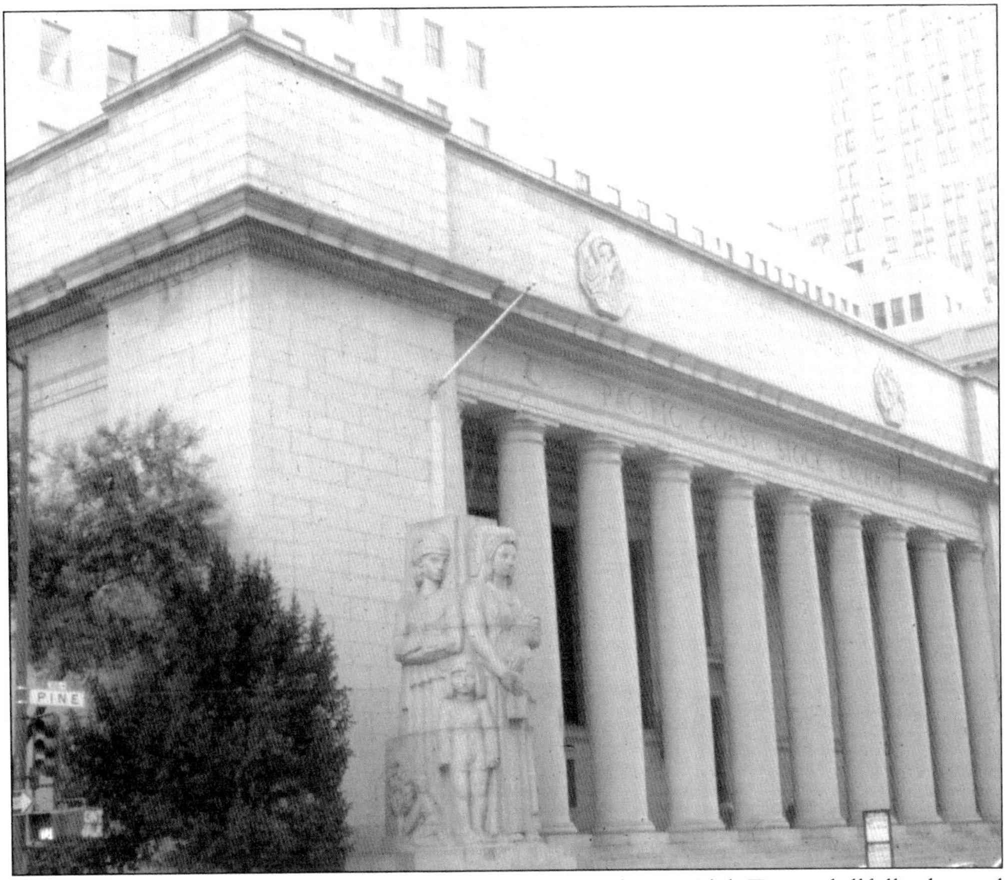

Timothy Pflueger, the architect for the adjacent Stock Exchange Club Tower, skillfully changed the older Federal Reserve Bank Building by the addition plinths for two large sculptures by Ralph Stackpole. The statue here depicts earth's fruitfulness embodied in the heroic figures of women, one holding a sheaf of wheat, and the other offering protection to a child. The interior of the Tower Building also has examples of the work of notable local artists. Most prominent, though, is the mural by the Mexican muralist Diego Rivera depicting the "golds of California." It was his first mural work in this country and one of three he completed in San Francisco.

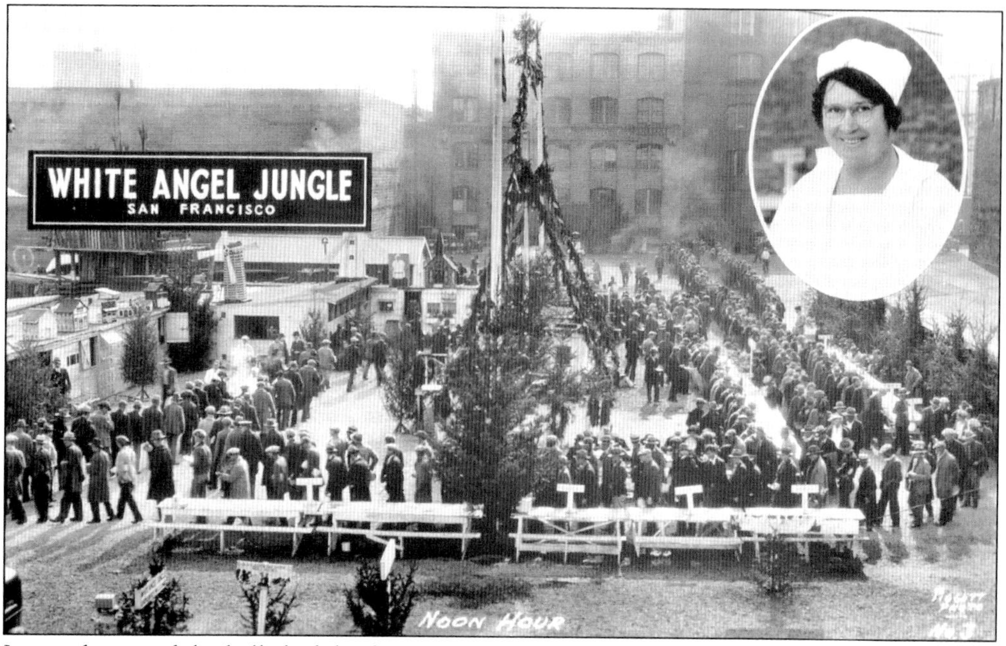

It was the era of the ballad of the forgotten man. The effects of the Great Depression in San Francisco can be seen in this J. K. Piggott photograph of the White Angel Jungle. "The Jungle," located on the Embarcadero near Filbert Street, was a soup kitchen. The self-proclaimed "White Angel" was Lois Jordan, a wealthy woman who served as many as 2,000 men a day on the principles of faith and no red tape. For supplies, Mother Jordan depended entirely on unsolicited donations of food and money.

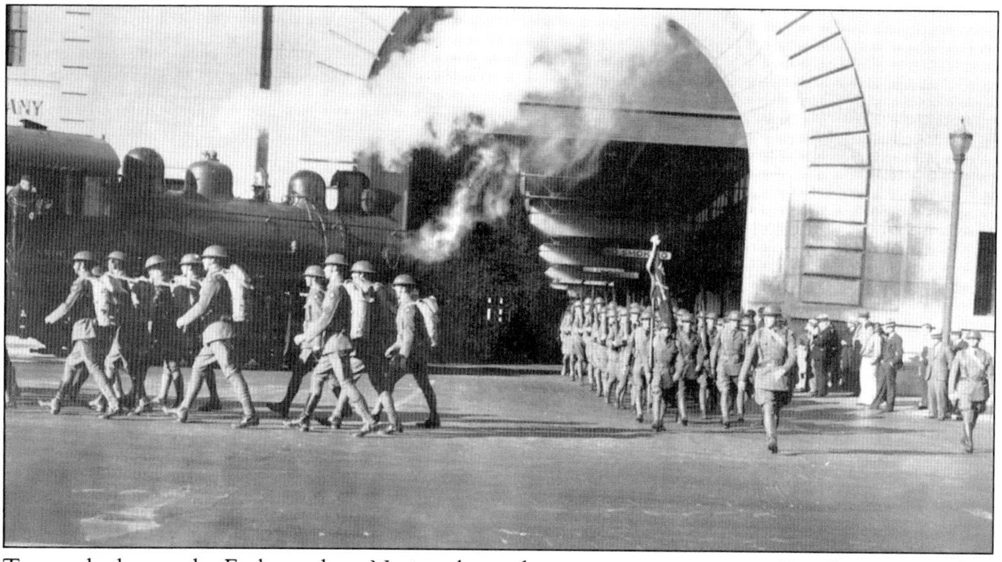

Troops deploy on the Embarcadero. National guardsmen were sent to assist San Francisco police in restoring order during a lengthy and violent waterfront strike. The strike reached a climax on Bloody Thursday, July 5, 1934. Police battled strikers with guns and tear gas, and two strikers were killed. On July 9, their funeral march went from the Embarcadero up Market Street to Valencia Street, sparking a four-day general strike of 127,000 workers throughout the city. Many local artists would use the strike as a theme in their artwork.

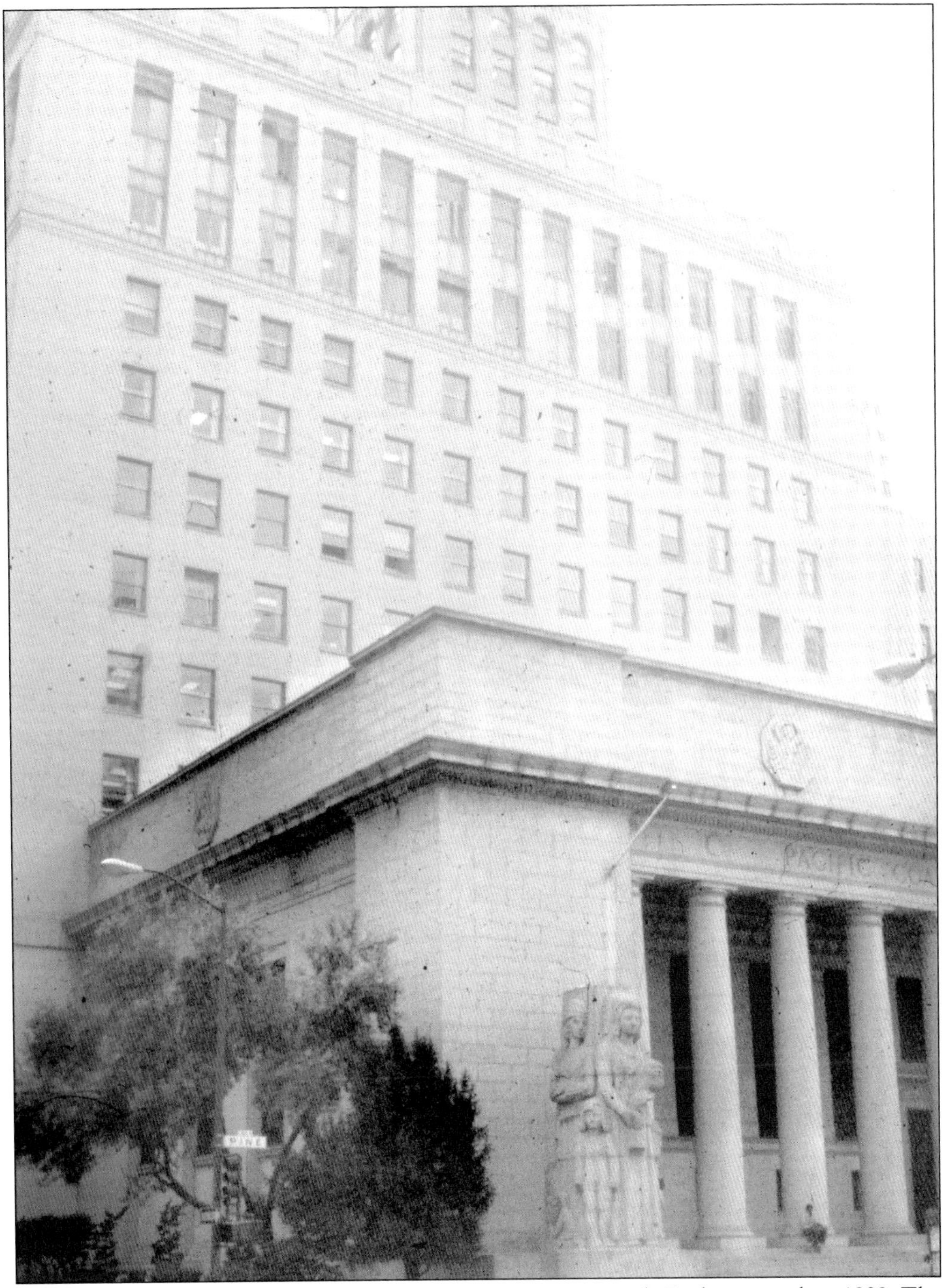

Timothy Pflueger won the design competition for a new Stock Exchange in late 1929. The Exchange decided then to acquire the former Federal Reserve Bank Building and commissioned Pflueger to come up with a new design integrating the older building with a new taller tower of offices. The tower has the same stone as the older building, and the piers at the top two floors echo the columns of the older building; the sparse and sleek look points to the new appearance of streamlining.

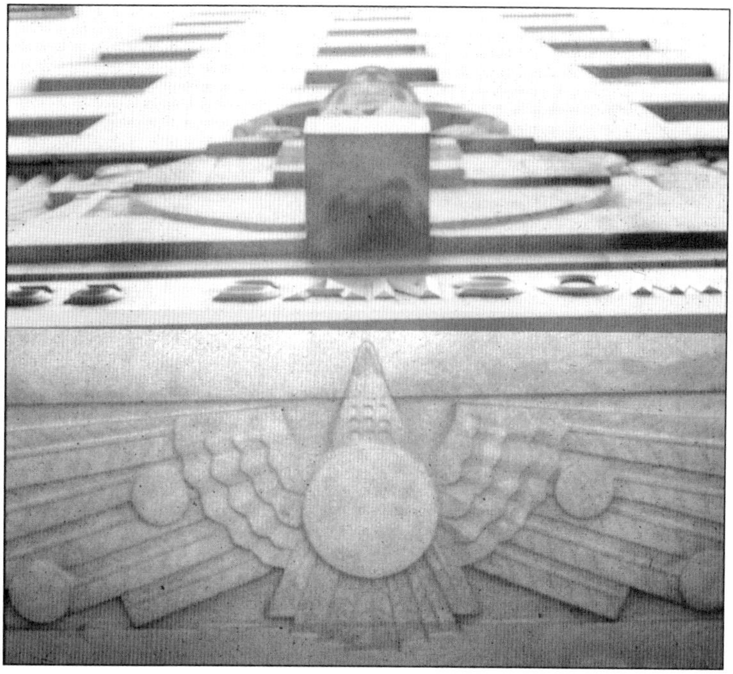

The underside of the entry to Stock Exchange Tower depicts an eagle, the symbol for commercial communication. The motif can be found on numerous older buildings in the financial district of the city. The bas-relief was completed by Ralph Stackpole, a friend of Pflueger. Particularly during the depths of the Depression, Pflueger was a strong supporter of using local artists.

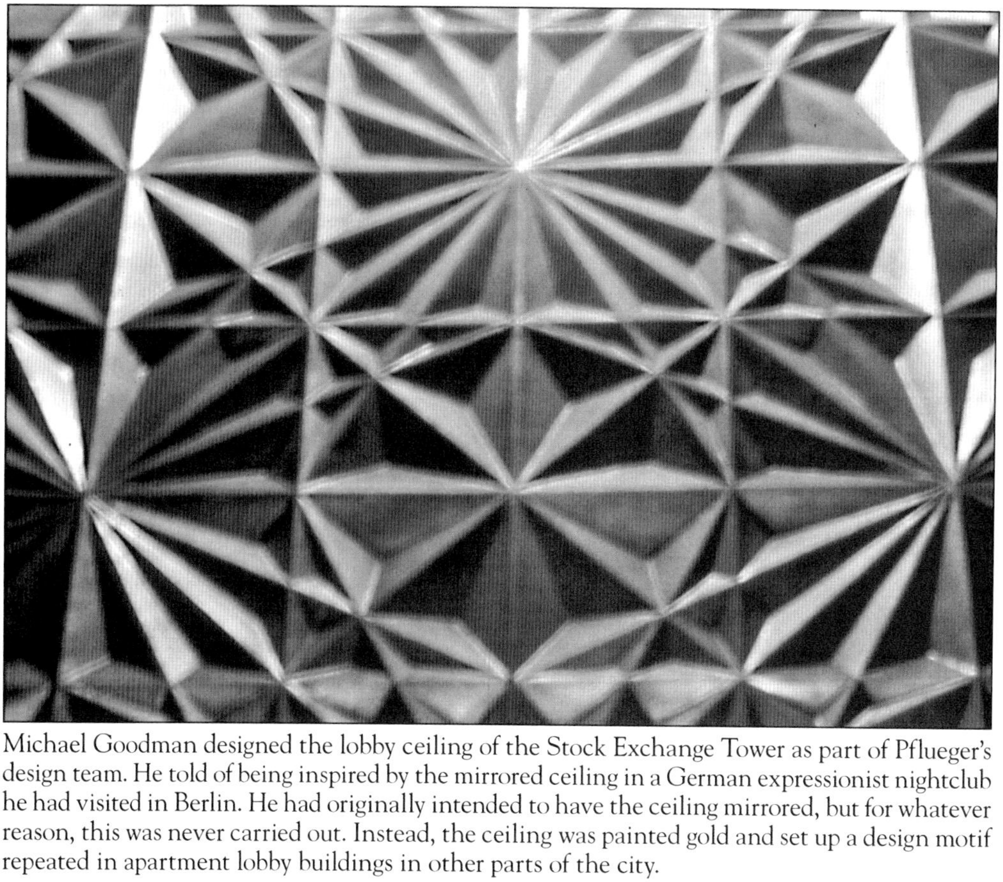

Michael Goodman designed the lobby ceiling of the Stock Exchange Tower as part of Pflueger's design team. He told of being inspired by the mirrored ceiling in a German expressionist nightclub he had visited in Berlin. He had originally intended to have the ceiling mirrored, but for whatever reason, this was never carried out. Instead, the ceiling was painted gold and set up a design motif repeated in apartment lobby buildings in other parts of the city.

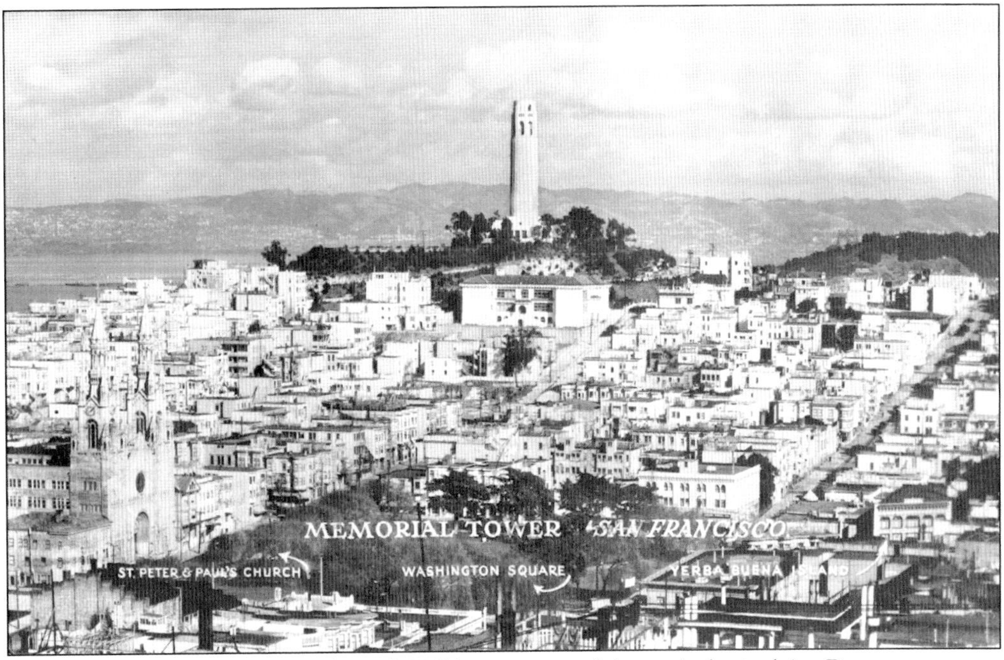

A sleek 180-foot column atop Telegraph Hill became one of the city's classical Art Deco monuments in 1933. Coit Memorial Tower was built as a legacy of Lillie Hitchcock Coit, who bequeathed $125,000 to San Francisco to be spent "for the purpose of adding beauty to the city which I have always loved."

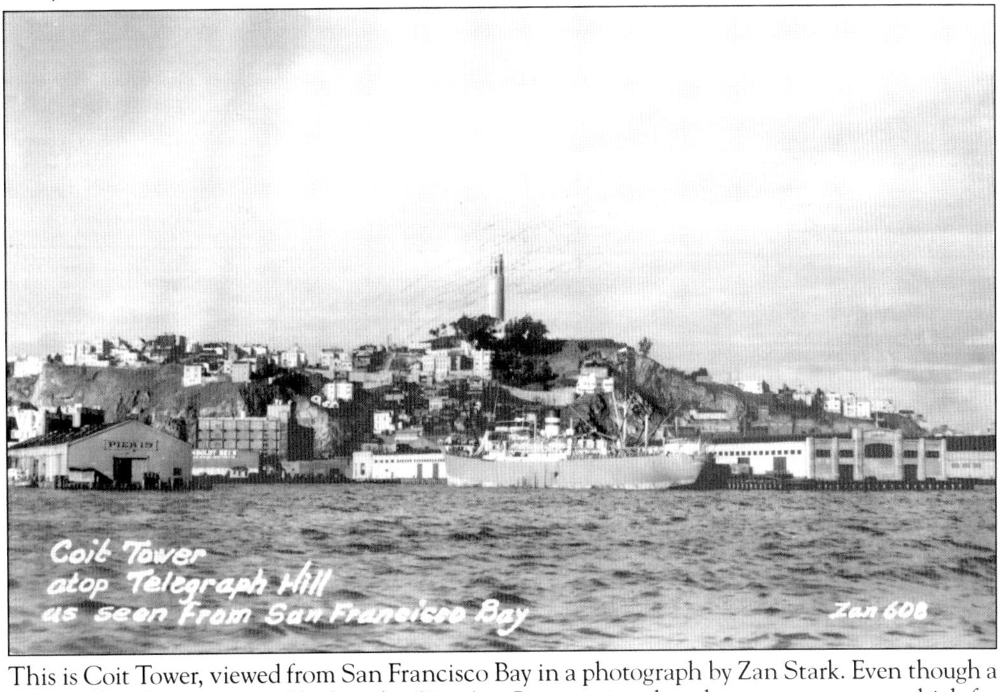

This is Coit Tower, viewed from San Francisco Bay in a photograph by Zan Stark. Even though a group of local artists argued before the City Art Commission that the structure was too high for the 228-foot hill, the board of supervisors voted to rezone Telegraph Hill "so that the skyscrapers of the future would not interfere with the view or detract from the beauty of Coit Memorial."

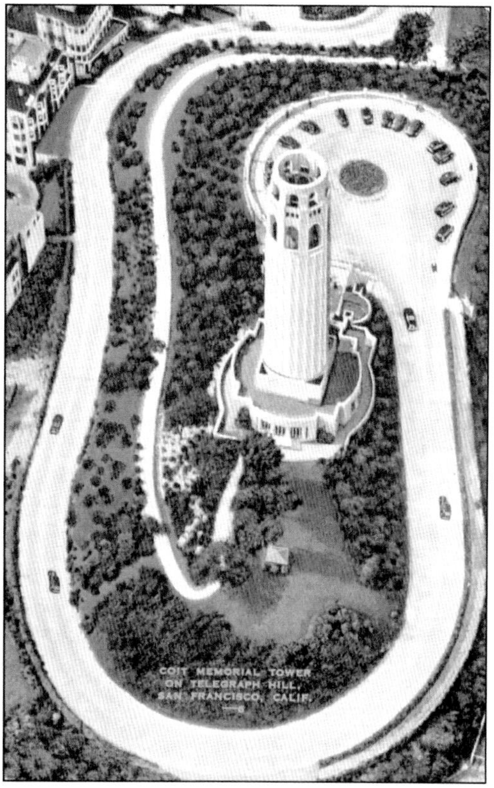

Coit Tower and Pioneer Park can be seen in this spectacular aerial of the crest of Telegraph Hill. The concrete tower, a memorial to the city's firemen, was designed by Henry Howard, an architect in the office of Arthur Brown Jr. It was not intended to look like a fire-hose nozzle. Howard's single, free-standing column was selected because it best fit on the small site and complimented the proportions of the hill.

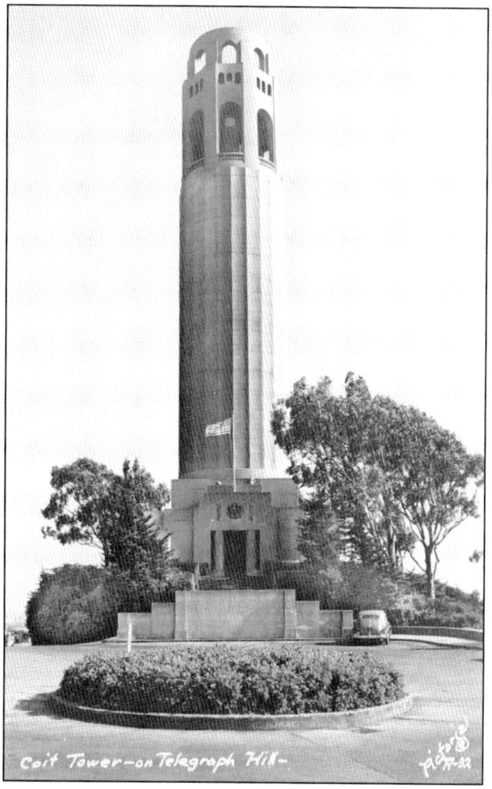

It was originally intended that the 20-foot-high base of Coit Tower would provide space for a restaurant. The observation gallery provides magnificent views of the Bay Area. To avoid looking top-heavy, there are three arched loggias in varying sizes, and it is narrower by 18 inches at the top. The exterior design consists only of rounded vertical parallel grooves and a bas-relief plaque by Robert B. Howard of a phoenix rising, flanked on either side by fasces, the ancient Roman symbol of authority.

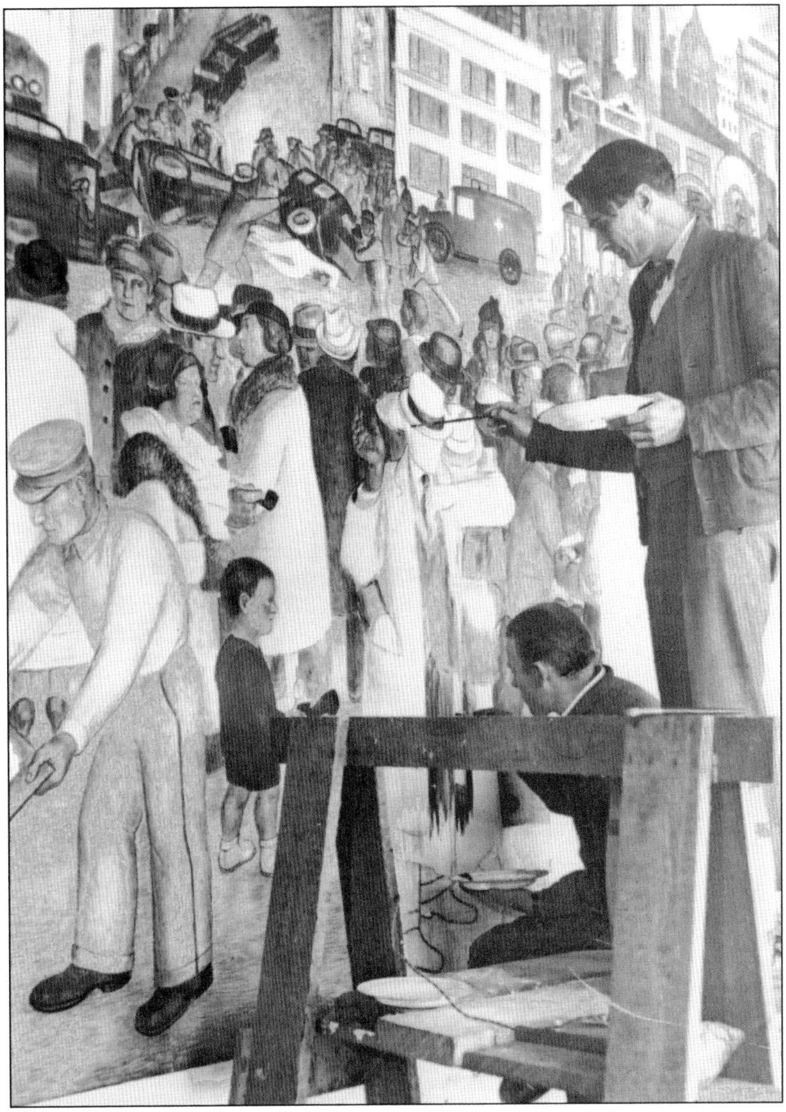

Victor Arnautoff (standing) and his assistant, Tom Hayes, are at work on a Coit Tower fresco. Dr. Walter Heil of the Legion of Honor Museum had the idea to have the tower's interior decorated with murals. The murals were one of the first federally funded Public Works of Arts Projects (PWAP), established to employ professional artists. In 1934, for six months, 25 master artists and 19 assistants painted 3,691 feet of wall space on the first floor, stairwell, and second floor. The work of the great Mexican muralist Diego Rivera influenced the technique and the content of many of the artists' work. Arnautoff was the project director and had previously worked with Rivera. Twenty-one artists utilized the fresco technique of applying dry paint directly on a thin coat of fresh plaster. Besides Arnautoff, the artists working with fresco were Maxine Alba, Raymond Bertrand, Ray Boynton, Ralph Chesse, Ben Cunningham, Mallette Dean, Parker Hall, Edith Hamlin, George Harris, William Hesthal, John Langley Howard, Lucien Labaudt, George Langdon, Frederick Olmstead, Suzanne Scheuer, Ralph Stackpole, Edward Takeo Terada, Frede Vidar, Clifford Wright, and Bernard Zakheim. Three artists, Rinaldo Cuneo, Jose Moya del Pino, and Otis Oldfield, did oil paintings for their Bay Area scenes, and Jane Berlandini used egg tempera. (Courtesy San Francisco History Center, San Francisco Public Library.)

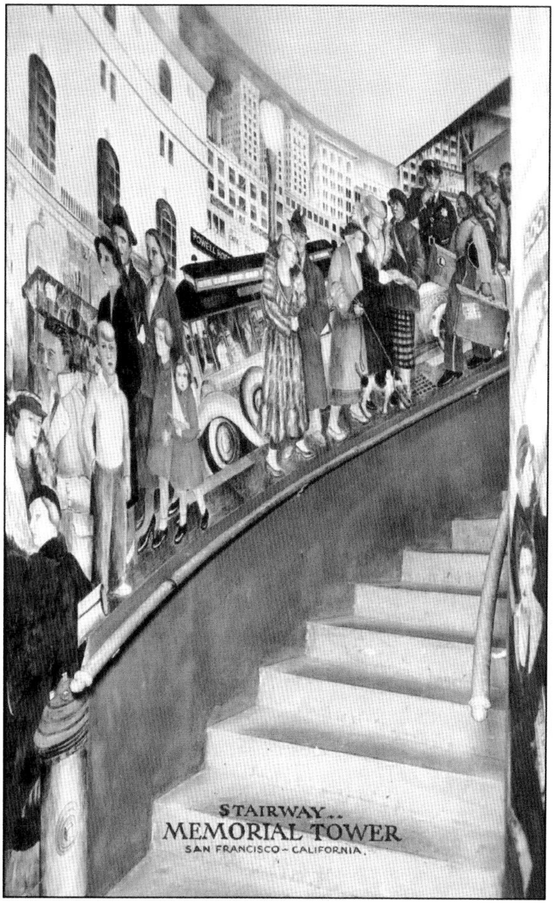

The stairway walls ascending to the second floor features Lucien Labaudt's mural of daily life on Powell Street. First Lady Eleanor Roosevelt, an early advocate of federal funding for the arts, appears near the bottom of the stairs. The faces of Coit Tower artists and some family members can be seen among the bystanders. The Labaudt mural and those on the second floor are more benign and apolitical then the works on the first floor.

The south corridor shows Arnautoff's 10- by 36-foot panoramic street scene. Next to the window is Malette Dean's 10-foot portrait of a stock broker. To the center rear is Frede Vidar's department store with its lunch counter of cheerless patrons and employees. The official opening of the gallery was delayed four months until October 1934, when artist Clifford Wright included a Communist hammer and sickle in his painting. No other murals were censored or repainted for political content.

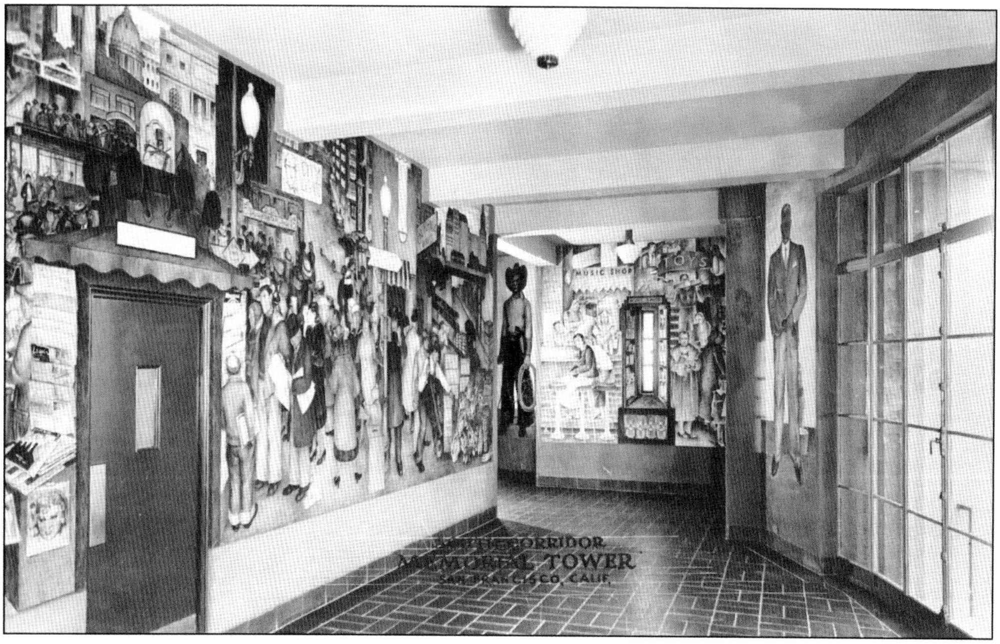

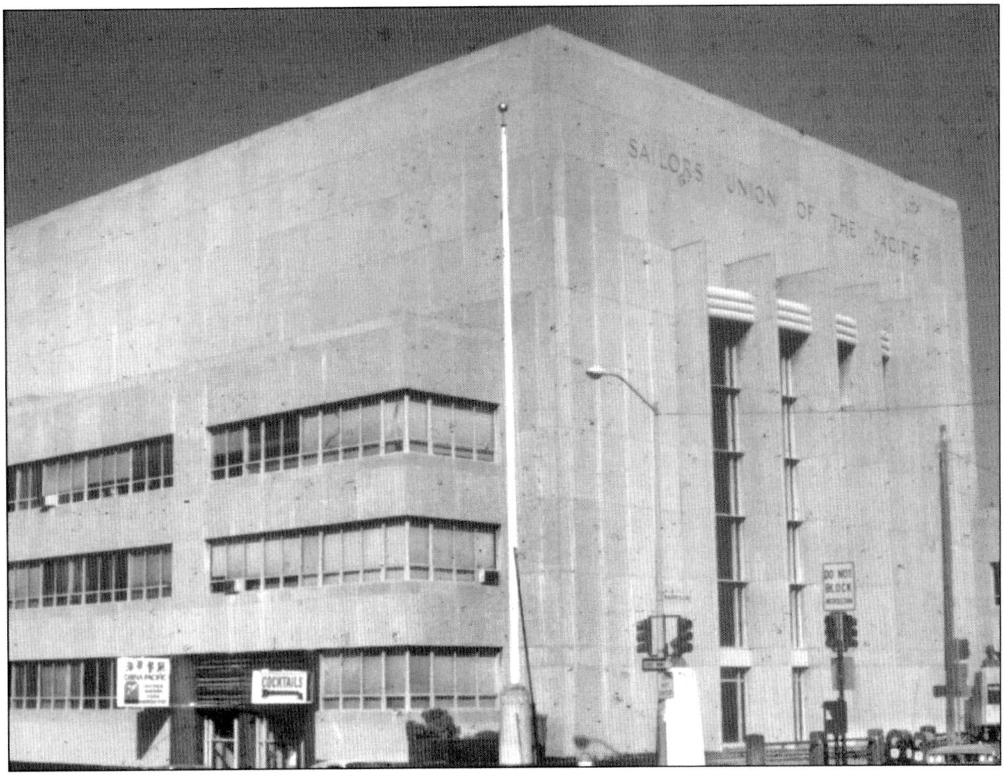

William Gladstone Merchant, who designed the Sailors Union of the Pacific Building at 450 Harrison Street, used the basic blueprint that he developed for his building at the Golden Gate International Exhibition on Treasure Island in 1939–1940. The central two-story entry section is flanked by lower side elements with three rows of ribbon windows that act as speed lines. The corner elevation shows all the design elements that the style took in the 1930s, but it was not constructed until 1950. It is a skillful, if late, example of streamlining.

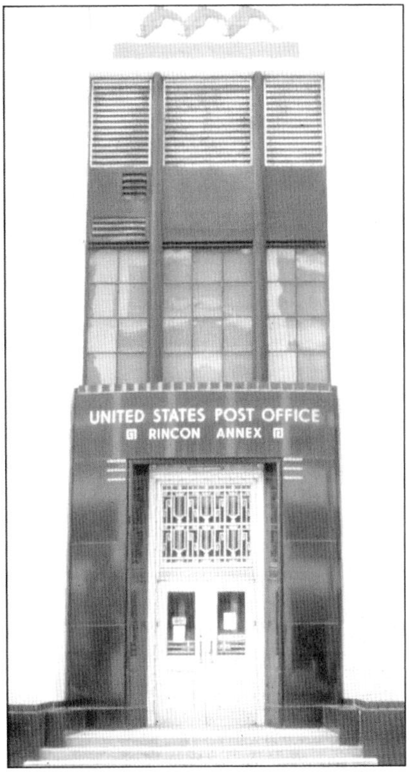

The Rincon Annex post office at 99 Mission Street is an excellent example of the streamlined phase of the style. Gilbert Stanley Underwood designed the building, which was constructed in 1940. The interior murals by Anton Refriger were completed in the early 1950s. Many of these kinds of public buildings were designed and completed under the public works construction programs started by Franklin D. Roosevelt to provide work for unemployed architects and construction workers.

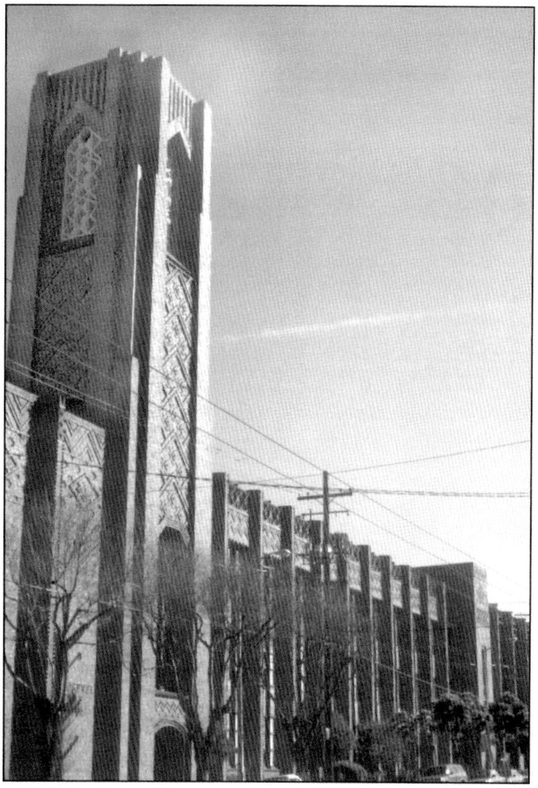

Timothy Pflueger designed the Roosevelt Middle School at 460 Arguello Avenue, built in 1928, to reflect the influence of European expressionism. He carried this out in the use of decorative brickwork set in a raised diaper (diamond-shaped) pattern and zigzags at the cornice. The bricks, in various reddish colors, are set at an angle at the pier ends, giving them prominence. The terra cotta trim is colored in harmony with the brick, and the angular design in the openings complements the brickwork. All of these designs, colors, and details can be traced to the work of expressionist architects in Germany and Holland.

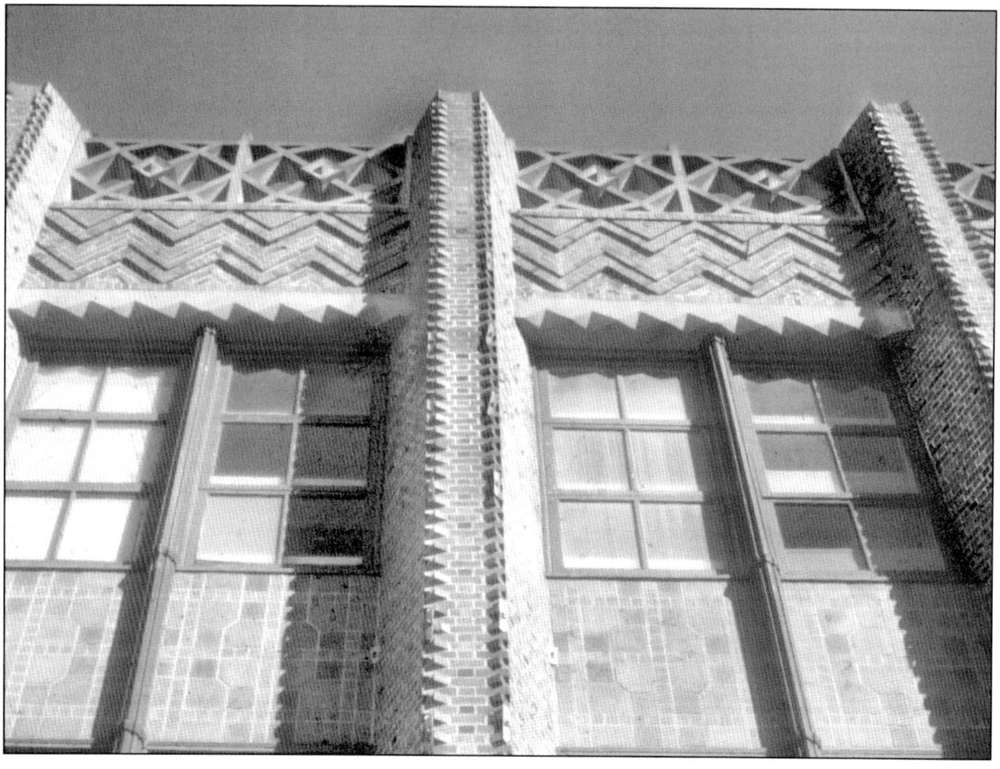

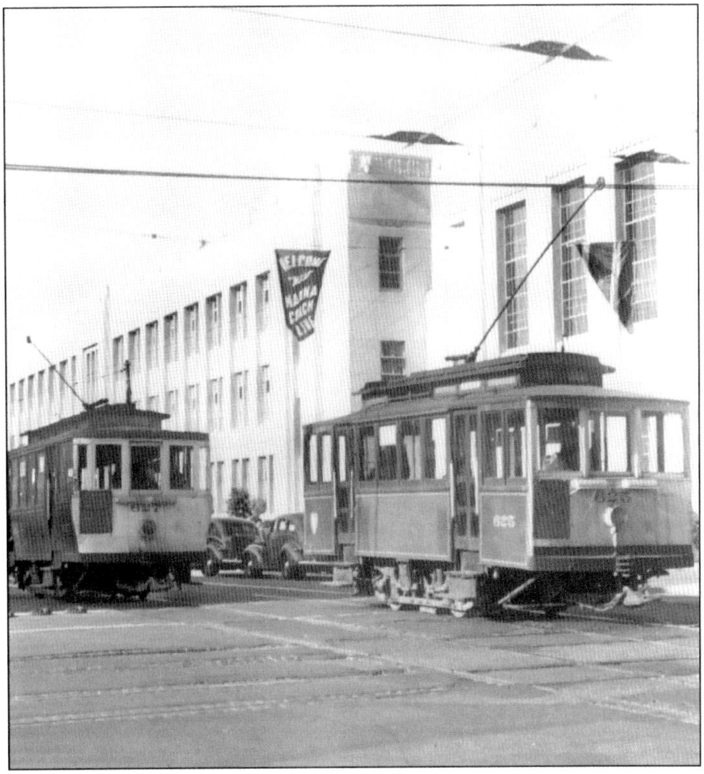

George Kelham and Will P. Day were the architects for the Marina Middle School at 3500 Fillmore Street. It was built in 1936 and shows the more streamlined look of the 1930s. Here the forms are stylizations of classical elements derived from the architecture of Greece and Rome. Maybe it should be called "Greco Deco." The auditorium wing has bronze transom grilles over the entries. The rest of the building has recessed, fluted pilasters and medallions of lions, rams, bears, and classical maidens. Cable car service ended in 1941 (Courtesy San Francisco History Center, San Francisco Public Library.)

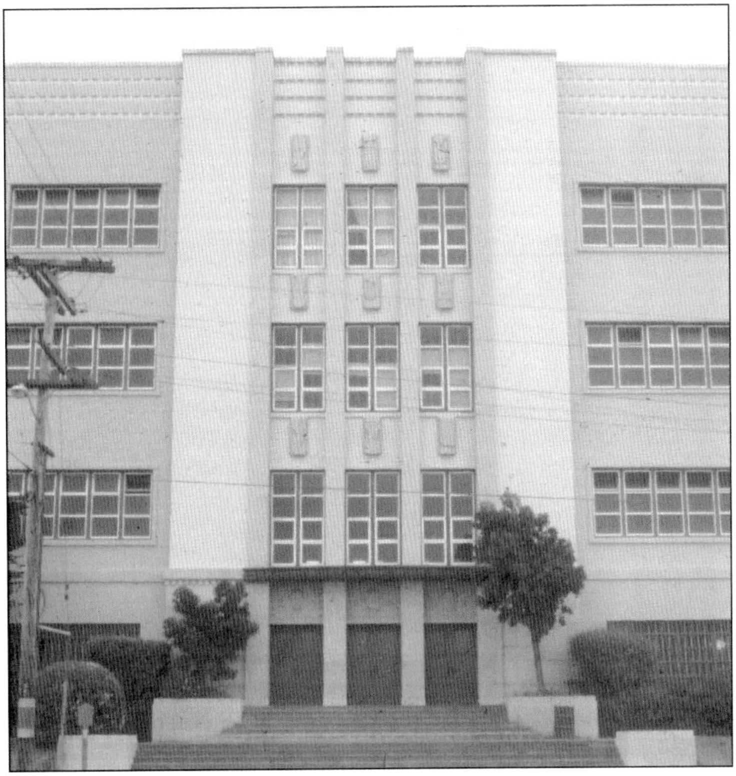

The George Washington High School, built in 1930 at 600 Thirty-second Avenue, shows that architect Timothy Pflueger was moving away from the highly decorative elements of his earlier Telephone Company Building. Here he uses a symmetrical central element, only minimally embellished with fluted speed lines and simple plaques. The triple-entry doors are surmounted by bas-reliefs of Washington, Lincoln, and Thomas Edison. Edison represented the epitome of modernism because of his inventions.

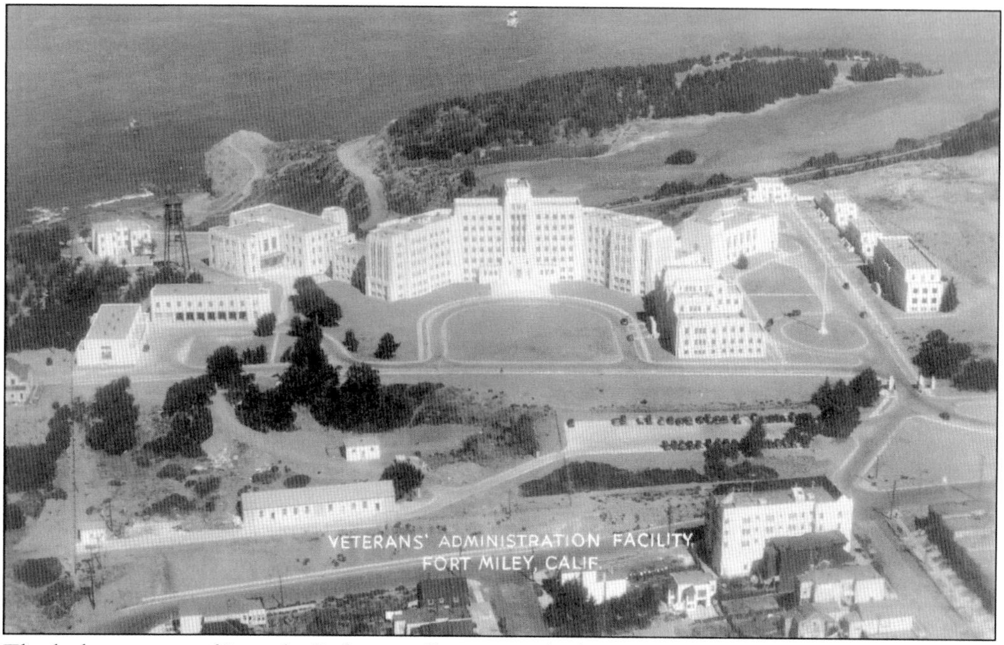

The lush greenery of Lincoln Park partially surrounds the Fort Miley Veterans Administration facility. In the 1890s, the site was taken over by the U.S. Army as part of its coastal defenses of the Golden Gate. In 1932, the Veterans Administration acquired 25 acres for construction of a medical center.

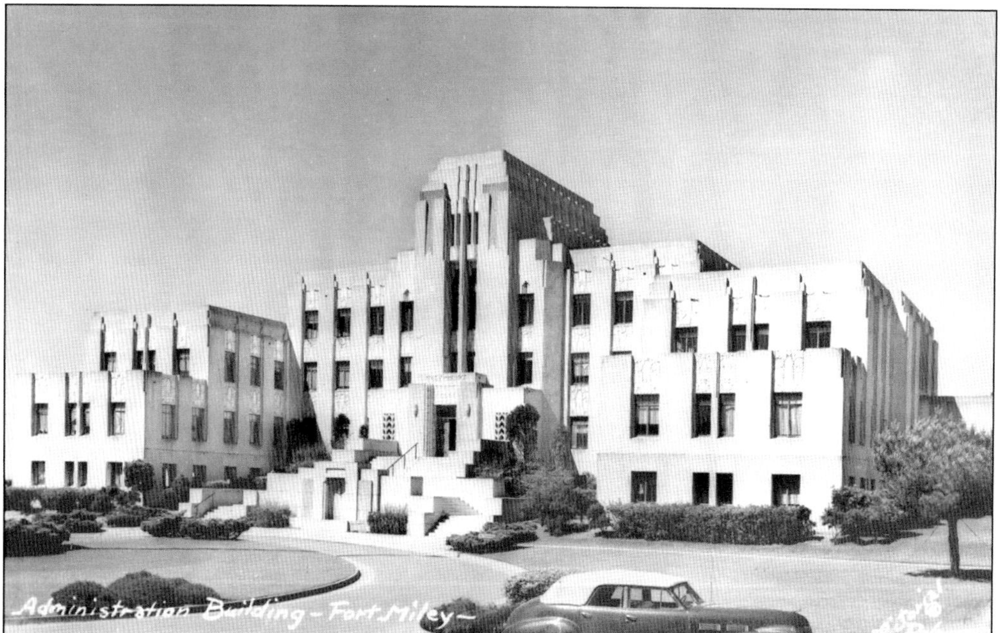

The Fort Miley facility had 21 buildings erected at a cost of $1,250,000 with a staff of 25 doctors. The Administration Building was molded in a pseudo-Mayan style reminiscent of the Yucatan pyramids. After Pearl Harbor, the U.S. Army reoccupied Fort Miley until the conclusion of the war.

The hospital buildings were designed by the Veteran Administration Construction Company and constructed in 1934. The central building has the classic elements that characterized high-rise structures throughout the city, with an emphasis on the vertical, decorative terra cotta panels in the window spandrels. Unfortunately, these panels have been painted so that the delicate coloration is lost.

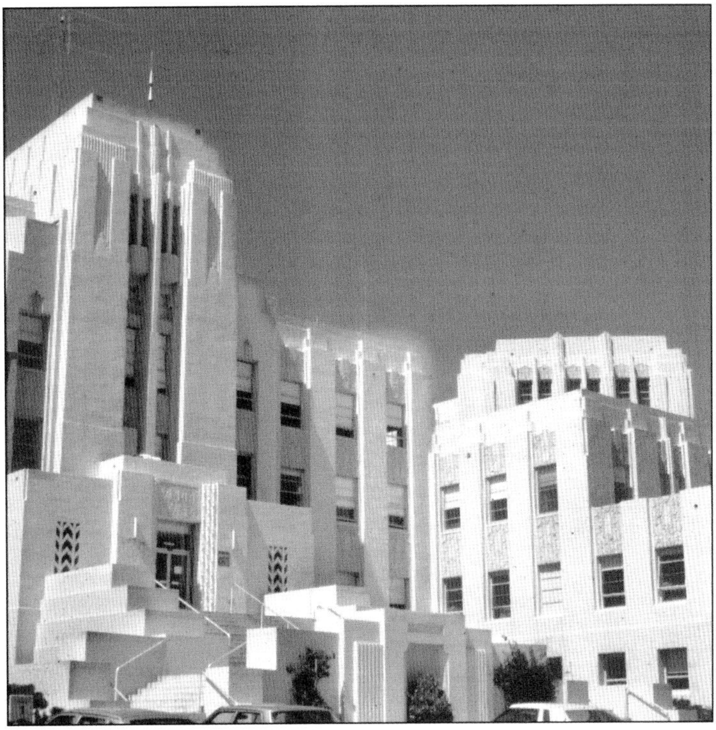

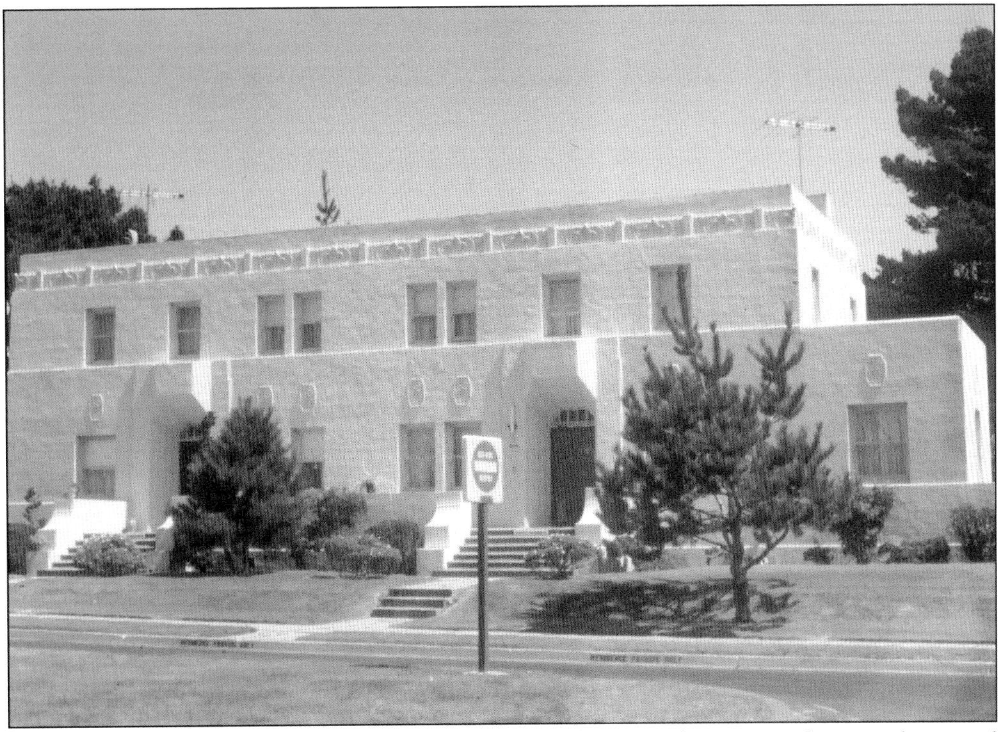

The other, smaller buildings in the complex carry out this same decorative scheme with stepped profiles, octagonal plaques over the windows, large hoods over the entry doors, and floral moldings at the cornice line.

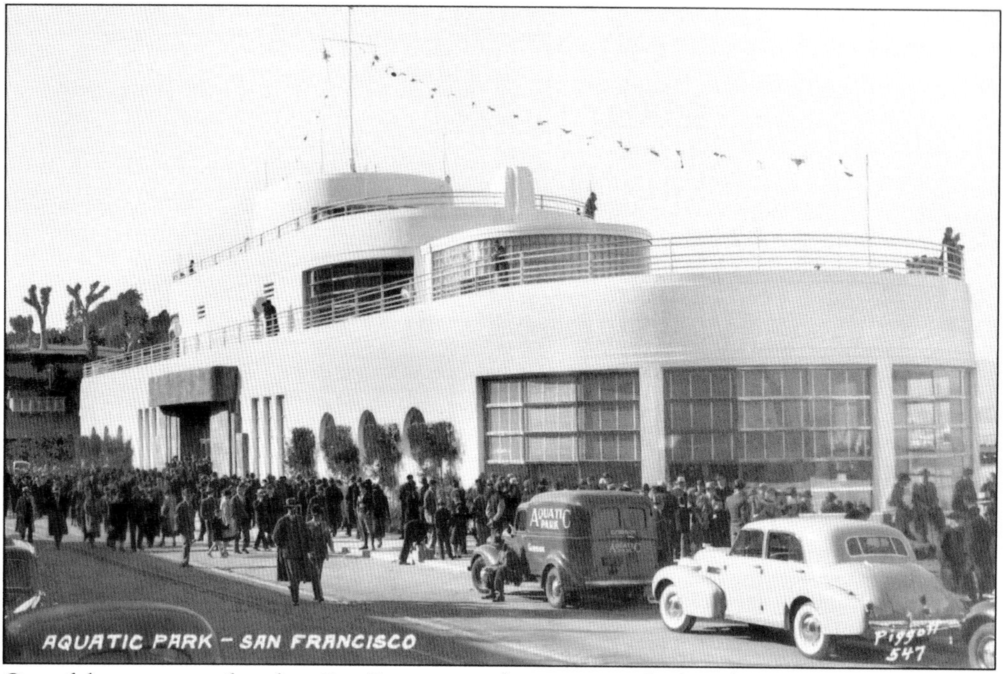

One of the treasures of modern San Francisco architecture can be found at the foot of Polk Street. Architect William Mooser III's nautical-looking structure was constructed as a Works Progress Administration (WPA) project in the late 1930s. Originally planned as a combination casino and bathhouse, the building has large wraparound windows on each end and splendid views of the Aquatic Park lagoon. Sargent Johnson handsomely decorated the main entrance with incised gray-green slate panels.

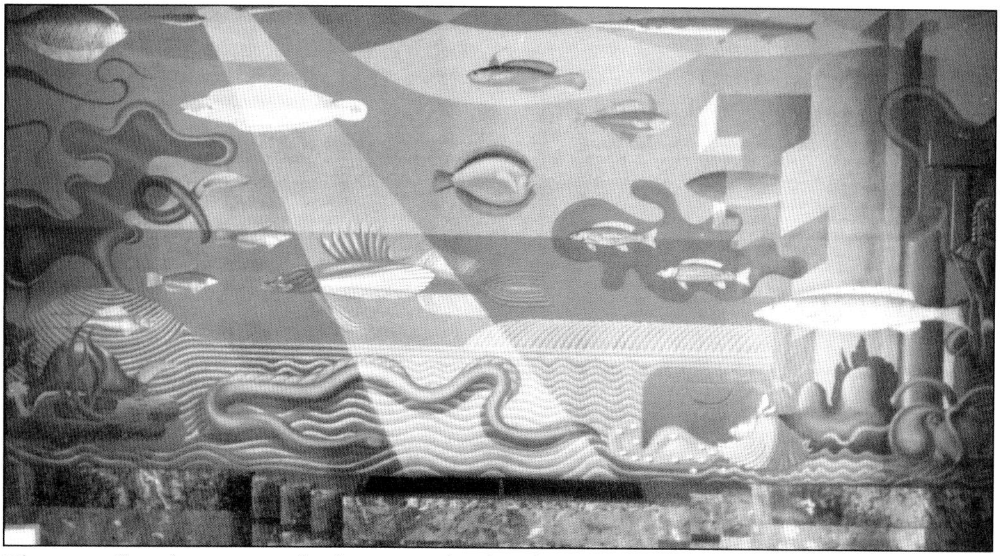

The main floor has spectacular large murals of undersea life created by Hilaire Hiler that were almost left unfinished when he threatened to leave unless plans were abandoned to install furniture not in keeping with his modern underwater scenes. On the outside gallery were sculptures by Beniamino Bufano of a toad, a penguin, and a seal. The artwork of the Aquatic Park Casino was considered by many to be one of the stellar achievements of the WPA program nationally.

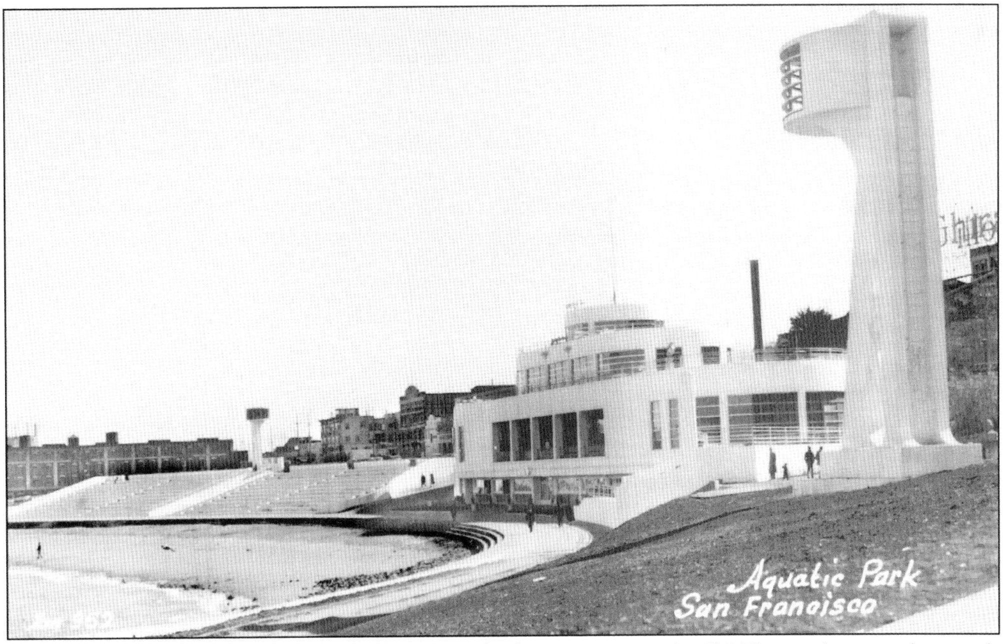

This modern ship-like structure was to provide dressing rooms for 5,000 people, complete with showers that were activated by electric eyes. A refreshment counter was also located downstairs. The building was flanked by two tall loudspeaker towers and a grandstand for viewing Aquatic Park events. The white beach sand brought from Monterrey washed away and was replaced by sand excavated for the Union Square Garage. The Belt Line Railroad continued to run along track between the beach and the building.

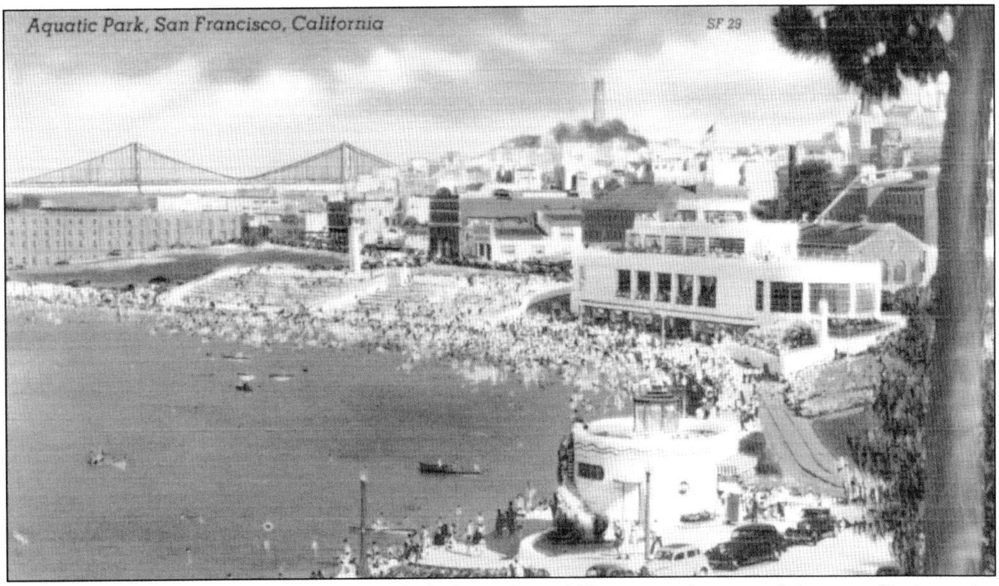

A drawing of the Bay Bridge was included on this 1939 postcard view of Aquatic Park at the height of its popularity. Architect William Mooser III designed the multipurpose round building in the foreground to house a food stand, restrooms, and a lifeguard station. During World War II, the U.S. Army took over Aquatic Park, and the area was off-limits to civilians. In 1951, the former casino-bathhouse became the site of the National Maritime Museum.

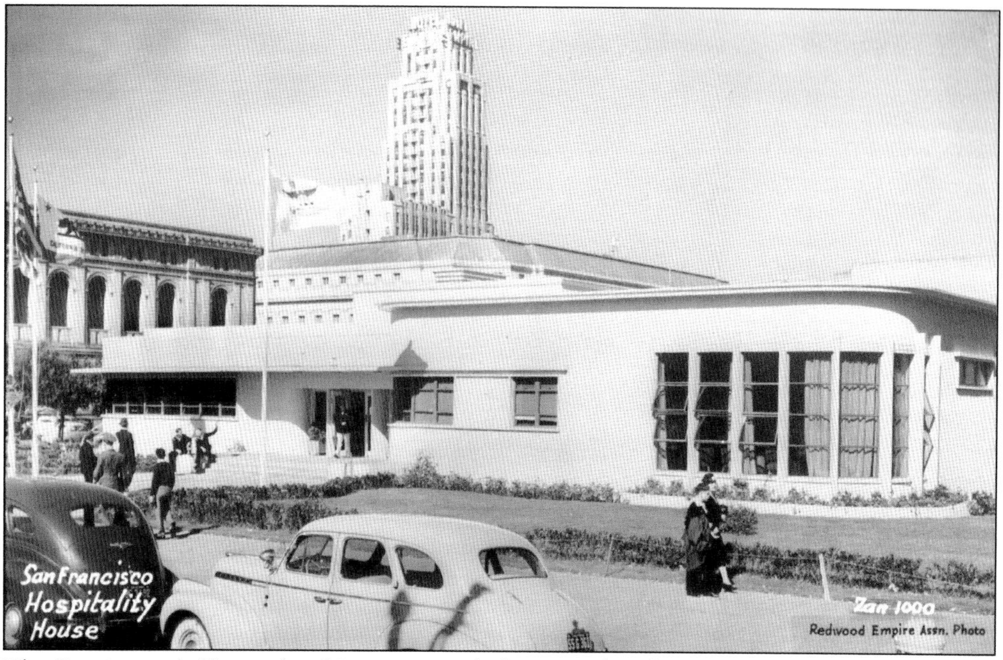

The Servicemen's Hospitality House was a sleek, streamlined-moderne, single-story structure with curving windows at 200 Larkin Street. Built in 1940, the Hospitality House was one of the last New Deal projects paid for with WPA funds. Labor-union volunteers from the local Building Trades Council, who wanted to show military personnel that San Franciscans really cared about them, constructed the building.

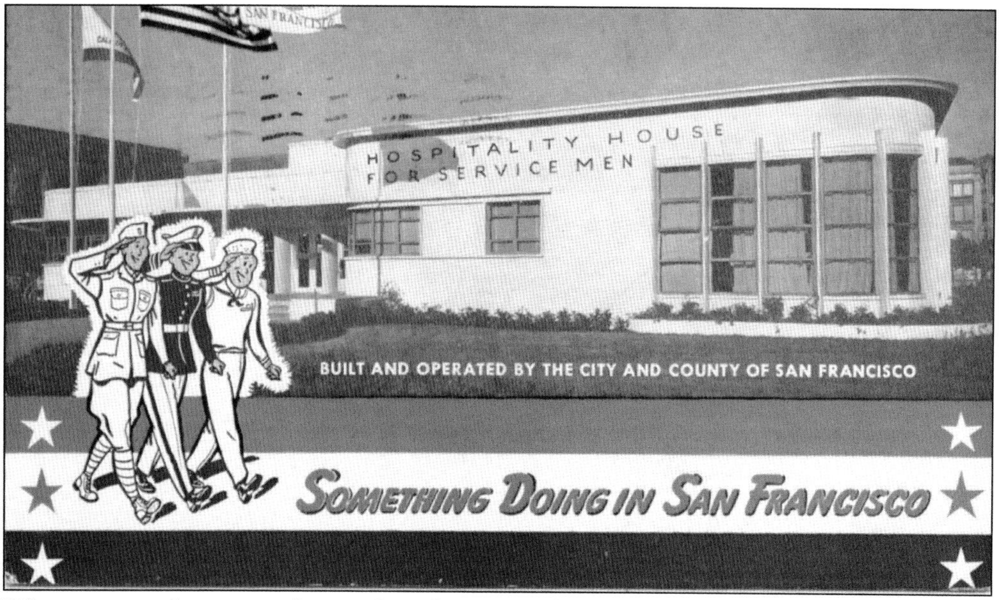

"This is a nice place to visit" wrote Pvt. Otto Paggoda in 1942. San Franciscans made sure off-duty soldiers, sailors, and marines had plenty of recreational activities at the Hospitality House. During World War II, young Bay Area females volunteered as hostesses for the nightly dances with a live band. There were plenty of free soft drinks, coffee, and snacks. Hollywood celebrities often stopped by to dance or just to chat.

Eight

MARVELS OF ENGINEERING

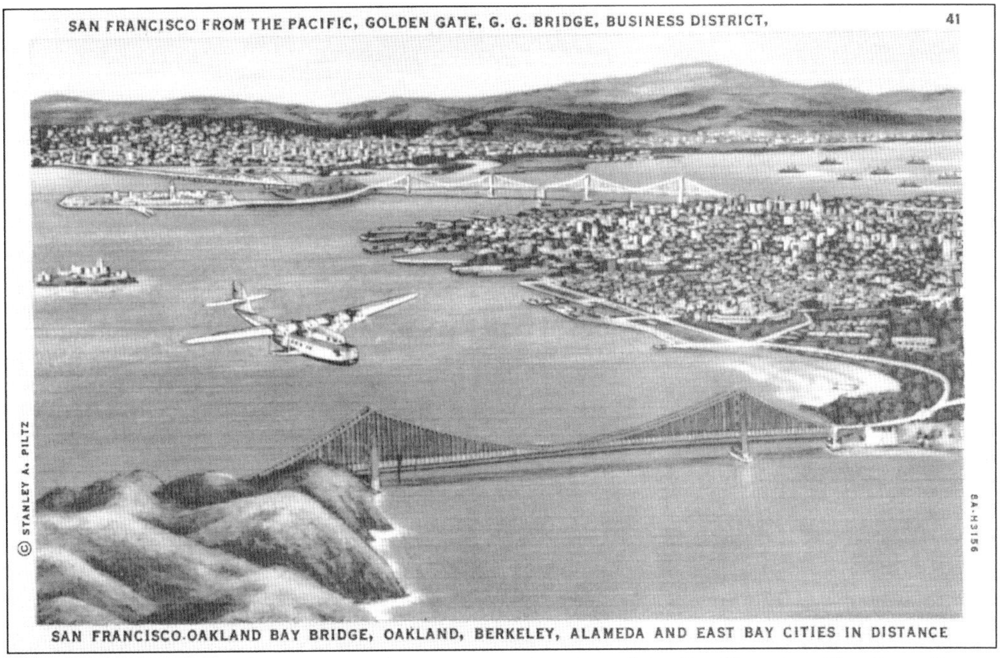

An anonymous postcard artist painted this spectacular view of the San Francisco Bay Area. Drawn about 1940, in his illustration the artist included battleships, Treasure Island, a China Clipper, and, most importantly, two new engineering marvels, the Golden Gate Bridge connecting the Marin and Northern Counties with San Francisco and the Bay Bridge connecting the City with Oakland, Berkeley, and other East Bay towns.

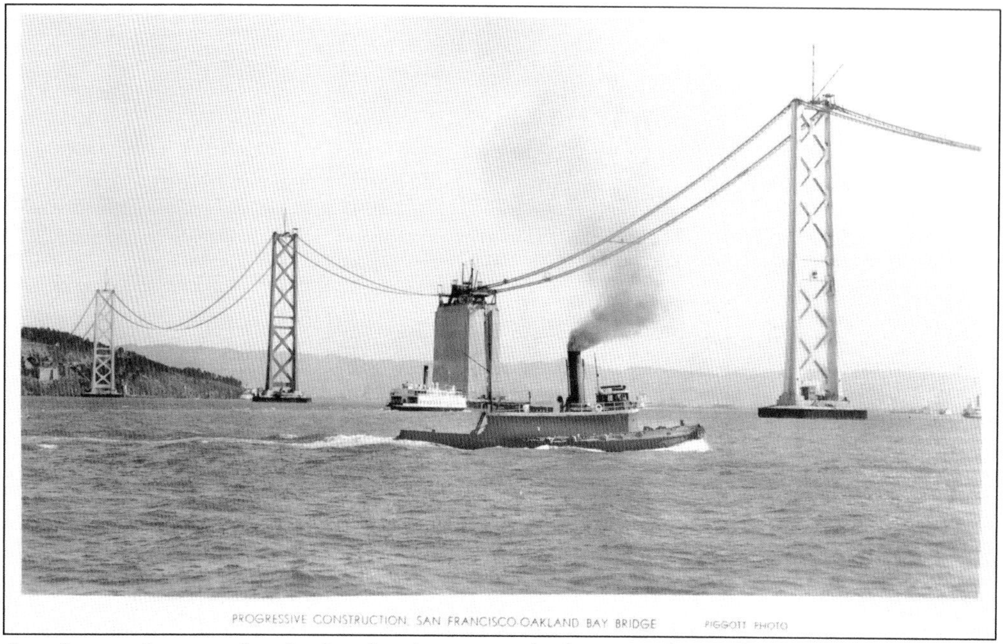

A tugboat and soon-to-be-obsolete ferryboat cross the bay near the newly constructed towers for the San Francisco–Oakland Bay Bridge. At $77 million, the new structure would become the costliest civil engineering project in the world.

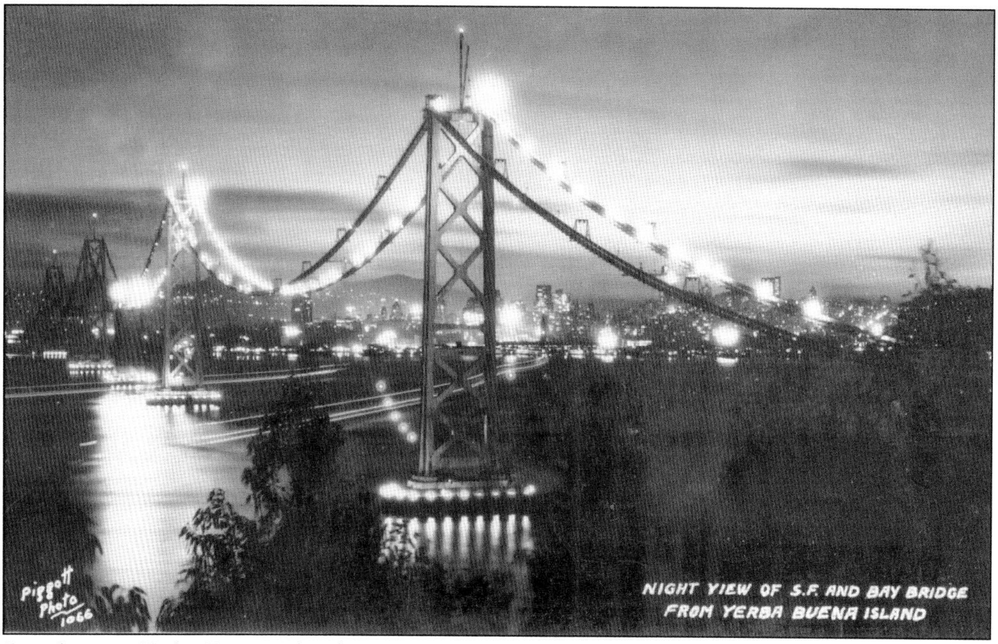

Standing on Yerba Buena Island, J. K. Piggott took a nighttime photograph of the unfinished suspension section of the Bay Bridge. Sodium lamps have already been attached to the cables and anchorages to provide an element of safety for passing ships and aircraft.

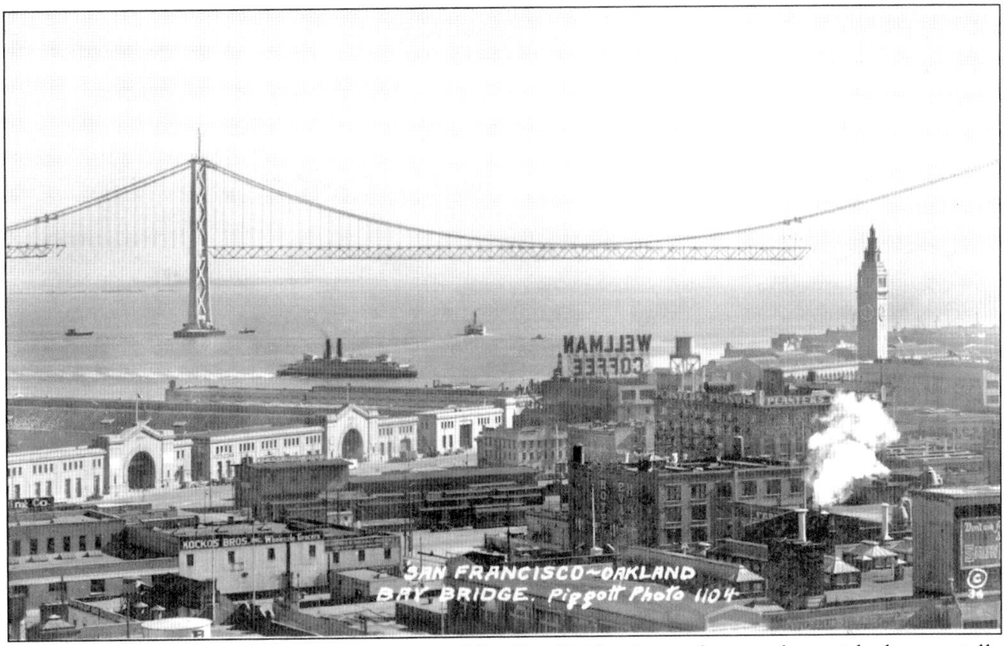

The final shape of the suspension portion of the Bay Bridge is nearly complete with the partially finished lower deck. The length of the suspension portion of the bridge was 10,450 feet, and the total length of the entire bridge structure came to 22,720 feet (8.25 miles).

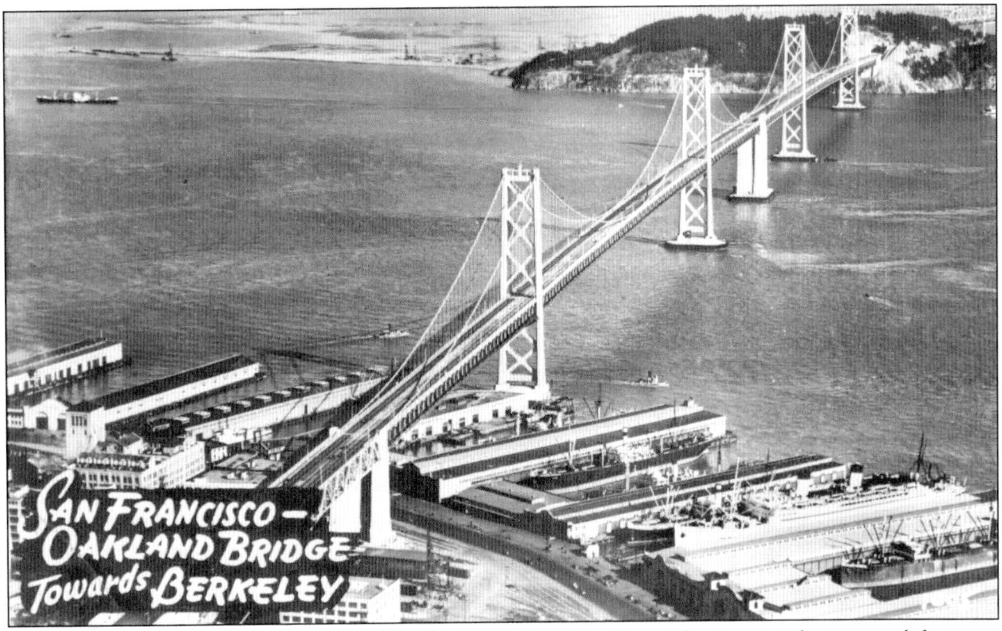

The completed Bay Bridge stands tall with towers 526 feet above the water. The original designer was engineer Ralph Modjeski. Governor Rolph appointed consulting architects Timothy Pflueger, Arthur Brown Jr., and John Donovan to assist engineers with the bridge design. It was Pflueger's recommendation to remove any extraneous design elements, utilizing only a stripped-away, well-proportioned steel design coated in silver-gray paint.

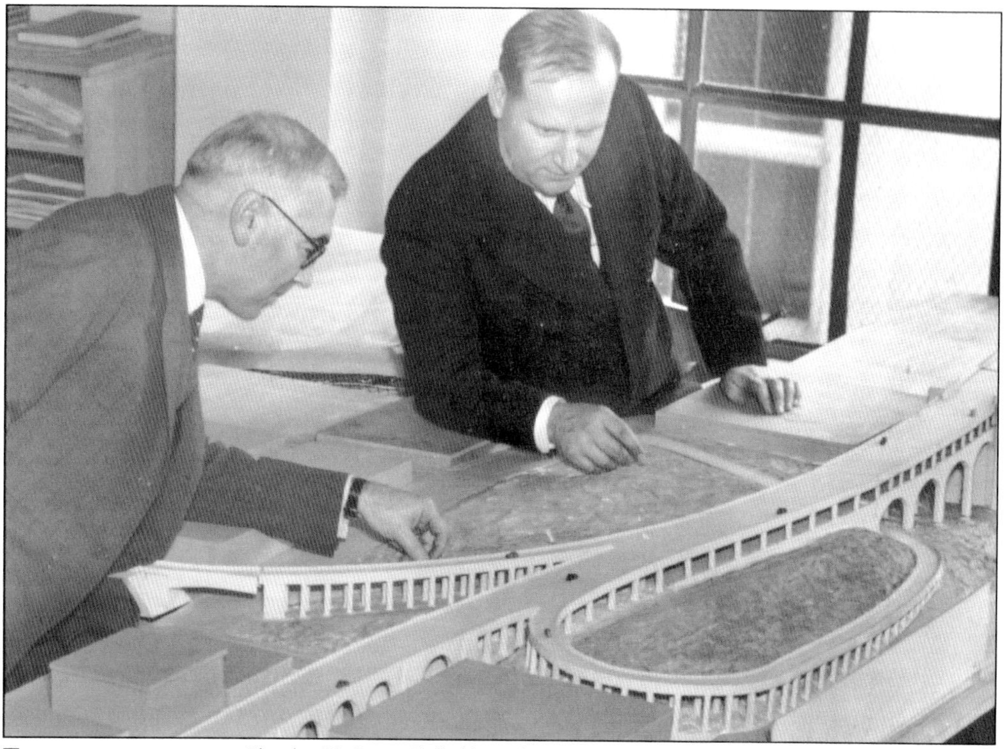

Two geniuses, engineer Charles H. Purcell (left) and architect Timothy L. Pflueger, look at a model of San Francisco approaches to the Bay Bridge. Purcell was chief engineer for the state division of highways and, along with consulting engineers Glen B. Woodruff and Charles F. Andrews, was a designer of the bridge and its approaches. (Courtesy San Francisco History Center, San Francisco Public Library.)

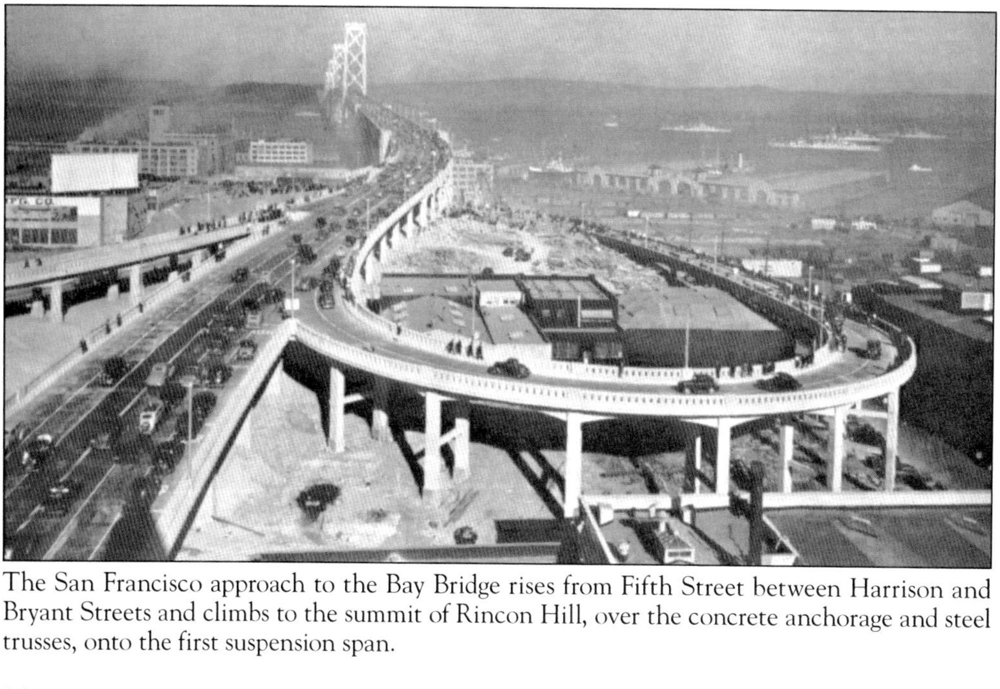

The San Francisco approach to the Bay Bridge rises from Fifth Street between Harrison and Bryant Streets and climbs to the summit of Rincon Hill, over the concrete anchorage and steel trusses, onto the first suspension span.

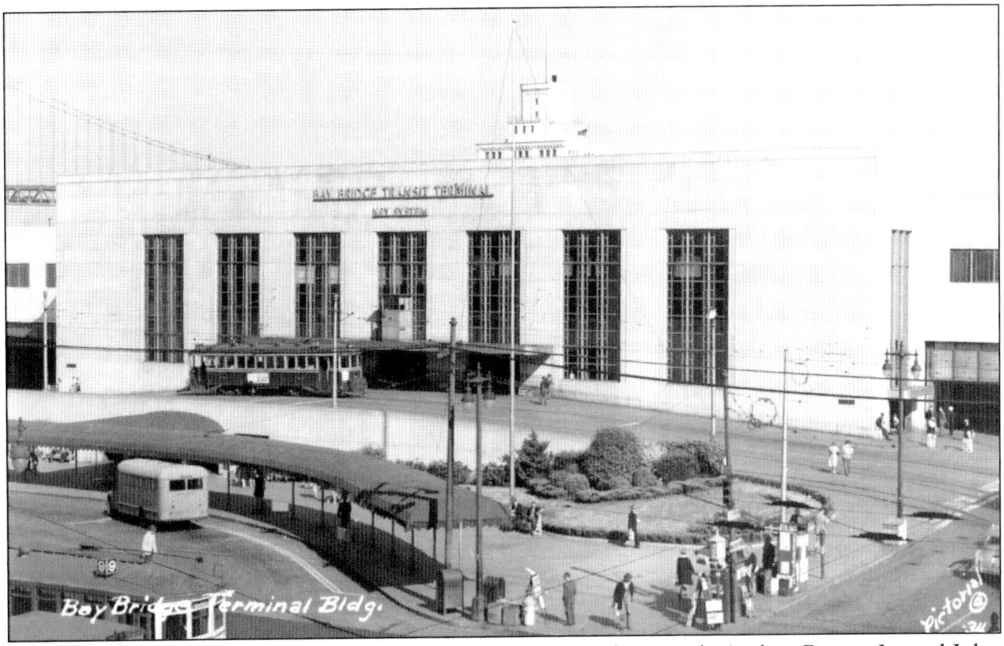

Timothy Pflueger was one of the supervising architects, along with Arthur Brown Jr. and John Donovan, for the terminus of the streetcar lines that arrived from the East Bay as part of the Key Route system. The interior of this 1937 building has a series of skylights that flood the waiting area with luminosity. Ramps allowed the commuter crowds to quickly access the waiting platforms and exit in large masses. The window design on the main elevation is similar to the windows Pflueger used on the Stock Exchange Club Building.

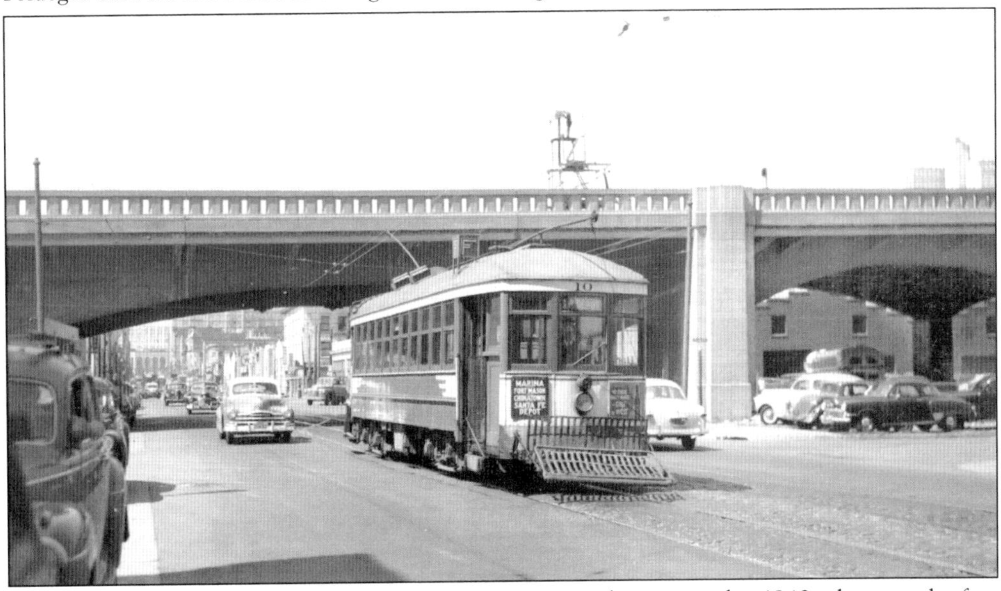

The bridge approach designed by Purcell and Pflueger can be seen in this 1940s photograph of an "F" line streetcar cruising down Fourth Street near Bryant Street. The municipal railway attempted to modernize the look of their trolleys with Art Deco–inspired wings painted on either side in a cream and green color scheme. The original "F" line closed January 1951 and was replaced by the 30 Stockton line buses.

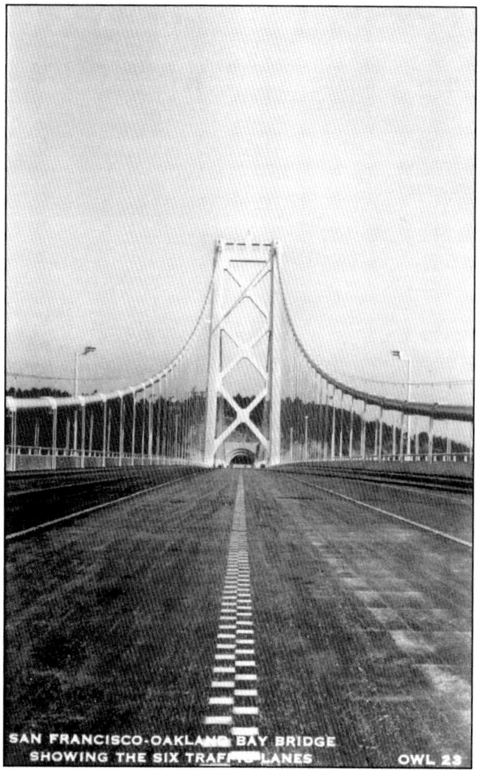

The upper deck of the Bay Bridge, seen near completion, had six traffic lanes with three eastbound and three westbound. The lower deck would have two lanes for trucks and buses and rail lines to be used by the Key System trains, the Sacramento Northern Railway, and the Interurban Electric Railway. In 1958, the train tracks were removed and each deck was reconfigured to one-way vehicular traffic.

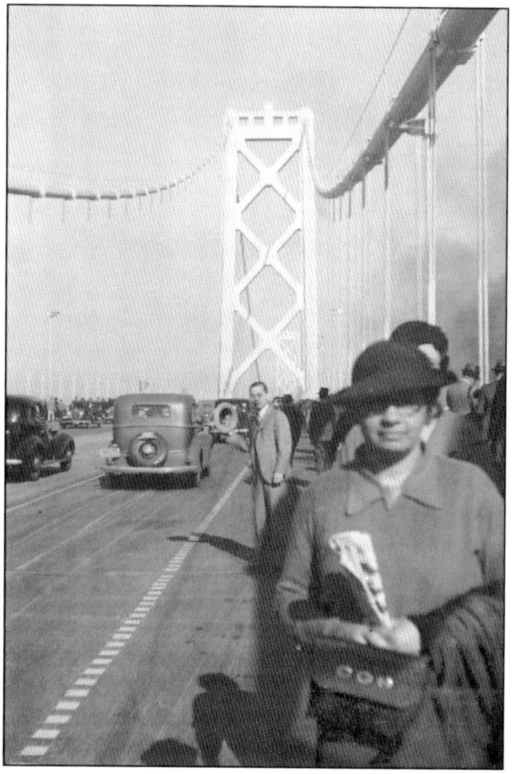

The Bay Bridge officially opened on Thursday, November 12, 1936, at 12:30 p.m. when Pres. Franklin Delano Roosevelt in Washington D.C. pressed a telegraph key opening the toll plaza to automobile traffic. Although they were not allowed, over 5,000 happy pedestrians strolled onto the bridge's upper deck and enjoyed the views as seen in this photograph by Anita Lum.

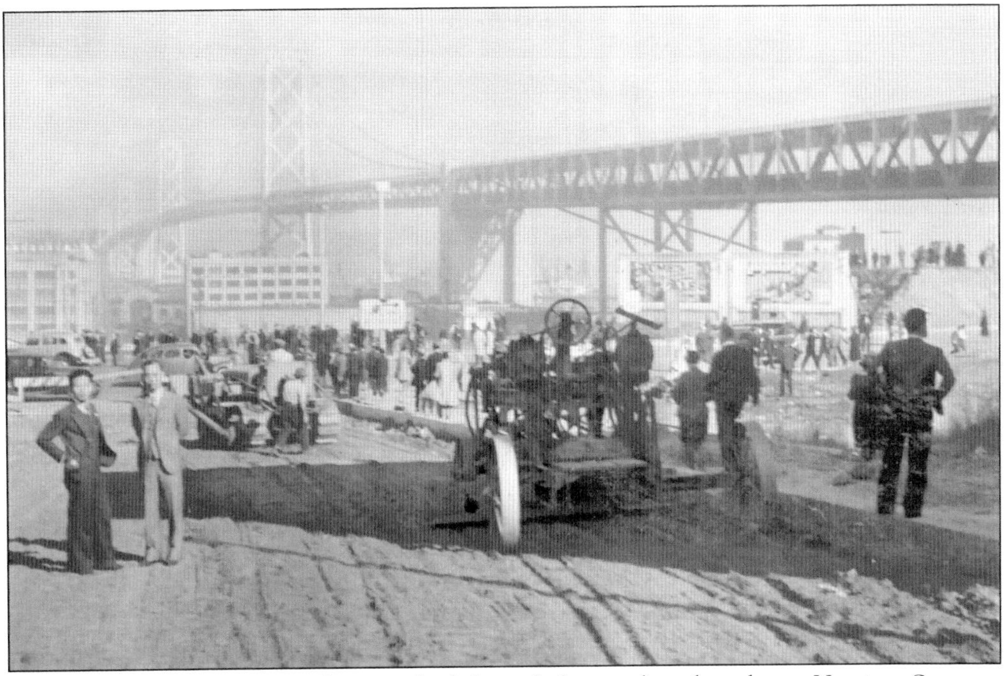

On opening day, Anita Lum photographed the orderly crowds gathered near Harrison Street to admire the Bay Area's newest engineering marvel. The bridge builders would still need several more months to complete laying tracks for the interurban electric trains on the lower deck.

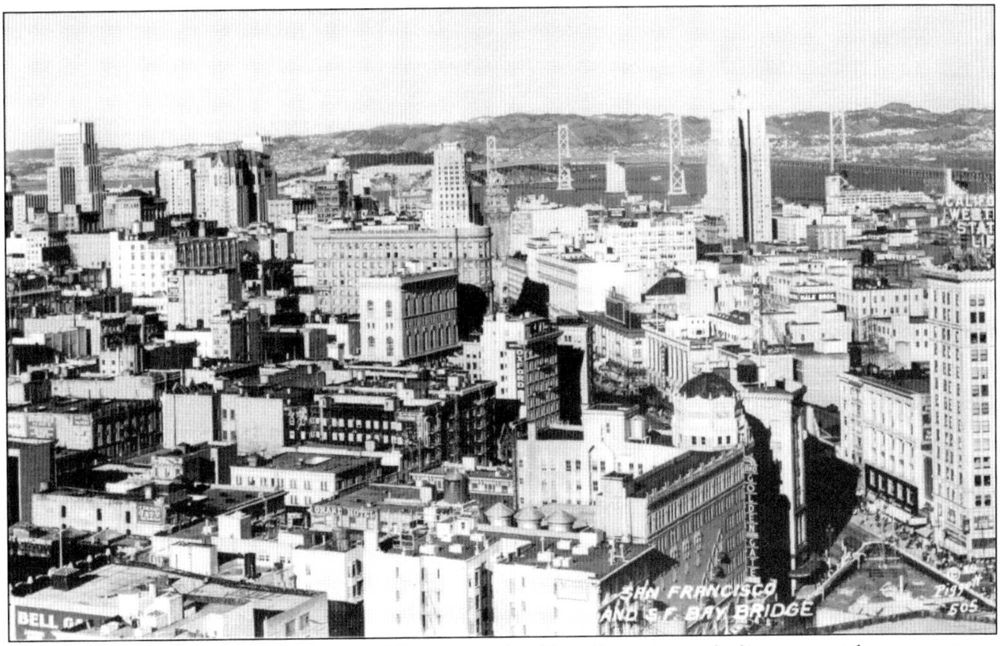

The Bay Bridge was an exciting addition to the San Francisco skyline, providing a unique background for the city's skyscrapers. The bridge would make its first appearance in the movies in 1941's *The Shadow of the Thin Man*, with actor William Powell as detective Nick Charles driving his roadster eastbound across the upper deck to solve a murder case.

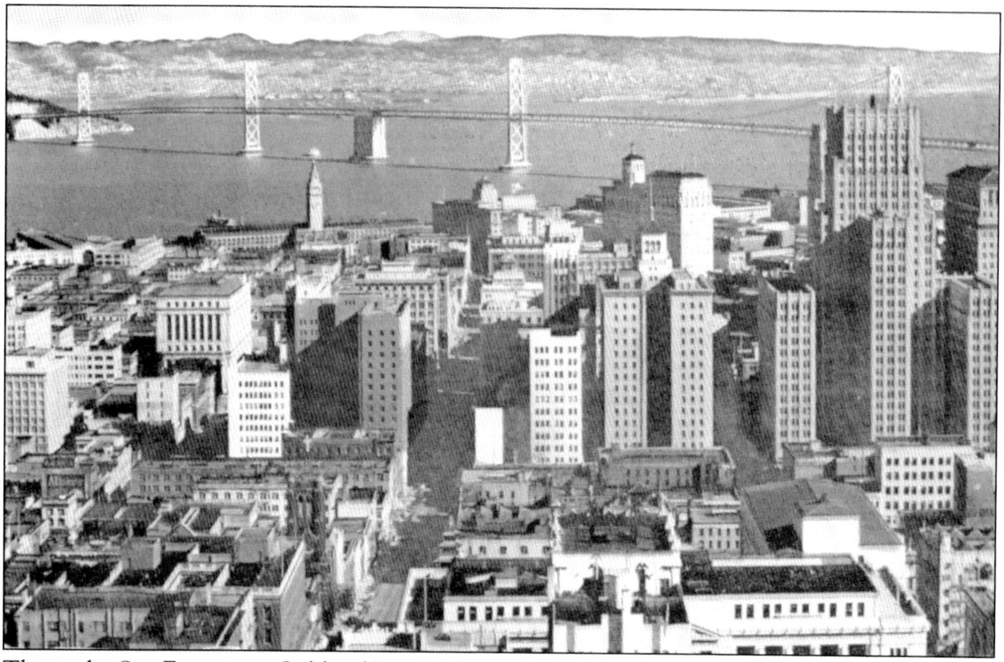

This is the San Francisco–Oakland Bay Bridge with the Russ Building on the right. The bridge's official name is the James Rolph Bridge in honor of the former governor and San Francisco mayor. The name never caught on with the public, who prefer to call the bridge by the names of the two cities it connected or just the Bay Bridge.

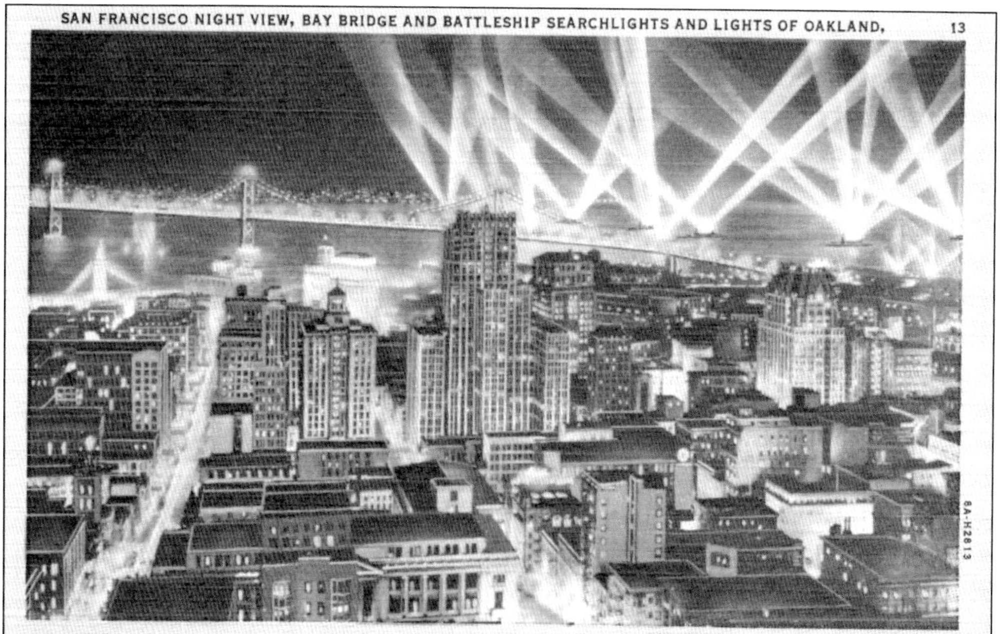

This is a postcard illustration of downtown San Francisco at night with the Bay Bridge illuminated by its sulfur lights and a dazzling display of rotating searchlights located on U.S. Navy ships of the Pacific Fleet. The original photograph of the searchlights on the bay was probably taken for the official 1936 opening of the bridge.

The venerable Hotel Californian superimposed a view of the San Francisco–Oakland Bay Bridge on this vintage postcard. The illustration also included directions to the hotel from the bridge. At the time, the Californian's room rate was $2.50 for a one person and $3.50 for two. A radio and tub and shower bath were included in every room.

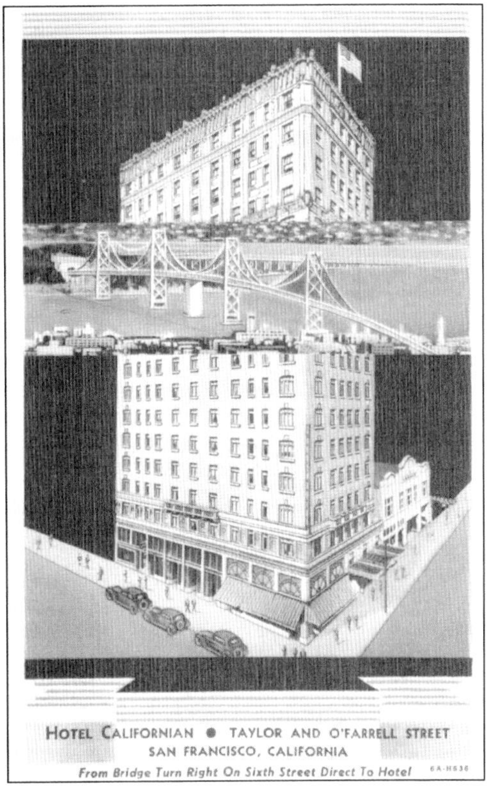

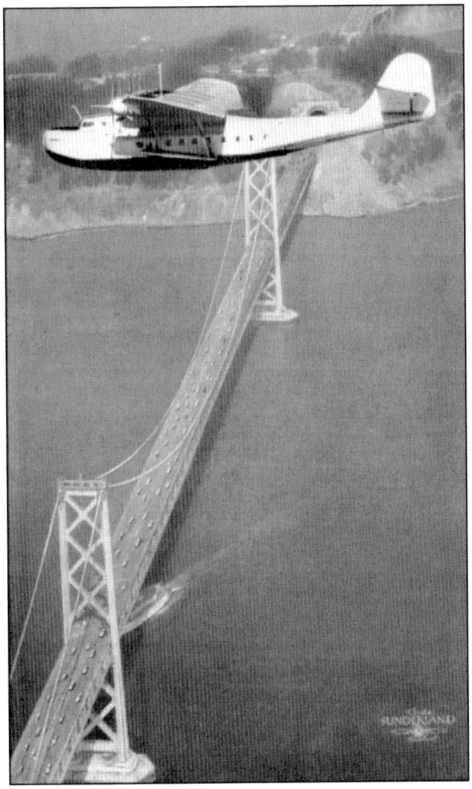

A Pan American Airlines Martin M-130 flies above the Bay Bridge in this image. Every Wednesday afternoon, one of the "China Clippers" headed westward 8,200 miles to Manila by way of Honolulu. Each Tuesday morning another Clipper passed eastward to the seaplane base in Alameda. Clippers were 90-foot-long, 26-ton giants carrying up to 74 passengers plus a flight crew. Service to Asia began in October 1936.

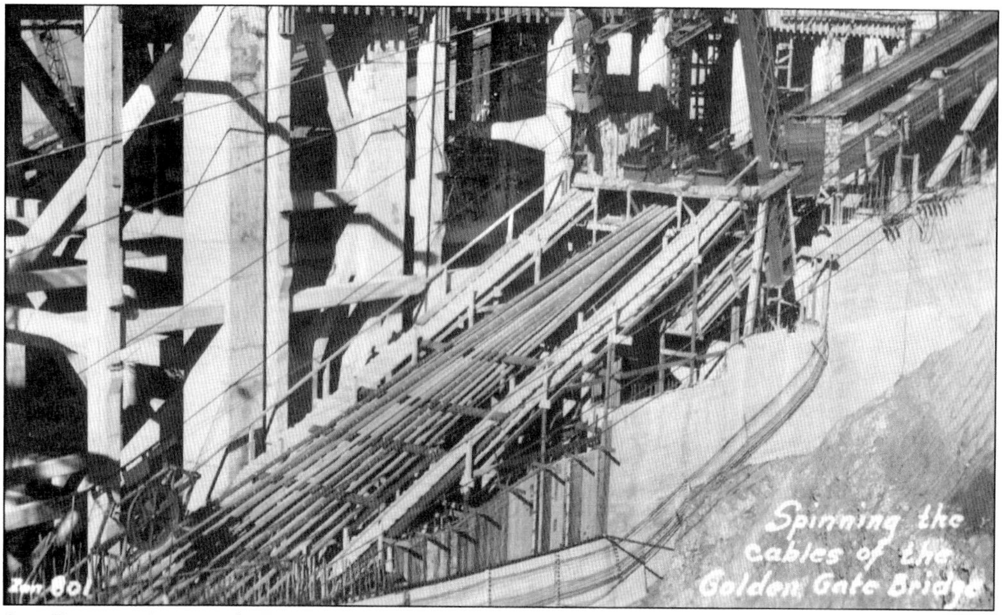

San Francisco's second "Engineering Marvel" would be the 6,450-foot, single-span suspension bridge across the Golden Gate entry into the bay. Construction began on January 5, 1933. For nine months, cable spanning began and ended at each of the anchor blocks, where the 1,600-pound coils of wire were spun across the Golden Gate. Eighty thousand miles of cable were used on the bridge's construction.

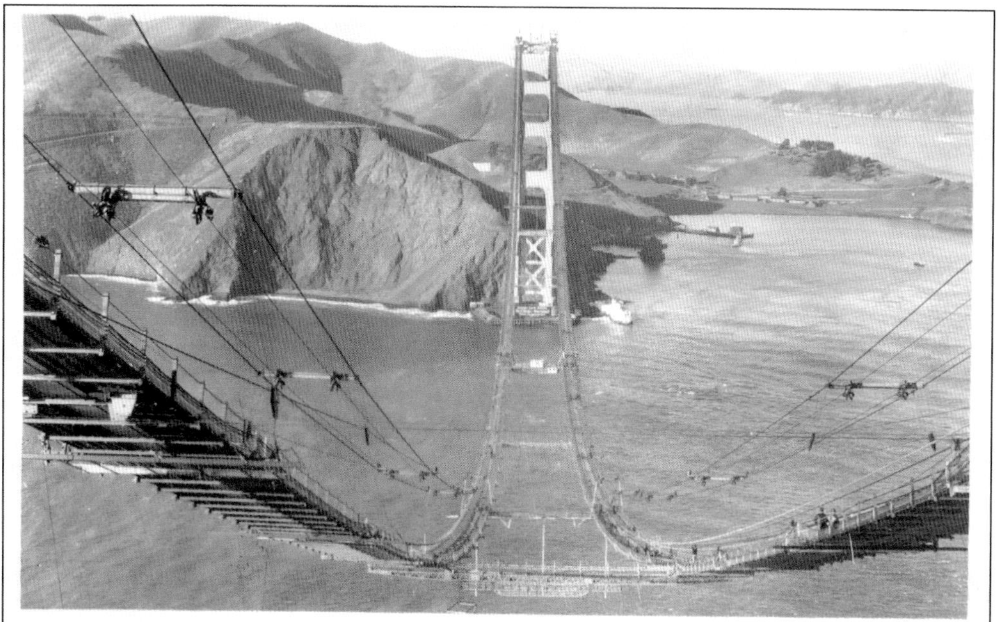

The Golden Gate Bridge under construction can be seen in this J. K. Piggott photograph taken from the south tower. Swift tides are visible beneath the suspension cables. The dangerous currents were a major obstacle for chief engineer Joseph B. Strauss, his principle assistant Clifford E. Paine, and resident construction engineer Russell B. Cone. When completed, the bridge towers reached a height of 746 feet above the water.

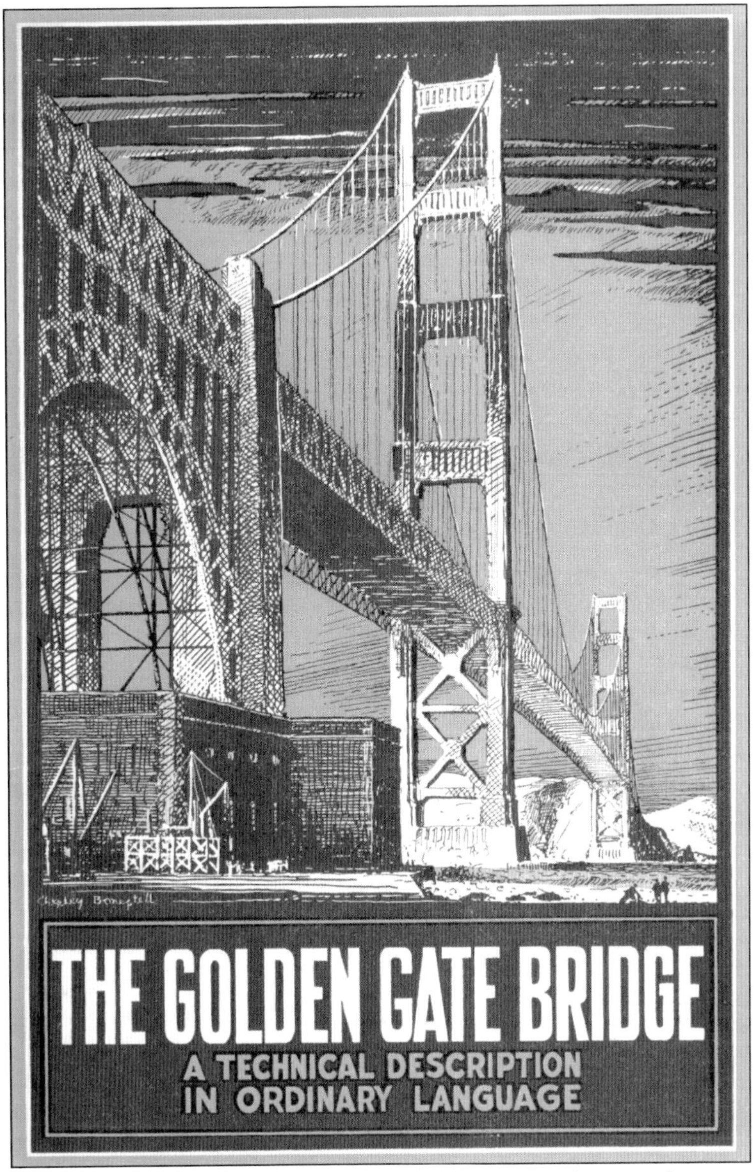

The work of visionary architectural designer Irving F. Morrow stands out in this cover illustration by Chesley Bonestell. Chief engineer Joseph B. Strauss hired Morrow as the consulting architectural designer responsible for every visible part of the Golden Gate Bridge above the waterline. When Morrow went to work in 1930, the structural concept of the bridge was already established, but it was the architect's designs that provided the bridge with its visual identity. With Strauss's approval, Morrow designed the tapering towers embellished with vertical fluting to accent their height, creating a graceful Art Deco look. Morrow's design simplified the railings to a line of waist-high uniform posts spaced slightly apart, allowing anyone crossing the bridge access to full, unobstructed views on either side. Morrow added angular decorative lampposts containing subdued sodium-vapor lights spaced along the bridge and overpasses. He also refined the bridge's appearance with his choice of Duclox International Orange (reddish orange) paint for its color. Cover illustrator Chesley Bonestell would become famous as an artist specializing in themes of outer space and science fiction.

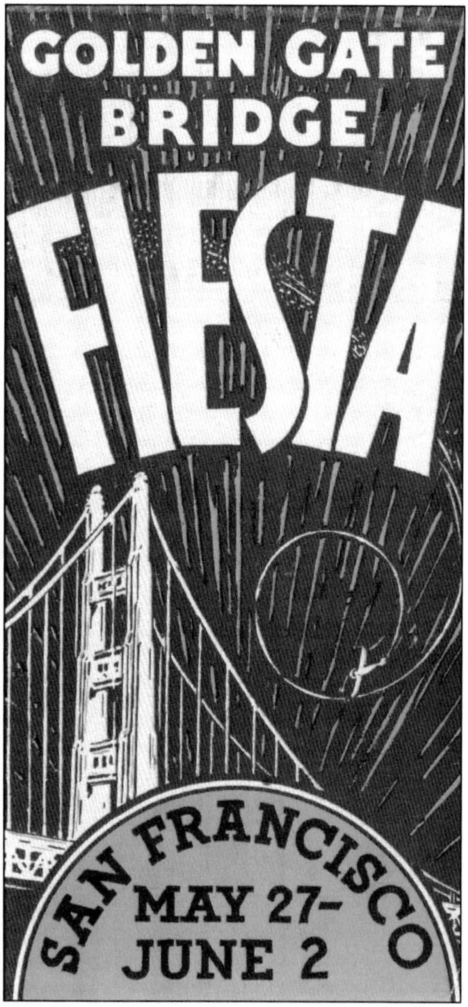

The completion of the construction of the bridge and official opening was celebrated with a week-long Golden Gate Bridge Fiesta. From May 27 to June 2, 1937, the San Francisco Bay Area celebrated with balls, fireworks, automobile caravans, yacht regattas, pageants, athletic events, massed airplane flyovers, navy ships cruising beneath the span, religious services, and memorial tributes to workers who died during construction of the bridge.

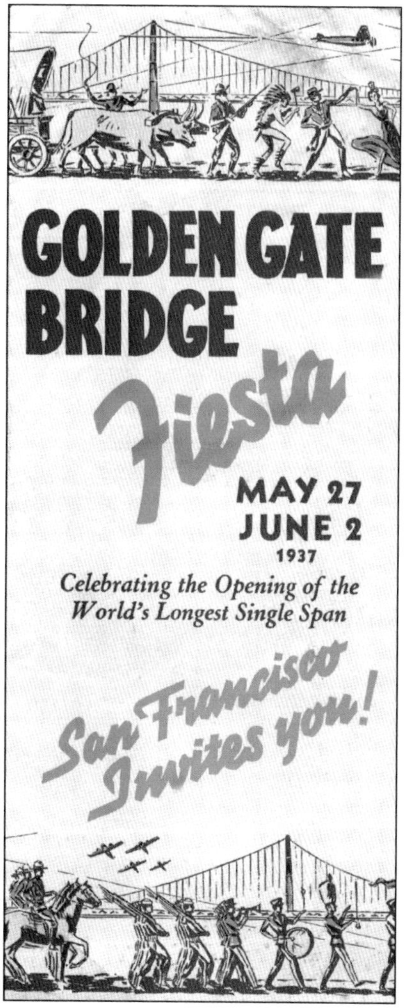

San Francisco invited everyone to join in the festivities of the Fiesta. The Queen Coronation Ball began the pre-fiesta events with "the most beautiful girls in nineteen counties ruling as Queens of the Festival." Celebrants marched on May 27 in a parade through San Francisco to Crissy Field, and the bridge was open for "Pedestrian Walks" across the span. On Friday, May 28, 1937, President Roosevelt pressed down a telegraph key to officially open the bridge to automobiles.

Anita Lum took this family photograph of her brother Gilbert, mother Chan Shee, and sister Ethel Lum walking across the bridge on Pedestrian Day. Local schools were closed for the day, and businesses closed or reduced their workforce to give as many people as possible an opportunity to cross the span. The *San Francisco Chronicle* estimated that 200,000 walkers made the trip between San Francisco and Marin County.

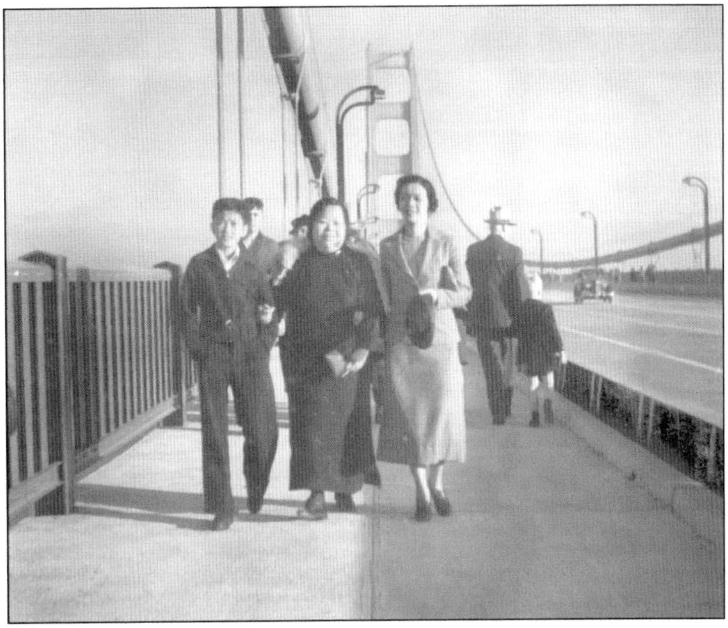

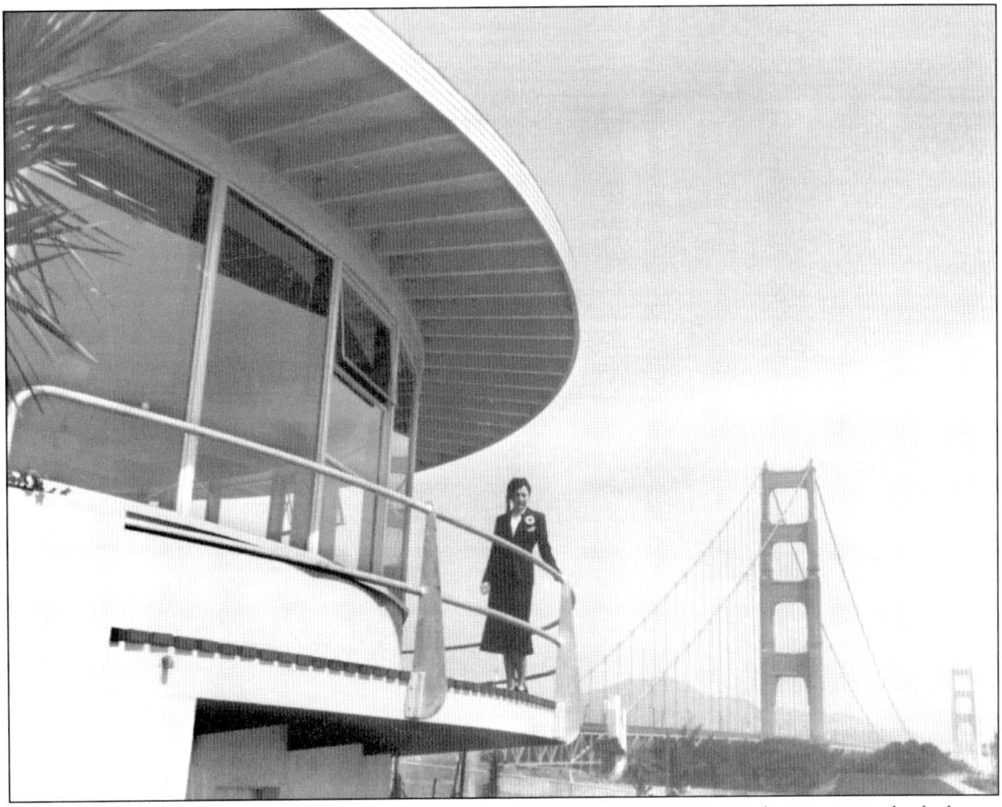

Stylish Mrs. Carl Wilke compliments the elegance of the bridge towers as she poses on the balcony near her husband's restaurant in this June 15, 1938, *San Francisco News-Call Bulletin* photograph. The Roundhouse Restaurant was an establishment known for its modest fare and panoramic views. (Courtesy San Francisco History Center, San Francisco Public Library.)

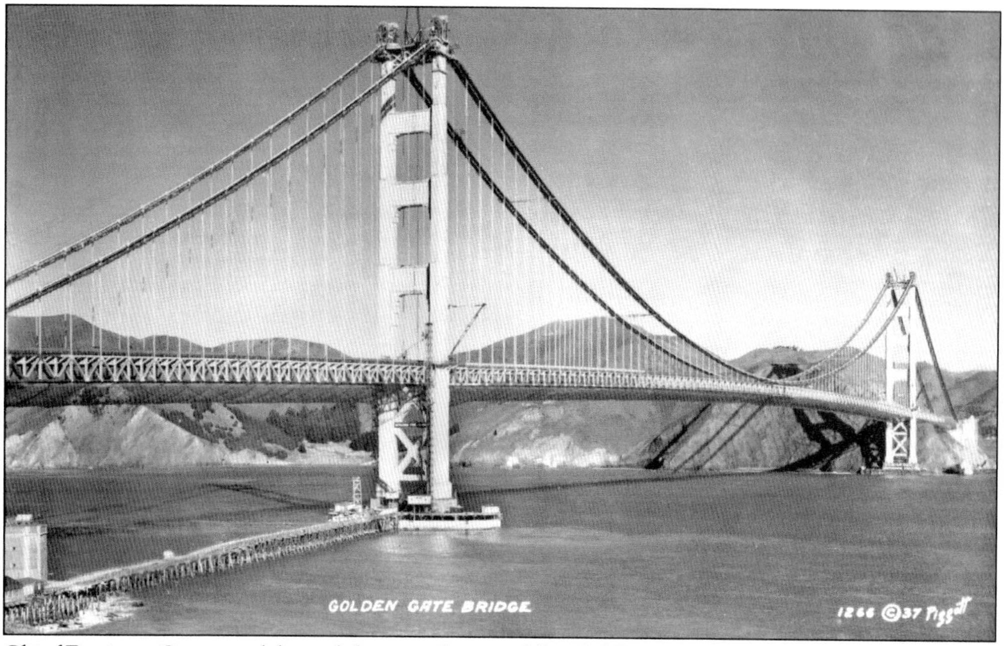

Chief Engineer Strauss celebrated the completion of the Golden Gate Bridge with a poem titled "A Symphony in Steel," which begins, "At last the mighty task is done / Resplendent in the Western sun / The Bridge looms mountain high / Its Titan piers grip ocean floor / Its Great steel arms link shore with shore / Its towers pierce the sky." Joseph B. Strauss died one year later.

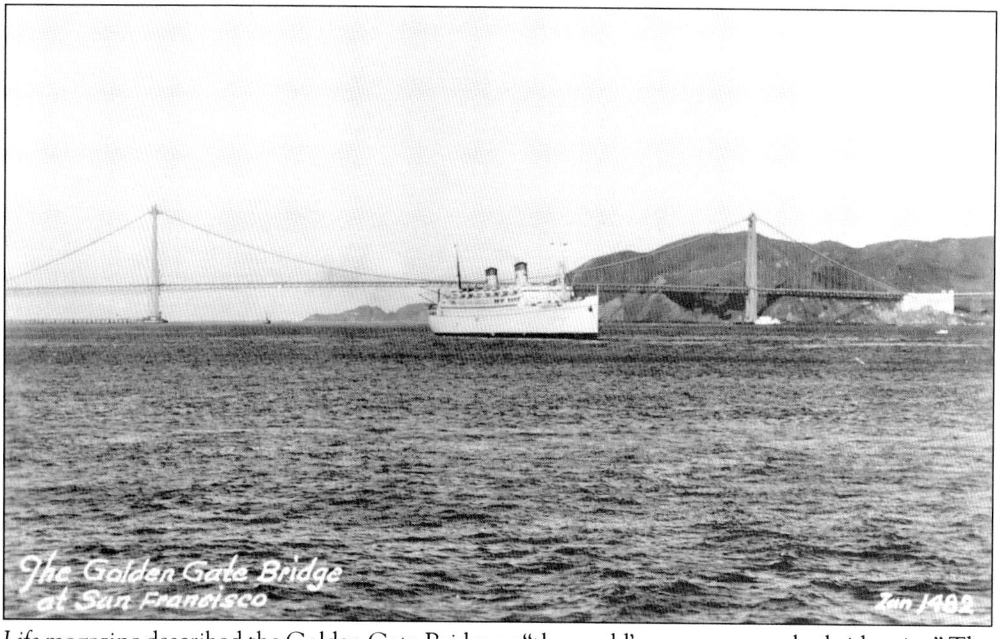

Life magazine described the Golden Gate Bridge as "the world's most spectacular bridge site." The first and last sight ship passengers and crew saw entering and leaving San Francisco Bay was the Golden Gate Bridge. For soldiers and sailors in World War II, viewing the bridge was for them a prominent symbol of America.

Spanning the mile-wide entrance to San Francisco Bay, the perfect symmetry of the Golden Gate Bridge can be seen in this vintage postcard view looking from the south tower towards the north tower and Marin Headlands. Engineers Strauss and Paine agreed with architect Morrow that the bridge should be functionally designed. The 90-foot-wide bridge was perfectly proportioned with six traffic lanes flanked by two 10.5-foot-wide sidewalks.

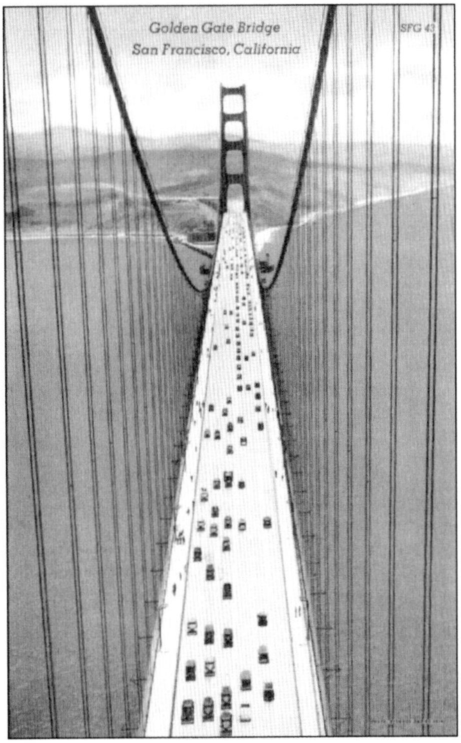

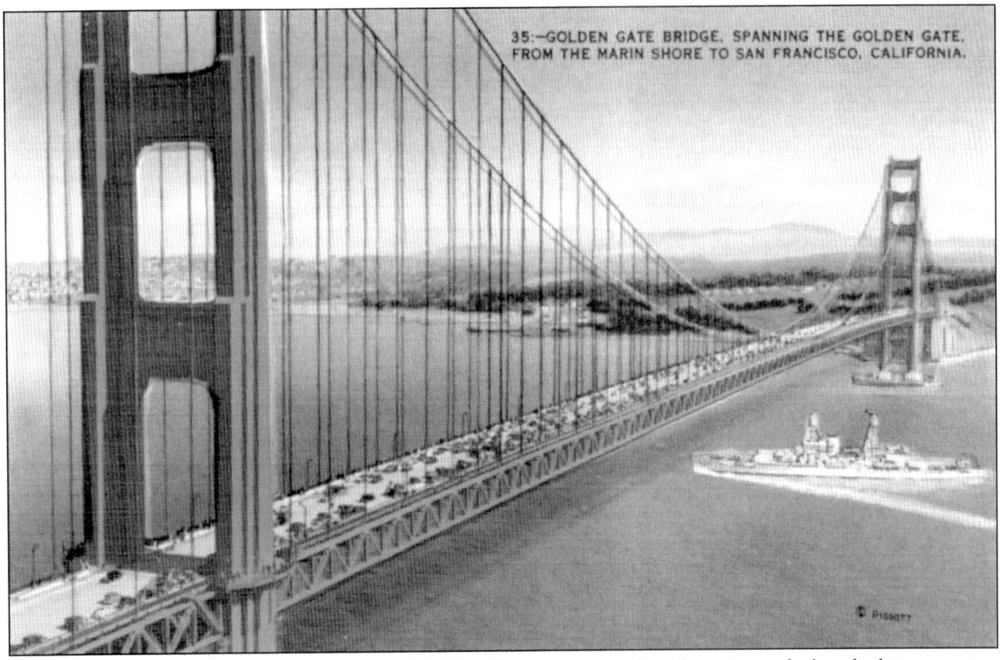

This is the "Gateway to Victory," a World War II–era postcard with a view of a battleship crossing underneath the bridge. With 220 feet of clearance between the trusses and the waterline, there was enough space for even the largest passing ships. *Life* magazine informed readers, "The Golden Gate Bridge is so designed that if it should be destroyed by an enemy fleet it would sink to the bottom of the channel and not bottle up the harbor."

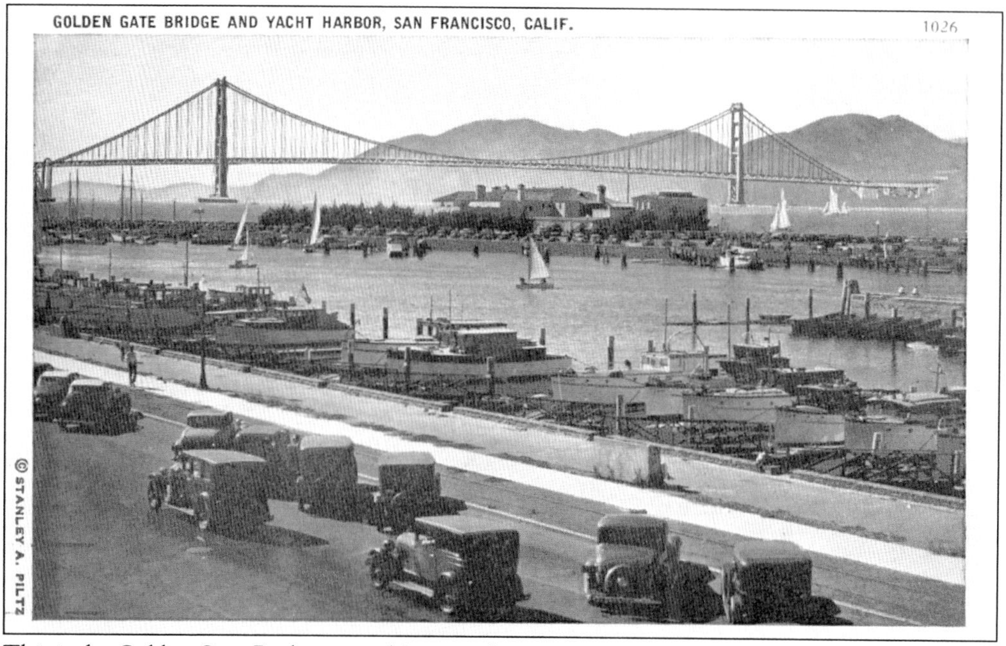

This is the Golden Gate Bridge viewed from Yacht Harbor and Marina Boulevard. The small-craft harbor was originally built for the 1915 Panama Pacific International Exposition. On the south side of the boulevard, large Mediterranean Revival–style houses were built in the 1920s, each with one of the most picturesque views in the city. In 1937, Marina Boulevard became one of the three primary approaches from the city to the bridge. (Published by Stanley A. Piltz.)

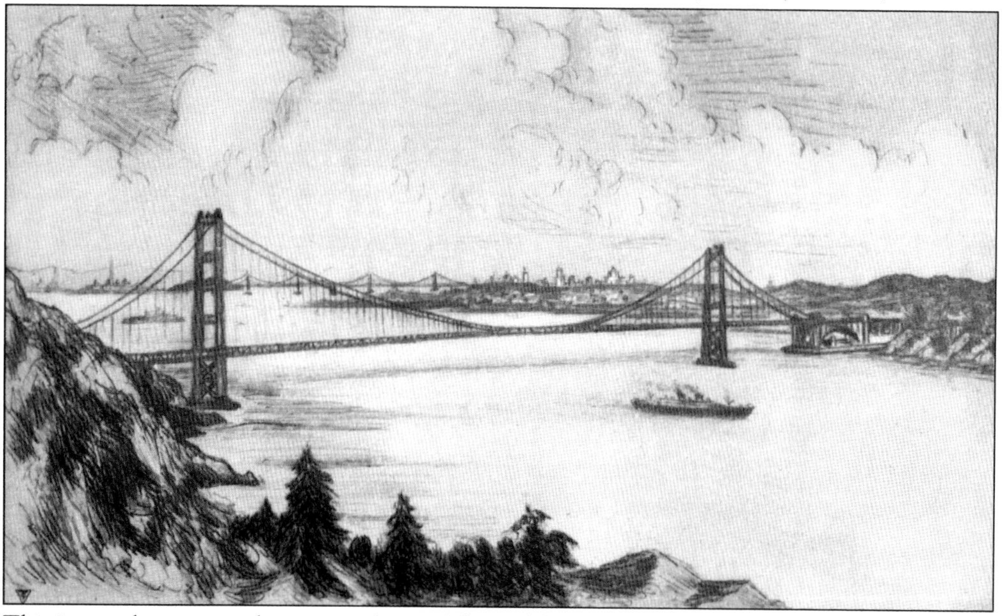

This image showcases a drypoint etching of the Golden Gate Bridge by (Arthur) Russell Wilson, an architect who studied painting and printmaking and later designed furniture. After moving from Southern California, he devoted his time to art and exhibited his work at the 1939 Golden Gate International Exposition. From its very beginnings, the bridge was a favorite subject of both amateur and professional artists and photographers.

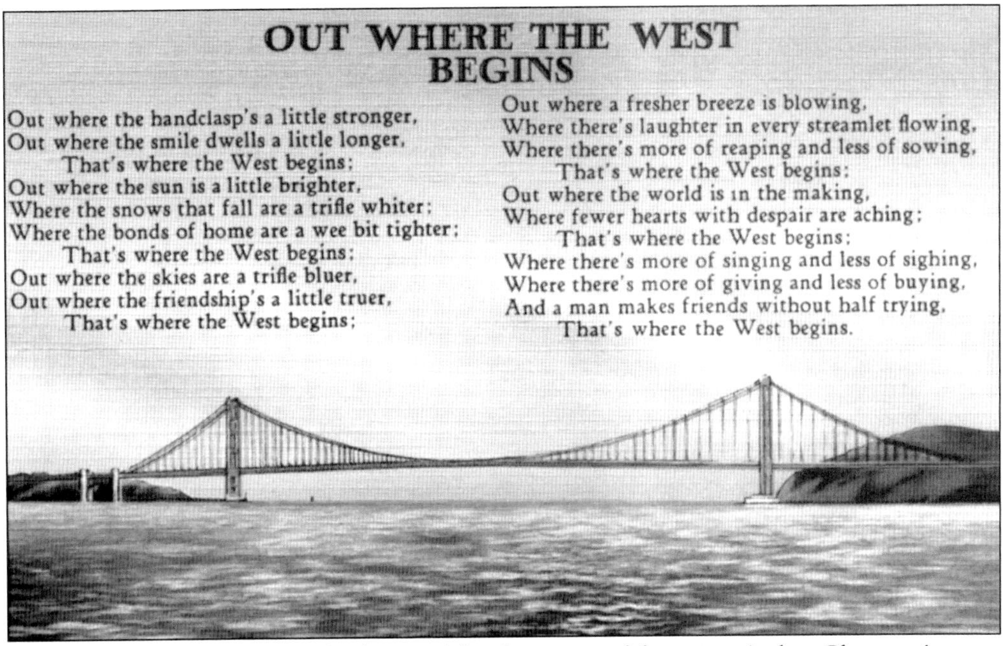

The bridge provided a unique background for this postcard featuring Arthur Chapman's poem "Out Where the West Begins." Newspaper columnist Chapman wasn't thinking of an Art Deco bridge spanning the Golden Gate when he wrote the poem in 1911 to commemorate the West of the American cowboy. It was considered the best-known verse in America during the 1920s and 1930s.

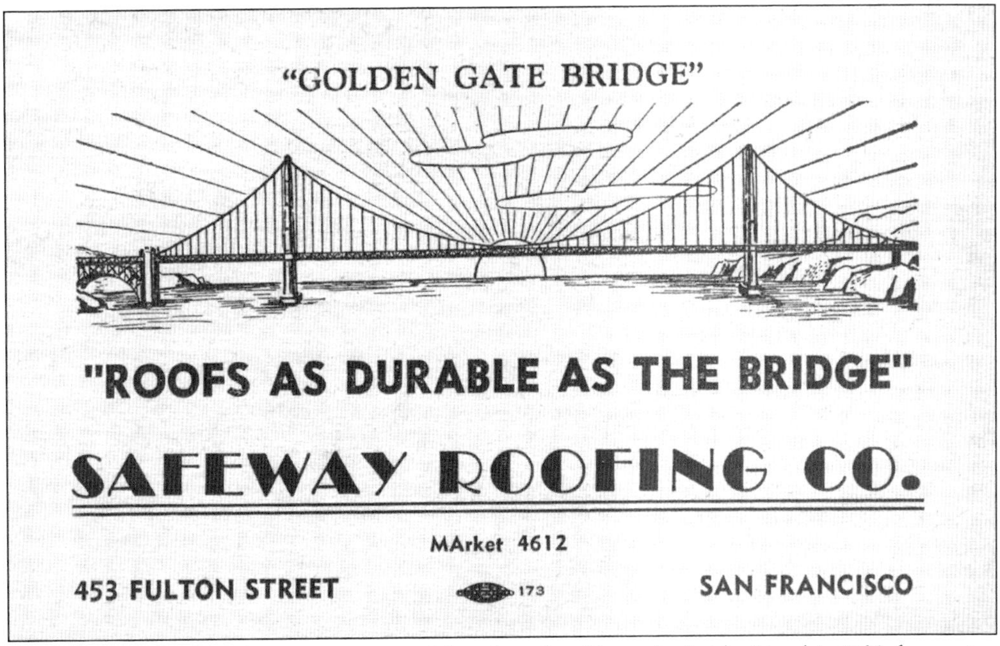

The Safeway Roofing Company promised "roofs as durable as the bridge" in this 1938 decorative illustrated advertisement. The Golden Gate Bridge immediately became the symbol of San Francisco, as well as its durability, and was featured in advertisements promoting everything from Lysol to the city water department.

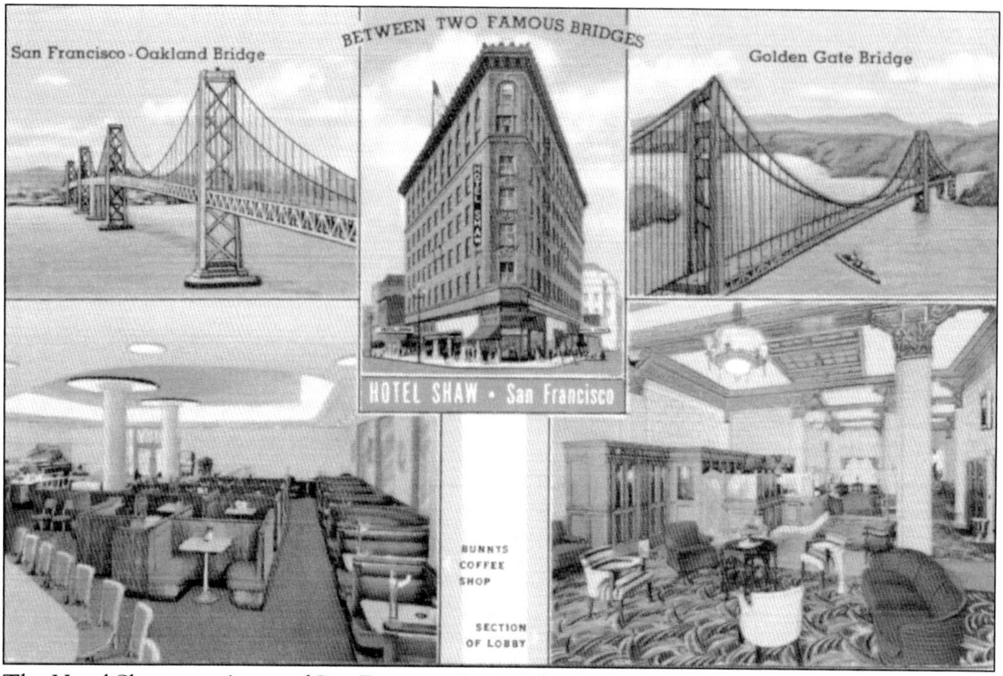

The Hotel Shaw wasn't one of San Francisco's more famous inns, so it was promoted as "Between Two Famous Bridges." Located at Market and McAllister Streets, near Jones Street, the hotel wasn't near either the Golden Gate or Bay Bridge. In 1939, the price of a room started at $2.50 and, best of all, guests could enjoy breakfast or lunch at Bunny's Coffee Shop.

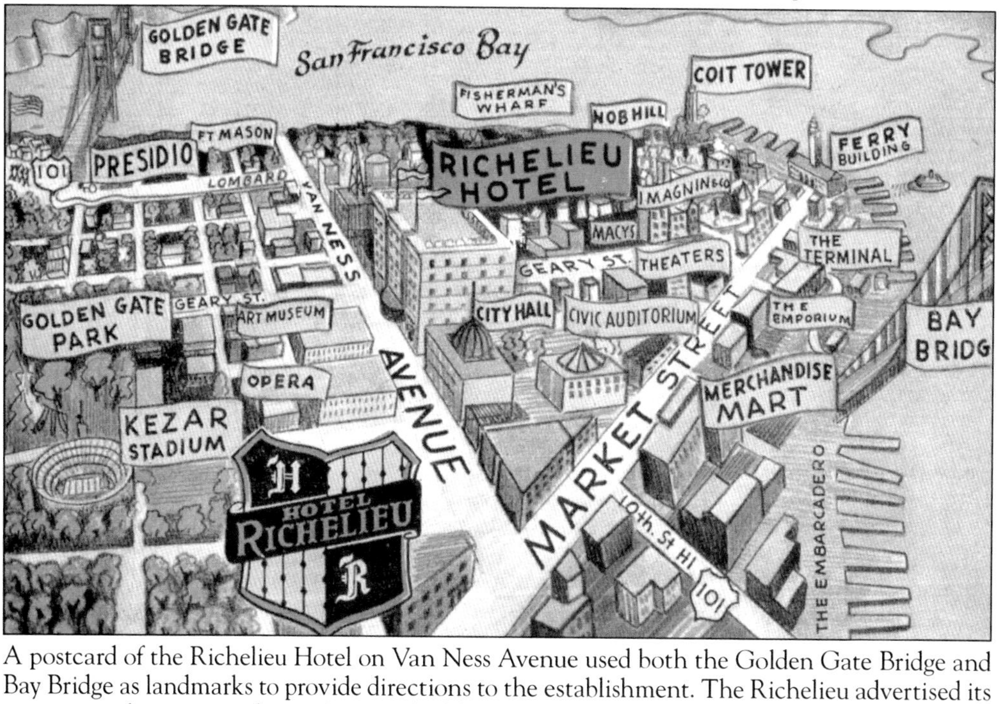

A postcard of the Richelieu Hotel on Van Ness Avenue used both the Golden Gate Bridge and Bay Bridge as landmarks to provide directions to the establishment. The Richelieu advertised its convenient location to the city's many highlights, including Kezar Stadium, the Opera House, and Emporium Department Store.

Nine

Golden Gate International Exposition

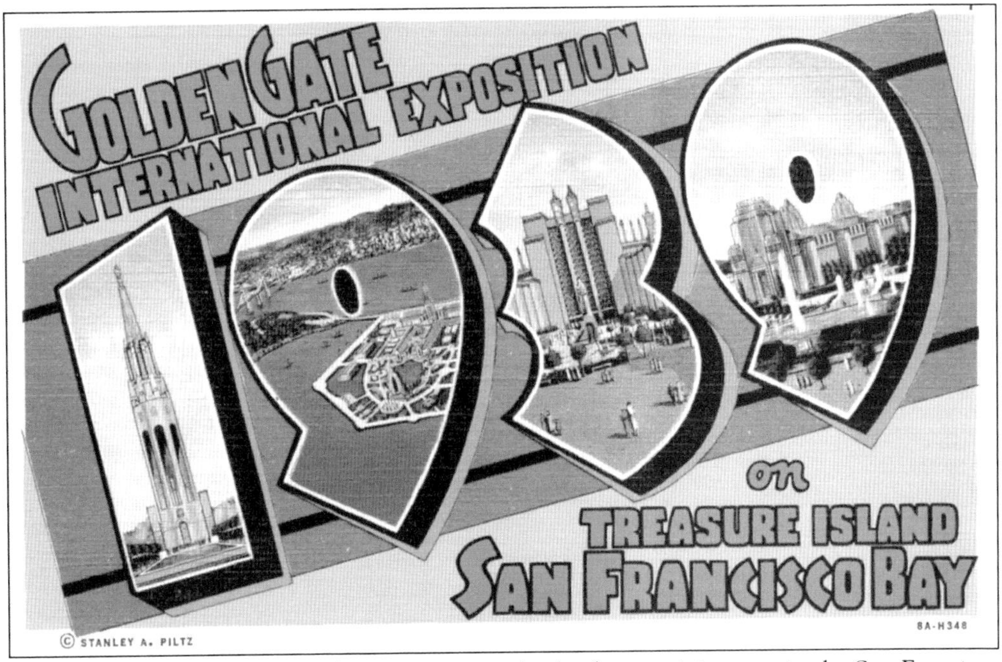

The Golden Gate International Exposition was the final great civic event in the San Francisco Bay Area before the United States became directly involved in World War II. Despite the looming battle clouds, San Franciscans wanted an opportunity to boost the Bay Area and to celebrate the completion of its two great bridges with a World's Fair. The exposition, located on Treasure Island in the center of San Francisco Bay, opened on February 18, 1939. (Published by Stanley A. Piltz.)

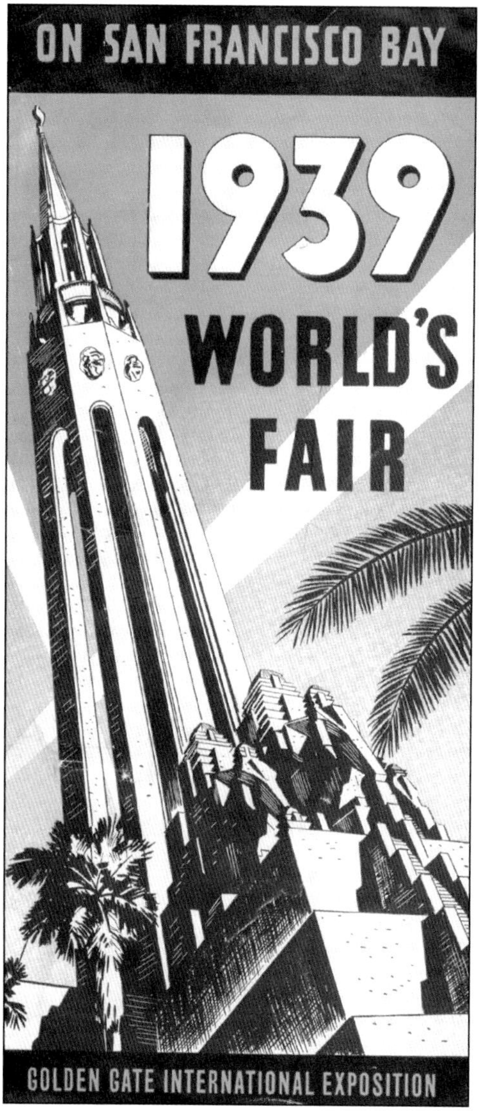

This illustration showing the Tower of the Sun and the Portal of the Pacific was featured on a promotional flier. The Golden Gate International Exposition (GGIE) was the third American World's Fair of the decade. The 1933 Chicago "Century of Progress" celebrated technological achievements of the past. The 1939 New York World's Fair emphasized the future with it's "World of Tomorrow," and in San Francisco, columnist Harold Gilliam noted that on Treasure Island, "The theme was the Pacific, which necessarily meant the future because America never before looked thoughtfully westward from these shores." An architecture commission, headed initially by George W. Kelham and after his death by Arthur Brown Jr., was responsible for overseeing the design of the buildings that provided the structural beauty and dominant features of the fair. Architects Lewis P. Hobart, William G. Merchant, Timothy L. Pflueger, and Ernest E. Weihe also served on the commission. Weihe designed the Portals of the Pacific with the elephant and howdah sculptures by Donald Macky. Arthur Brown Jr designed the Tower of the Sun. In 1939, the Art Deco era in San Francisco was drawing to a close, and the GGIE, with its blending of modern art, architecture, and gadgetry with the arts and cultures of the nations of the Pacific basin, provided a spectacular exclamation point to commemorate the end of an era.

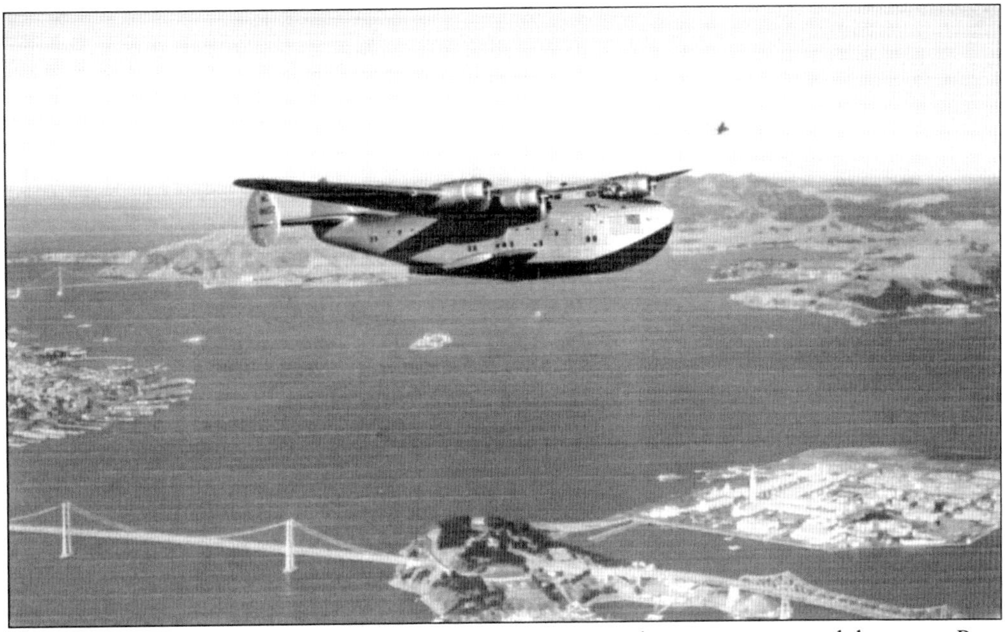

"Watched the take-off this afternoon" was the comment on this picture postcard showing a Pan-American Trans-Pacific Clipper returning to its seaplane port located at Treasure Island. The creation of the man-made island had a dual purpose as a site for the World's Fair and to provide an international airport in the Bay Area. There were three permanent buildings constructed on the island, all designed by George W. Kelham: two 300-foot-long hangars and the administration building (main terminal). During the fair, visitors could watch the complete overhaul of the large seaplanes.

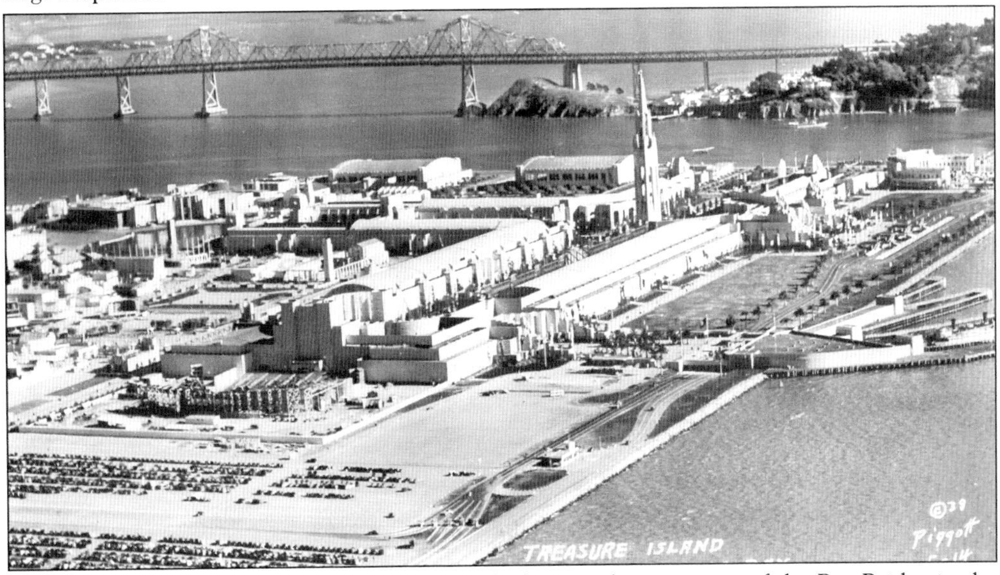

A J. K. Piggott view shows Treasure Island with the cantilever section of the Bay Bridge in the background. About a mile long and two-thirds of a mile wide, the 400-acre island was constructed mostly of mud dredged from the bay on a shallow shoal by the U.S. Army Corps of Engineers at a cost of $3,719,800 footed by the Works Progress Administration plus $760,780 in additional funds from business sponsors in San Francisco.

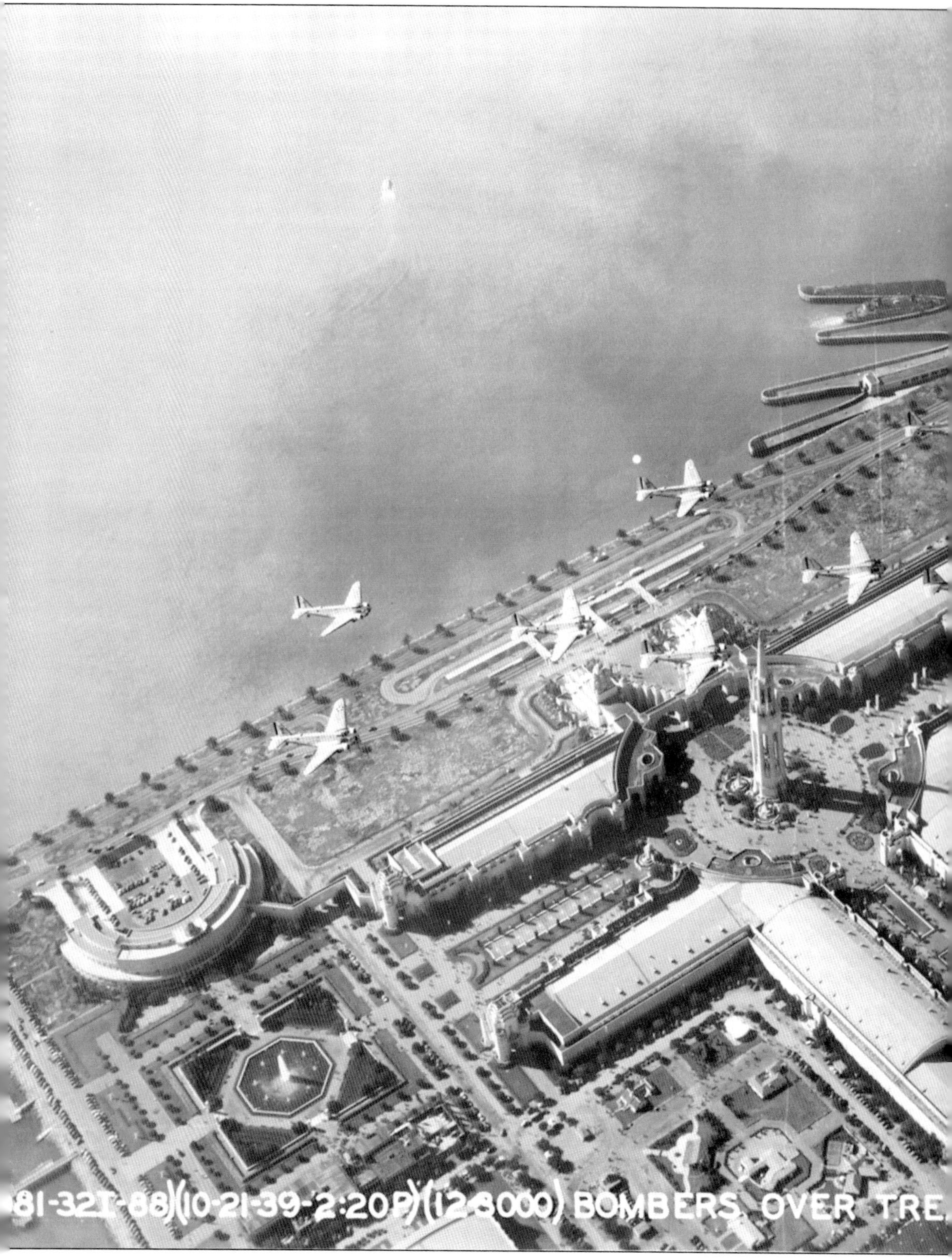
81-321-88)(10-21-39-2:20P)(12-8000) BOMBERS OVER TRE.

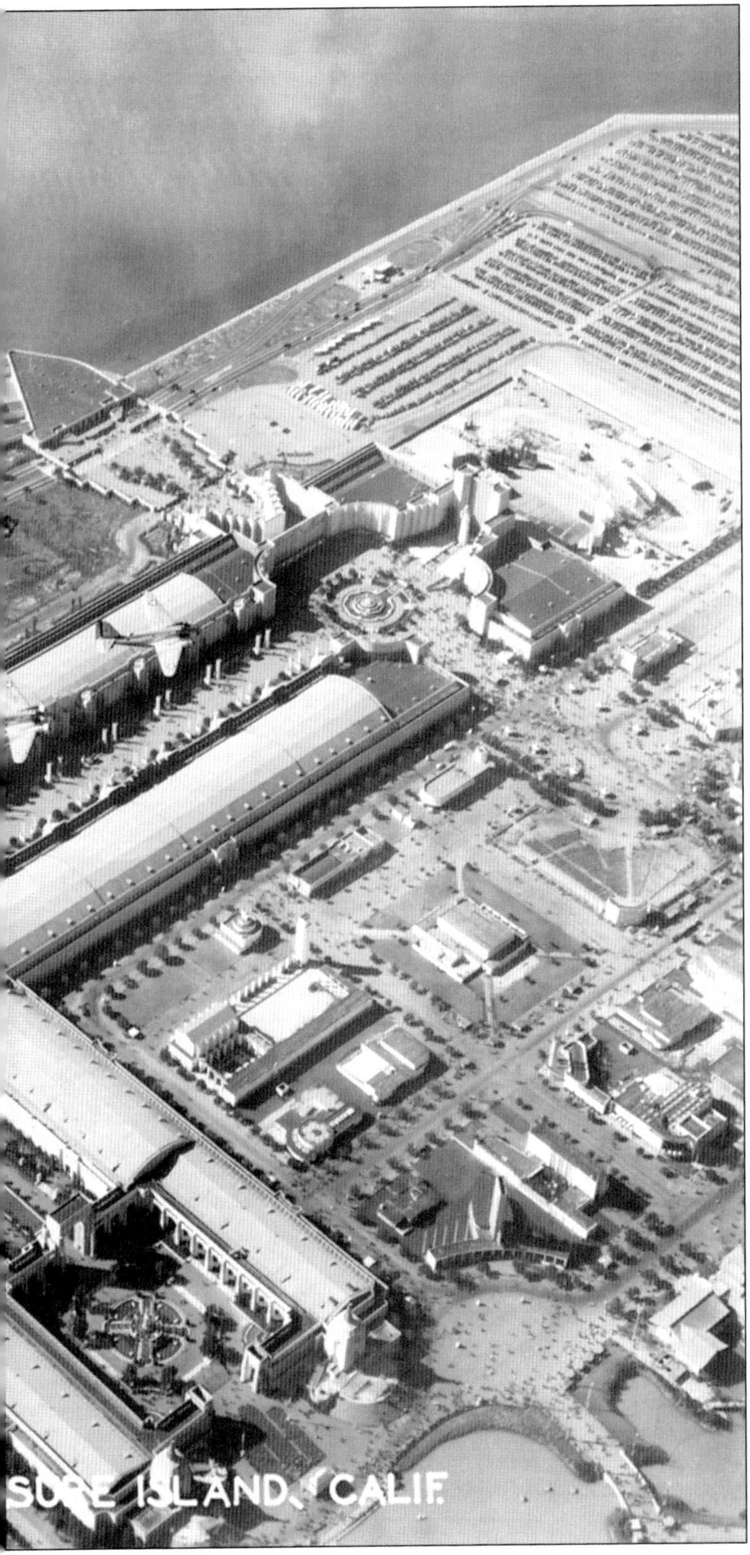

U.S. Army Air Corps bombers fly over Treasure Island in this aerial view taken October 20, 1939. The semicircular Administration Building is the first structure on the left and directly behind it is the Treasure Garden with its octagonal pool designed by George W. Kelham. The Court of Honor and 400-foot-high Tower of the Sun are in the center, and to the right is the Court of Pacifica. While most structures look sturdy, the pavilions were wood framed, covered with laths, and then sheathed in burlap and stucco. The 12,000-car parking lot is located in the upper right, or north side, of the island; an area considered unsafe for buildings because of the base of spongy mud underneath.

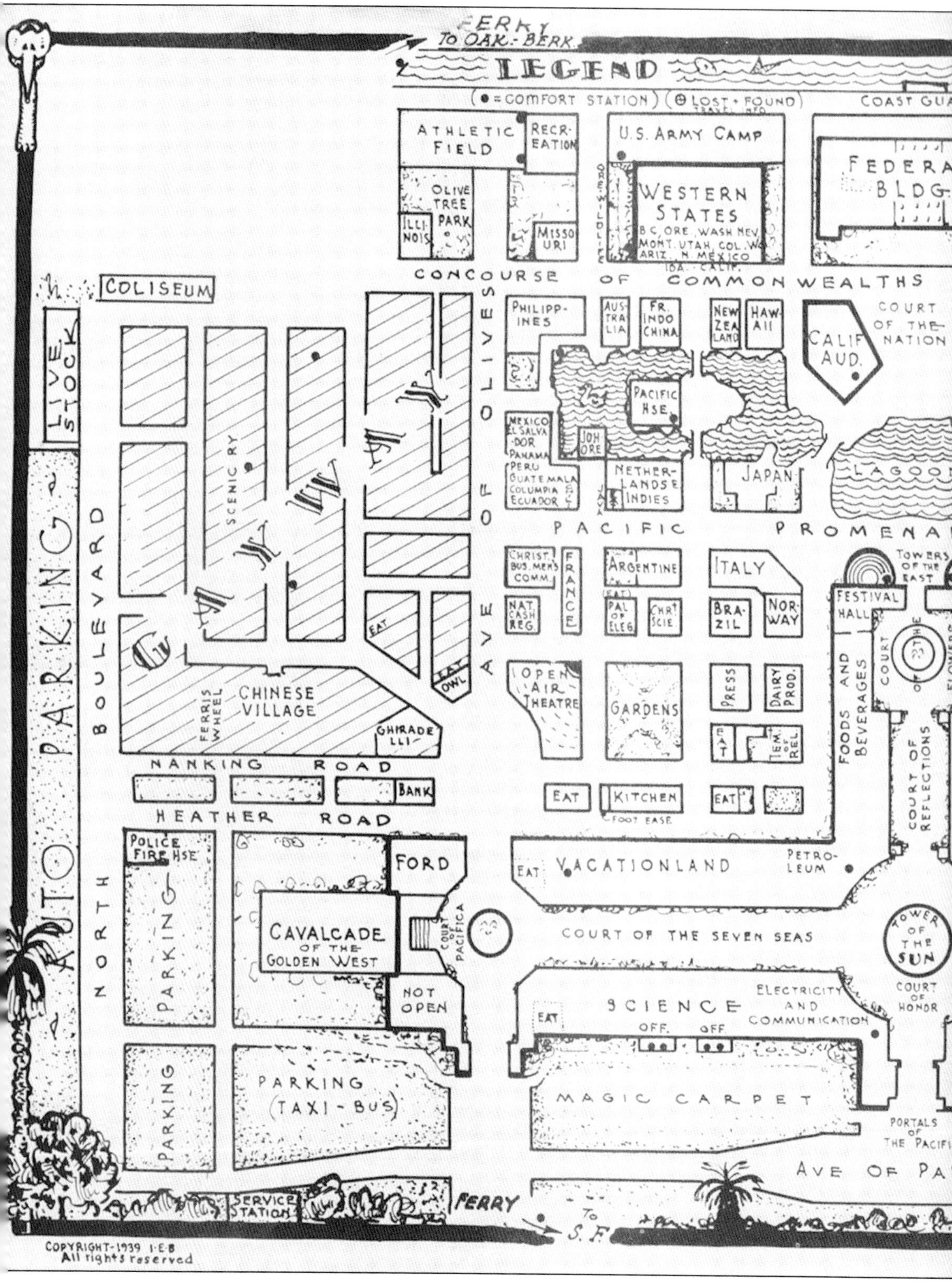
FERRY TO OAK.-BERK.
LEGEND
(● = COMFORT STATION) (⊕ LOST + FOUND TRAVEL INFO)
COAST GUA
ATHLETIC FIELD
RECR-EATION
U.S. ARMY CAMP
FEDERAL BLDG
OLIVE TREE PARK
ILLI-NOIS
MISSOURI
WESTERN STATES
B.C. ORE. WASH. NEV. MONT. UTAH. COL. WY. ARIZ. N. MEXICO IDA. CALIF.
OREWILDLIFE
CONCOURSE OF COMMONWEALTHS
COLISEUM
LIVE STOCK
PHILIPPINES
AUSTRALIA
FR. INDO CHINA
NEW ZEALAND
HAWAII
CALIF AUD.
COURT OF THE NATION
PACIFIC HSE.
MEXICO EL SALVADOR PANAMA PERU GUATEMALA COLUMPIA ECUADOR
JOHORE
NETHERLANDS INDIES
JAVA
JAPAN
LAGOON
SCENIC RY
GAYWAY
AVE OF OLIVES
PACIFIC PROMENADE
CHRIST. BUS. MEN'S COMM.
FRANCE
ARGENTINE
ITALY
TOWERS OF THE EAST
NAT. CASH REG.
PAL OF ELEG
CHR'T SCIE
BRAZIL
NORWAY
FESTIVAL HALL
EAT
EAT OWL
OPEN AIR THEATRE
GARDENS
PRESS
DAIRY PROD.
TEM. OF REL
FOODS AND BEVERAGES
COURT OF THE FLOWERS
COURT OF REFLECTIONS
BOULEVARD
FERRIS WHEEL
CHINESE VILLAGE
GHIRADELLI
NANKING ROAD
BANK
KITCHEN
FOOT EASE
HEATHER ROAD
POLICE FIRE HSE
FORD
VACATIONLAND
PETROLEUM
CAVALCADE OF THE GOLDEN WEST
COURT OF PACIFICA
COURT OF THE SEVEN SEAS
TOWER OF THE SUN
NOT OPEN
SCIENCE
OFF.
ELECTRICITY AND COMMUNICATION
COURT OF HONOR
NORTH
PARKING
AUTO PARKING
MAGIC CARPET
PARKING (TAXI-BUS)
PORTALS OF THE PACIFIC
AVE OF PA
SERVICE STATION
FERRY TO S.F.
COPYRIGHT-1939 I-E-B
All rights reserved

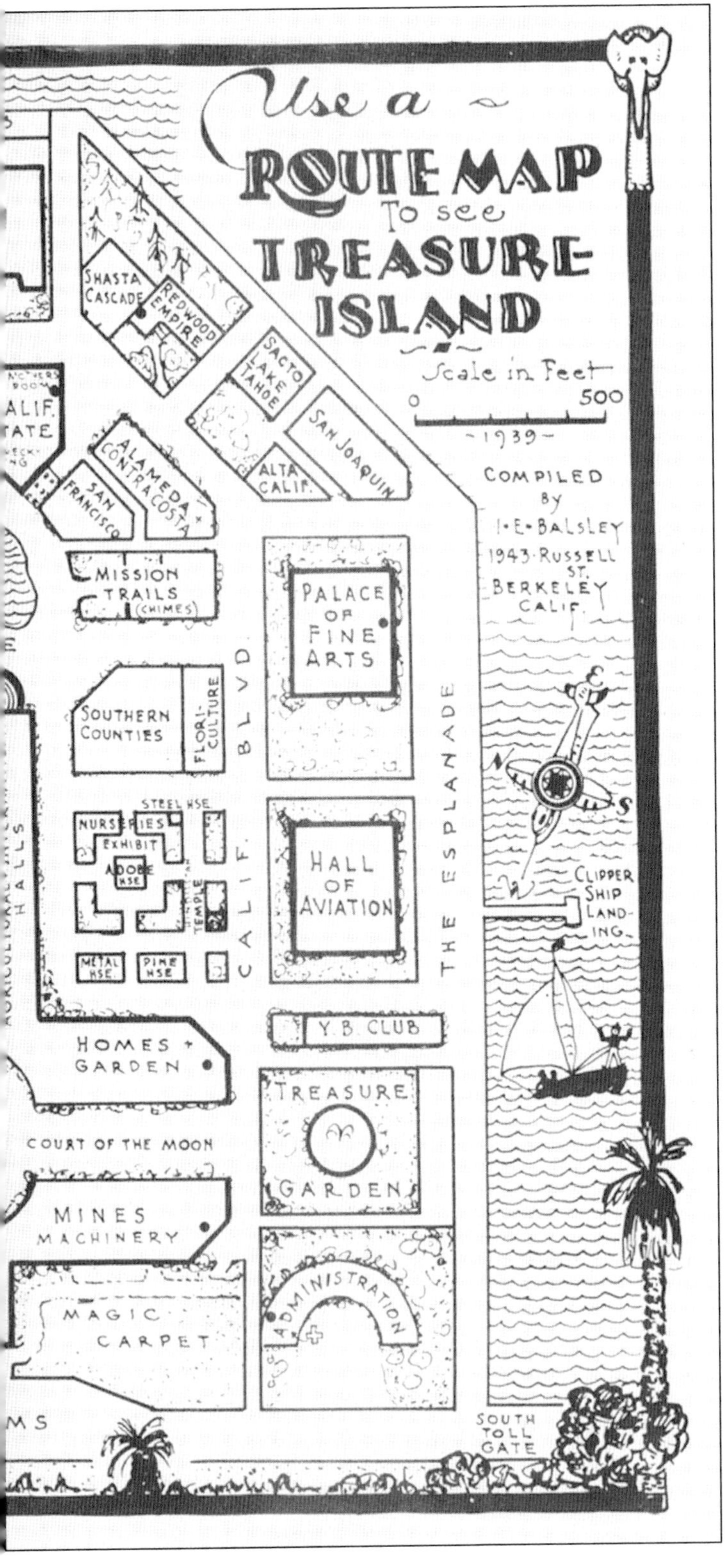

This is a map of the fairgrounds on Treasure Island drawn by I. E. Balsley. If a person wanted to see "Wrong Way," Douglas Corrigan's famous airplane, he or she could visit the Hall of Aviation, one of the fair's permanent buildings. Another lasting structure, going up the Esplanade, was the Palace of Fine and Decorative Arts, where visitors could see Sandro Botticelli's *Birth of Venus* and rare works of art. The Gayway, not shown in detail, was the fun zone of Treasure Island, where more than 50 exhibits and amusement concessions were located. It featured the Sally Rand Nude Ranch, with cowgirls wearing only Stetsons, boots, bandanas, and strategically placed holsters; the Holy Land Building, a non-denominational religious voyage; the Incubator Babies, Inc.; and a deep-sea diver fighting an octopus in a transparent-walled pool.

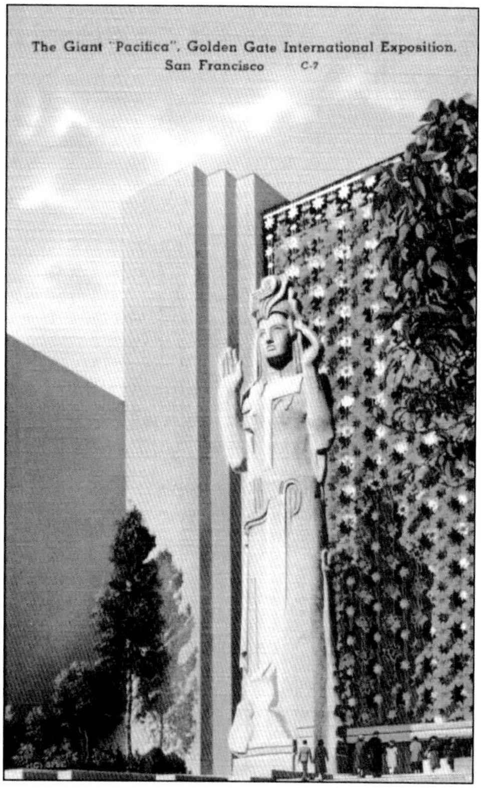

Pacifica was a themed statue of the exposition. Sculptor Ralph Stackpole took two years to shape the 80-foot-high plaster female figure. The statue stood in front of a 100-foot-high by 48-foot-wide "prayer" curtain of connected metal stars and small tubes, which produced wind chimes with movement of the sea breezes or when assisted mechanically. At night, theatrical lighting produced a rotation of colors varying from dark blue to pale apricot, creating an ethereal background of color for *Pacifica*.

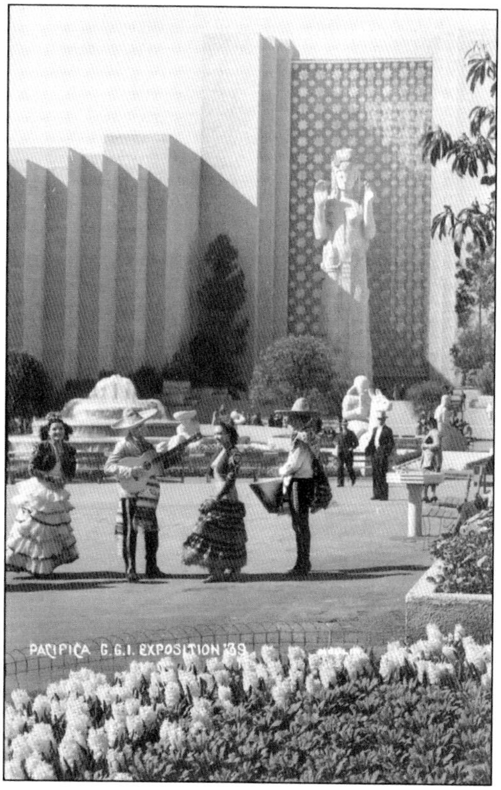

Mexican entertainers stroll in the Court of Pacifica. Designed by Timothy L. Pflueger, the court represented the fair's underlying motif—Pacific peace and unity. *Pacifica* stands at the head of a grand staircase behind a fountain surrounded by smaller sculptures representing the people of the Pacific Basin, including the *Modern American Woman* by Carl George. In the foreground are a few of the 14,310 flowers planted in the courtyard in a blue and gold color scheme.

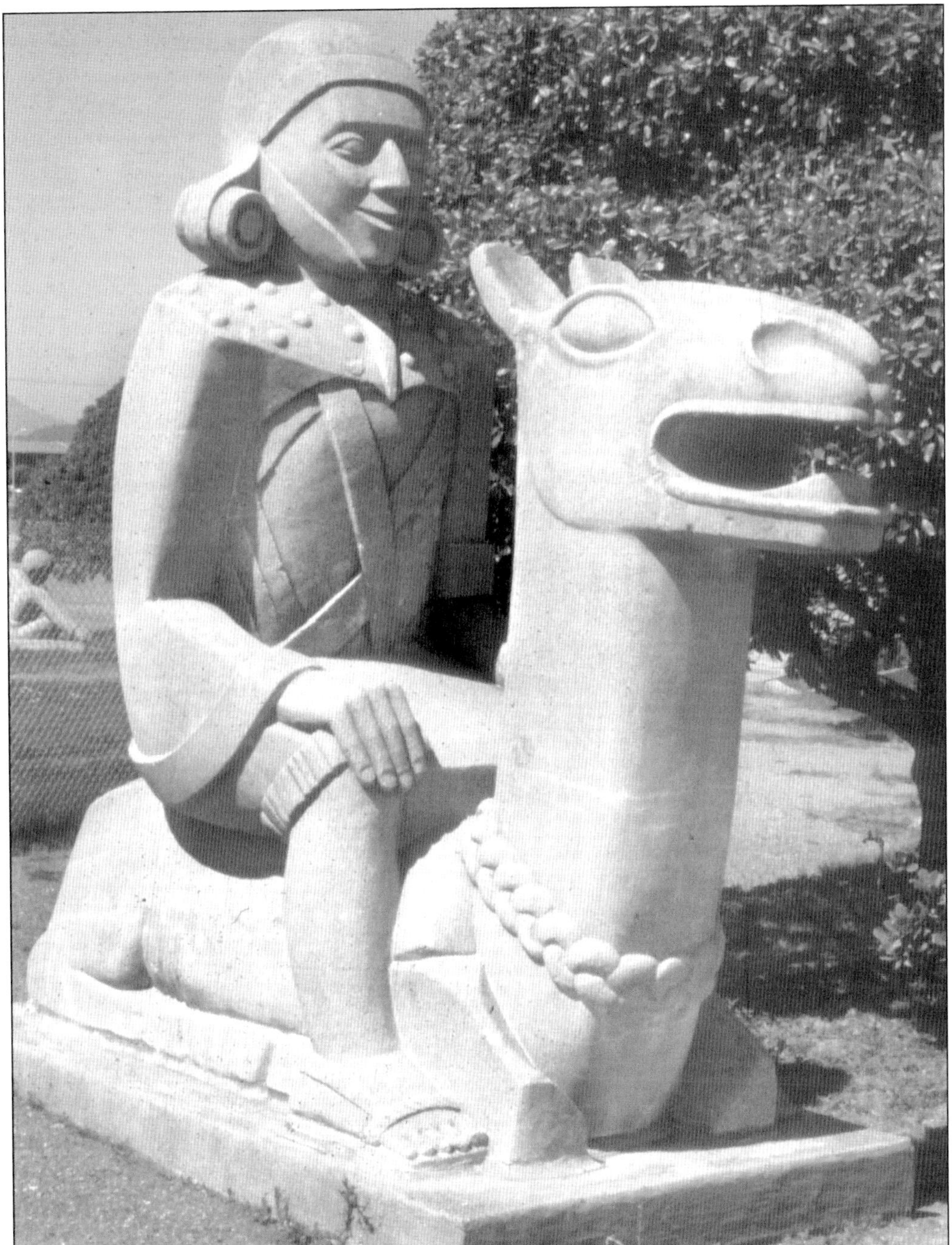

This sculpture is a remnant of the Court of Pacifica, which featured not only the statue *Pacifica* but also a series of statues illustrating the various nations and cultures that rimmed the Pacific Ocean. In this case, Sargent Johnson sculpted an Inca astride a llama to depict the South American country of Peru, which borders the South Pacific. Johnson, a Boston-born African American sculptor, was part of the Federal Art Project in the Bay Area during the Depression. He sculpted the stonework around the entrance to the Aquatic Park Casino, now the San Francisco Maritime Museum.

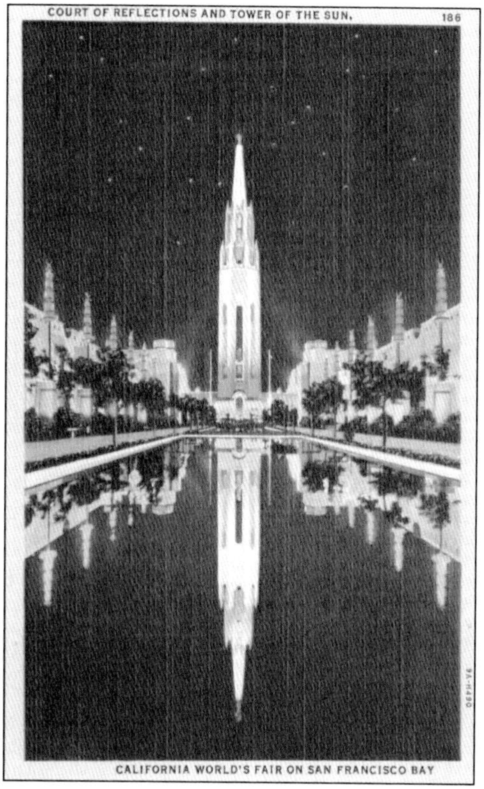

This is a nighttime view of the Tower of the Sun with its reflection mirrored in the still pool of the Court of Reflections. The tower was illuminated with shades from amber to white with mercury green highlights. The golden phoenix at the top was spotlighted in red. Floodlights bathed Lewis P. Hobart's Siesta Pool with pink light, and everyone agreed this was one of the great views of the fair. Jess Stanton was the exposition director of color in charge of this color decoration and night lighting.

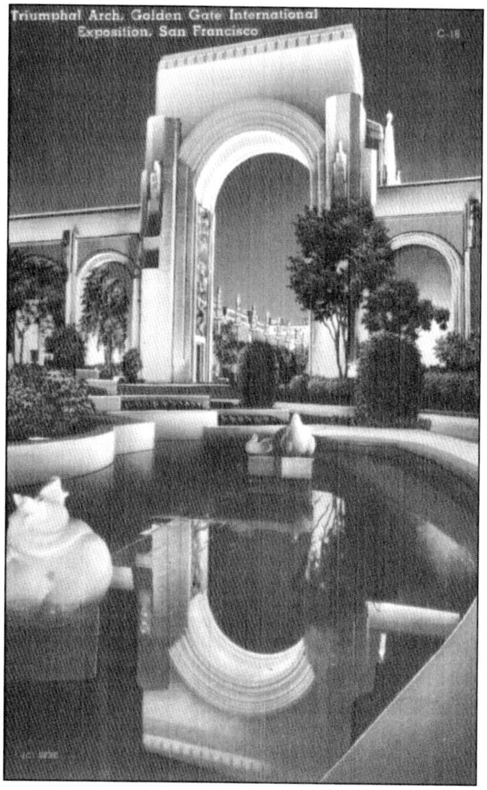

Lewis P. Hobart designed the graceful 105-foot-high Arch of Triumph to provide a passageway between the fountains of the Court of Reflection and Court of Flowers. Sparkle was added to the buildings with "Zonalite," a decorative process that involved spraying the wet stucco surfaces with heated flakes of mica in 1 of 19 official tints. The night lighting of the arch stressed green highlights and shadows of mauve under the arches and pink above.

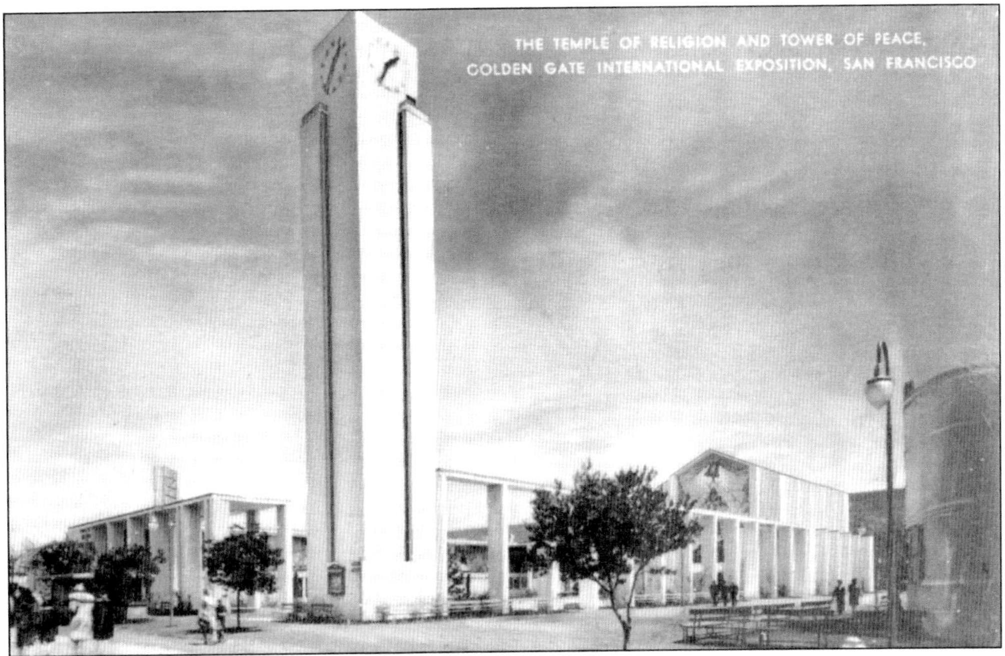

Architect Edward G. Bolles designed the Temple of Religion and Tower of Peace. A clock topped the tall unadorned non-sectarian column, and in the neo-Gothic Hall of Religion, exhibits portrayed the faiths. The hall murals included Peter Illyin's *The Rise of Religious Freedoms*, Jose Moya Del Pino's *Man in Relation to God*, and Franz Bergmann's *Religion on the Pacific Coast*. In the garden were 200 varieties of flowers mentioned in the Old and New Testaments.

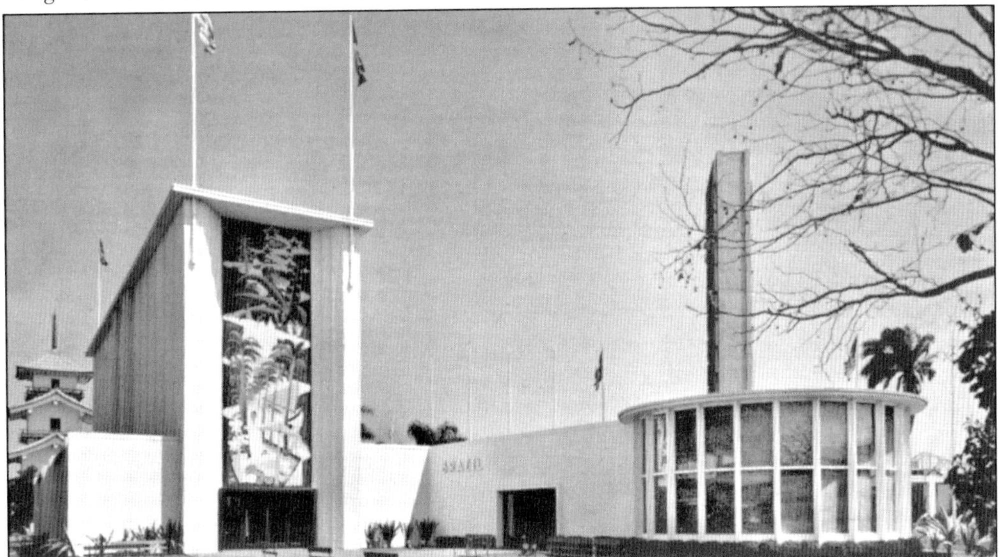

The Pavilion of the United States of Brazil was a popular destination at the fair. Designed by San Francisco architect Gardner A. Dailey, the building had two 40-foot-high murals by Robert B. Howard and two large murals by Jane Berlandina. The pavilion displayed handmade and manufactured Brazilian products. The patio area, Café Brazil, had tables for 200 persons and served Brazilian coffee and tea (maté). An orchestra played the latest popular music in Brazil for the crowds.

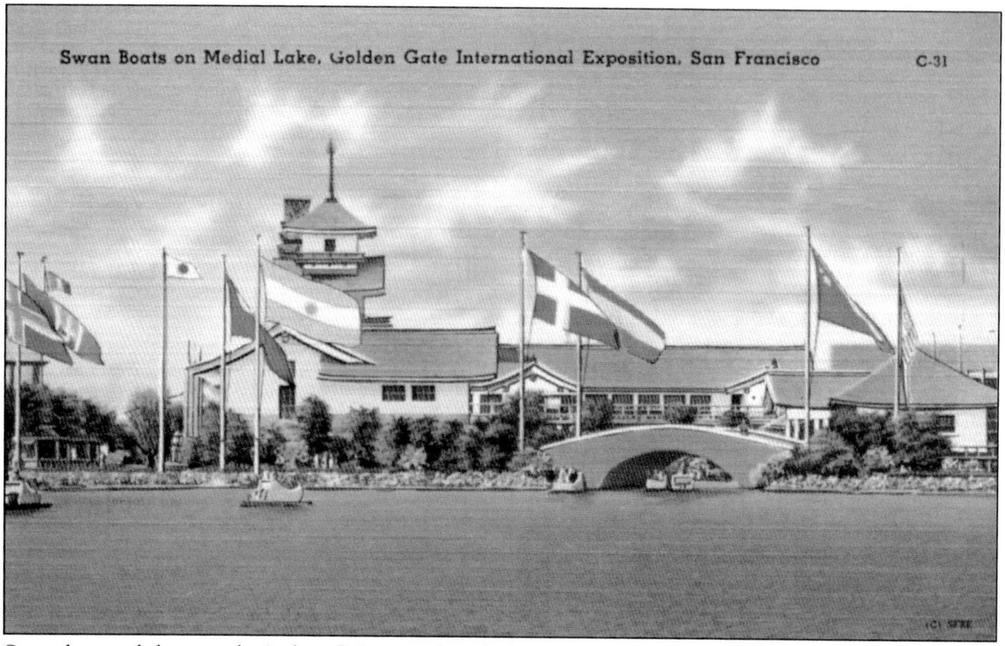

Swan boats glide over the Lake of Nations (Medial Lake) past the Crescent Bridge and a display of flags of the 30 nations represented at the fair. The Japanese pagoda stands out in the background. The Japan Pavilion was the most extensive foreign pavilion and included a samurai castle, Buddhist shrine, and terraced gardens enclosed by a picturesque pool and drum bridges.

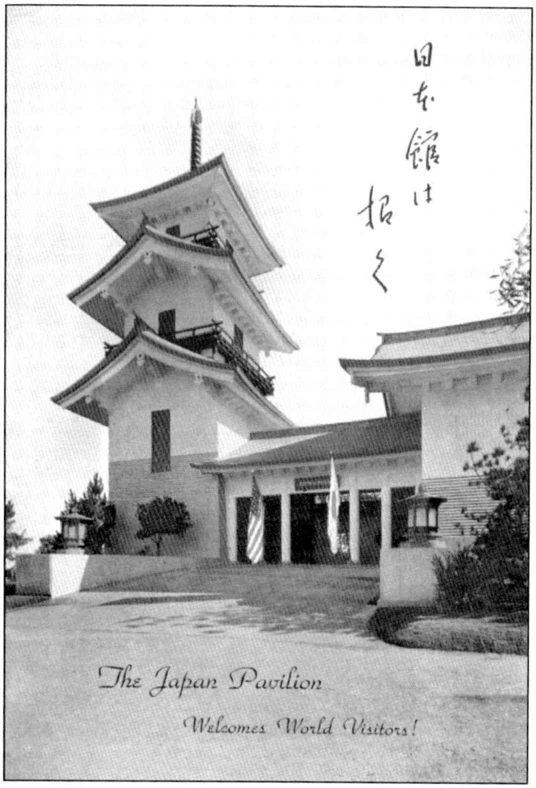

"The Japanese Pavilion welcomes world visitors," states this exhibit pamphlet featuring both the United States and Imperial Japanese flags at the pavilion entry. Despite the continually worsening relations between the United States and Japan, the Japanese exhibits were well received by the fair's visitors. For Japan, it was not only an opportunity to promote better relations but also an opportunity to propagandize their ongong war with China.

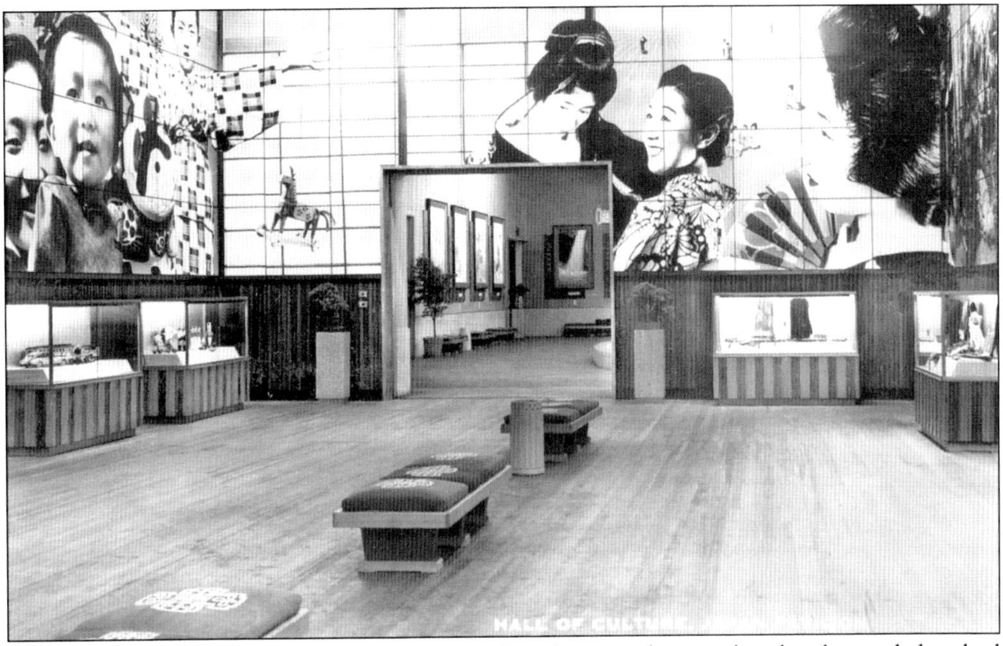

In Japan, there was an appreciation of classical moderne and streamlined styles, and they had adapted these styles to their arts, fashions, and designs (Taisho Chic). At Treasure Island, though, the exhibits focused on showcasing Japan's traditional art, crafts, and products. The Hall of Culture was a large, uncluttered, open space decorated with huge wall transparencies showing representative images of typical Japanese people that included those from the conquered provinces of Chosen (Korea), Manchoukuo (Manchuria), and Formosa (Taiwan).

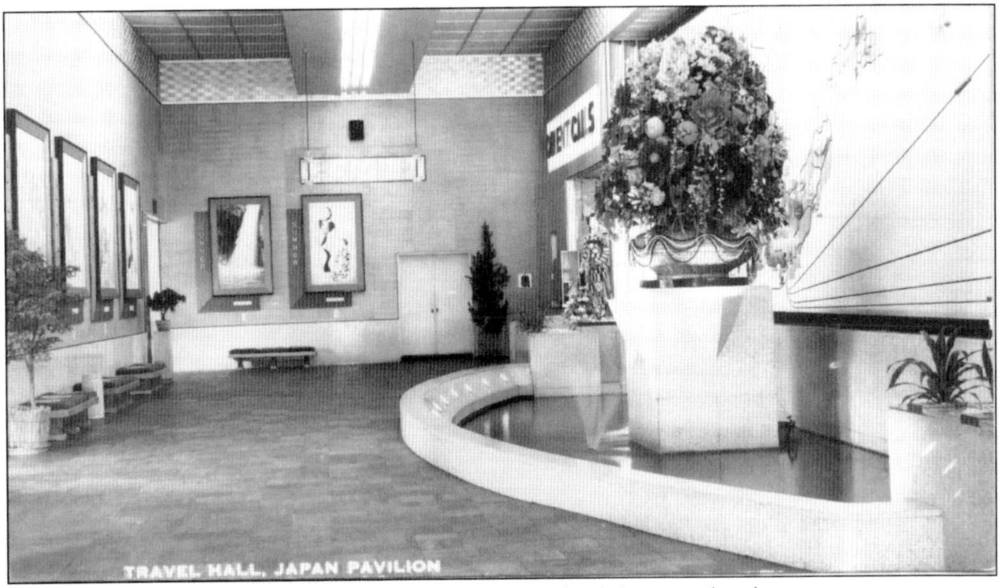

Architect Yoshizo Utida and his associate, Tatunao Toki, did not use local carpenters to construct the pavilion but brought Japanese men to construct the buildings and grounds using traditional materials, tools, and techniques. The modern interior of the Travel Hall provided a particularly serene environment with a fountain and bonsai trees while one took time to view the large panoramic wall map.

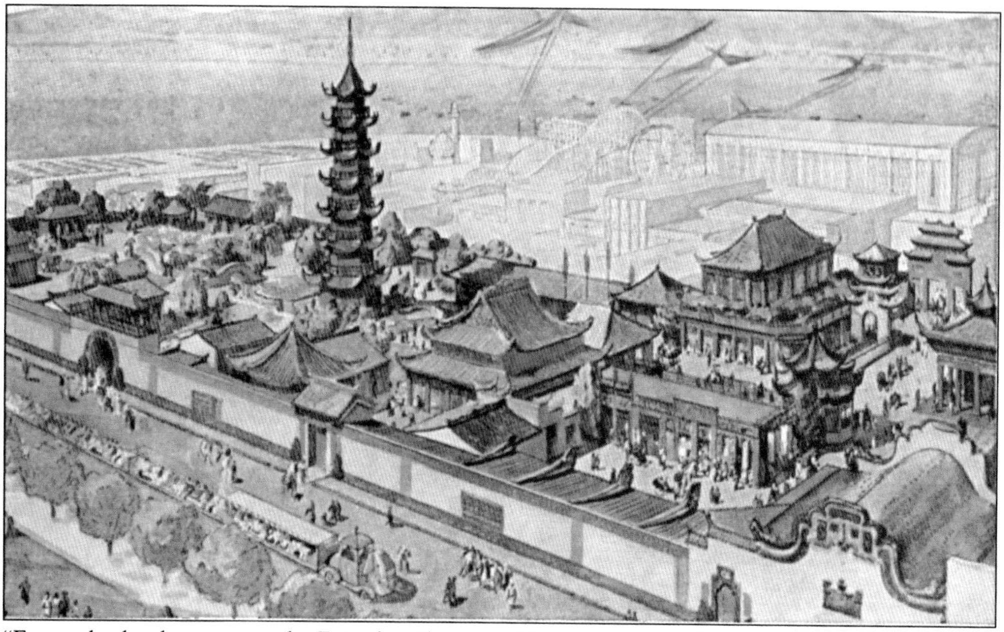

"For anybody who came to the Fair, the Chinese Village was a must," said San Franciscan George Jue. China had been at war with Japan since 1936 and was unable to provide the assets for a national pavilion, so Jue raised $200,000 in funds and then managed the Chinese Village built on three acres and surrounded by a 45-foot-high wall to provide security for the display of rare ivory and jade art treasures.

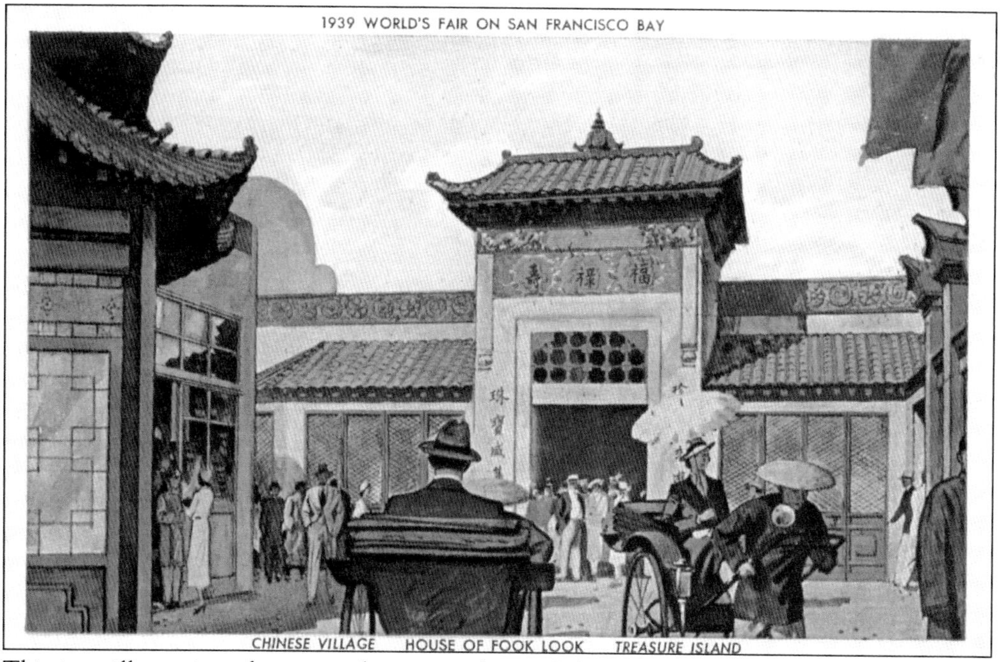

This is an illustration of a man and woman riding rickshaws on their way to the House of Fook Look, where they could shop for silk and jade merchandise or play games of chance. At the Fong-Fong Restaurant and Tom Wing Kong, visitors could purchase reasonably priced meals. According to George Jue, the Chinese Village lost money and had only enough to pay employee wages.

San Francisco Chinese community leaders selected local architect Mark Daniels to design the Chinese Village. The signature landmark was a 150-foot-high pagoda, a reproduction of one in Shanghai that cost $75,000 to build. Daniels studied the construction of buildings in China and integrated elements of Feng Shui into his design to create favorable influences on the pagoda that was used to house objects of art.

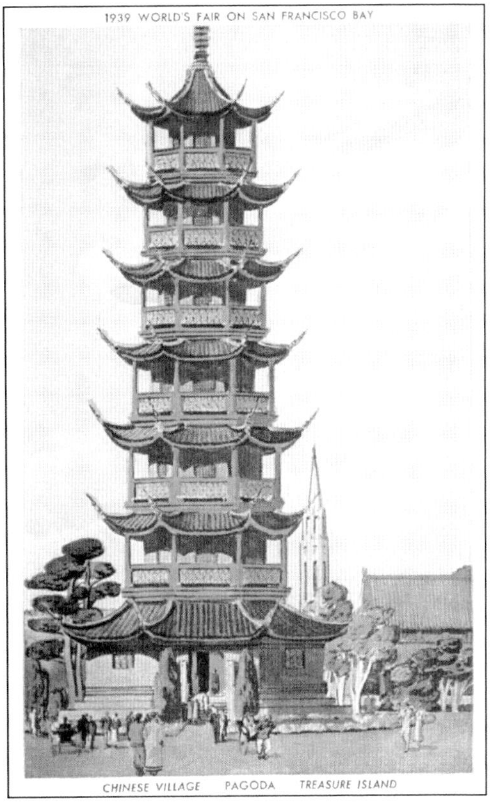

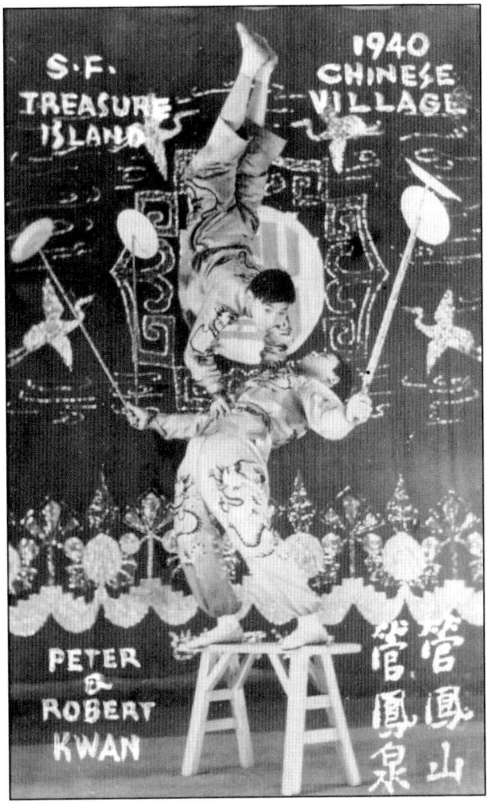

Brothers Peter and Robert Kwan were part of an acrobatic troupe performing three shows daily at the Chinese Village, doing somersaults, spinning plates, and jumping through hoops of fire. Young ladies sang Chinese opera and performed traditional dances as part of the show. General admission to the village was 25¢.

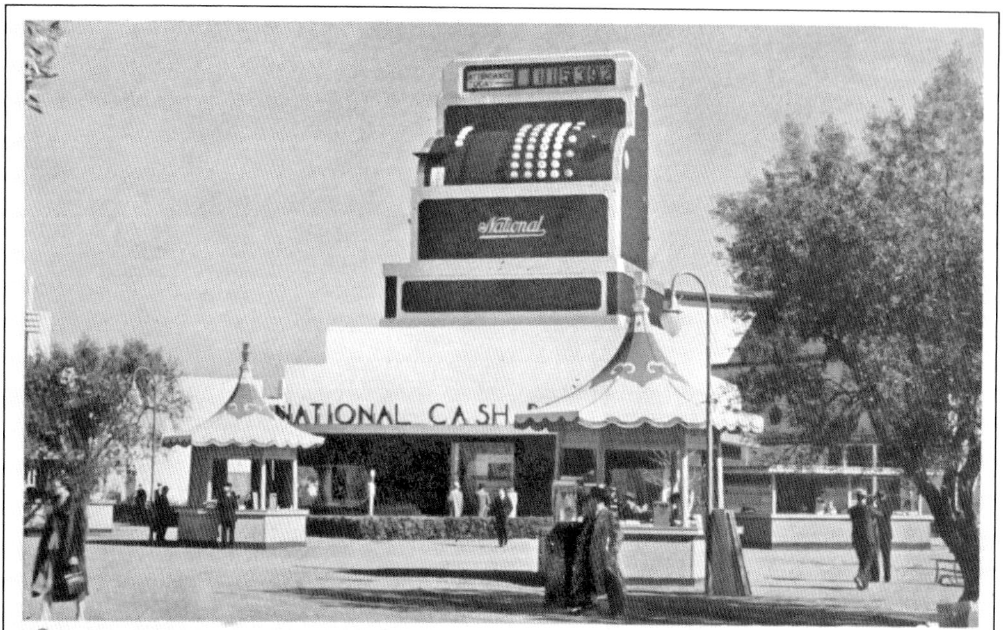

© STANLEY A. PILTZ

Every half hour, every day the fair was open, the daily and total attendance was displayed with numbers 2 feet 4 inches high on a giant National Cash Register model. On opening day, February 18, 1939, the mammoth cash register tallied fewer then 130,000 visitors, but on the last day of the fair in 1940, over 200,000 visitors were counted.

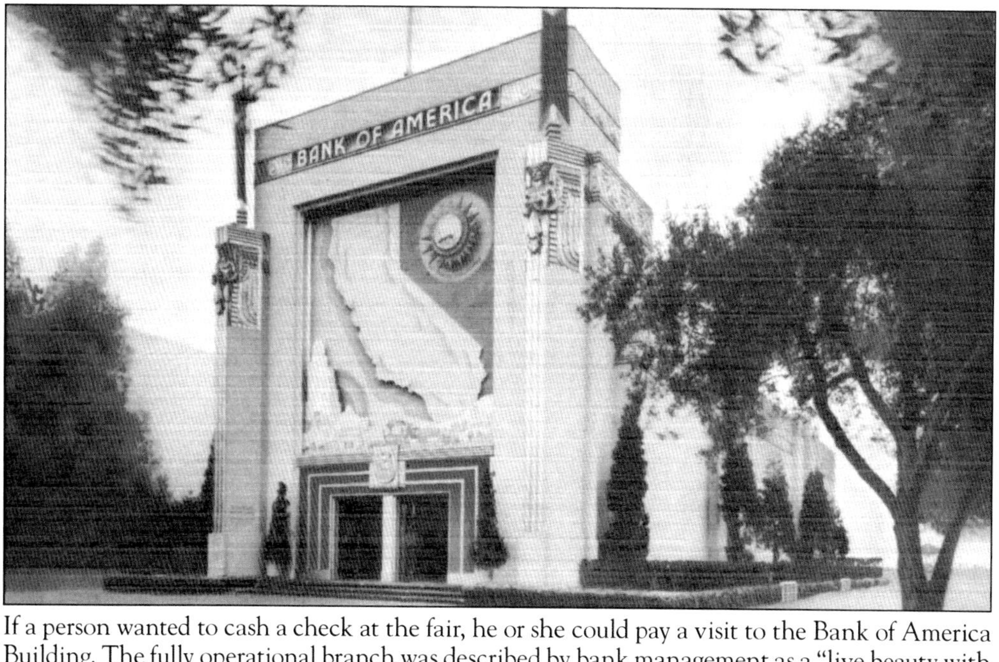

If a person wanted to cash a check at the fair, he or she could pay a visit to the Bank of America Building. The fully operational branch was described by bank management as a "live beauty with real eye appeal." The colorful but windowless building was 45 by 110 feet in size and featured a giant frieze map above the entrance showing the locations of 495 bank branches.

Here is a stylish Art Deco advertising postcard for the Chicago and Northwestern Railway exhibit, which was located in Vacationland. The official guidebook claimed, "All out doors brought under one roof." The giant building, 900 feet long and 200 feet wide (4 acres), ran along the length of the Court of Seven Seas and was home to 31 different vendors promoting travel, vacations, and related products. Postcards were popular free souvenirs given away by exhibitors at the fair.

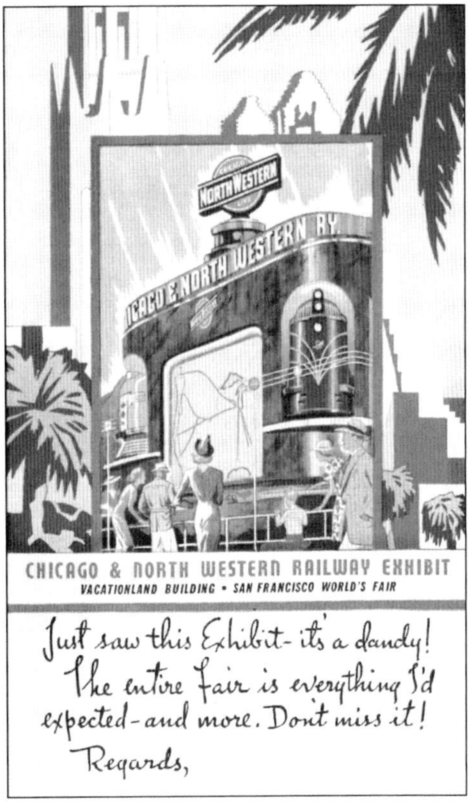

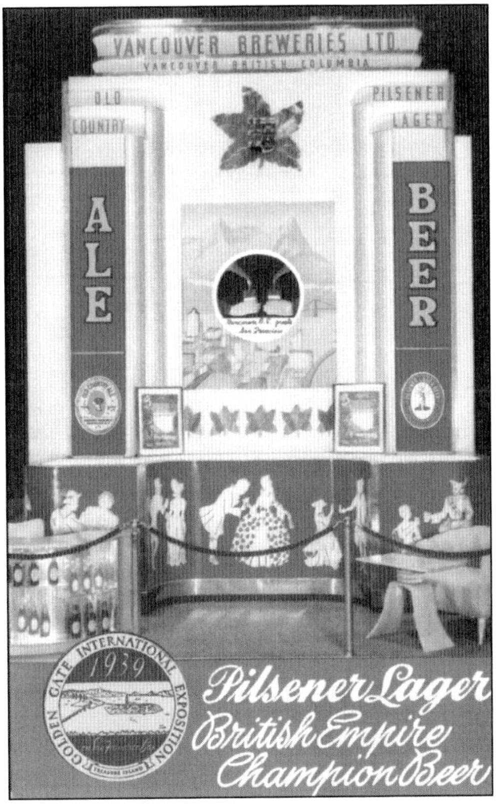

"The Pride of British Columbia," Canada's Vancouver Breweries promoted prize-winning Pilsner Lager at their exhibit in the Food and Beverages Building, where visitors could sample a cold bottle of beer or Old Country Ale. From the over 30 vendors in the Food and Beverages Building, visitors could pick a full-course dinner literally from soup to desserts.

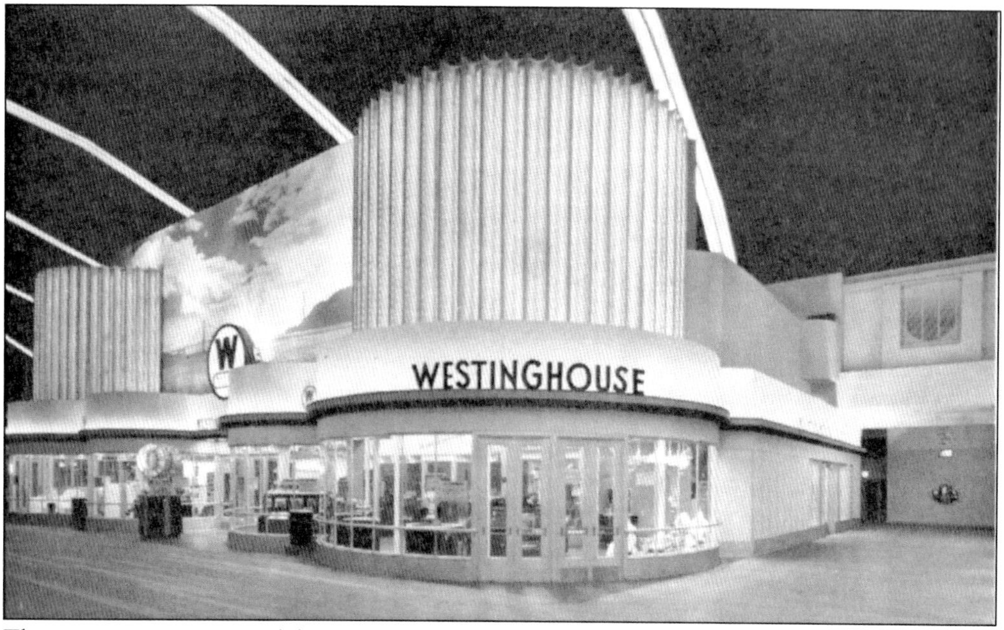

The newest inventions and developments in the field of electricity were exhibited in the Hall of Electricity and Communication. The Westinghouse exhibit featured a television demonstration, displays of modern electric kitchens and laundries, and Willie Vocalite, an electric robot who could sit down, rise, smoke, and talk.

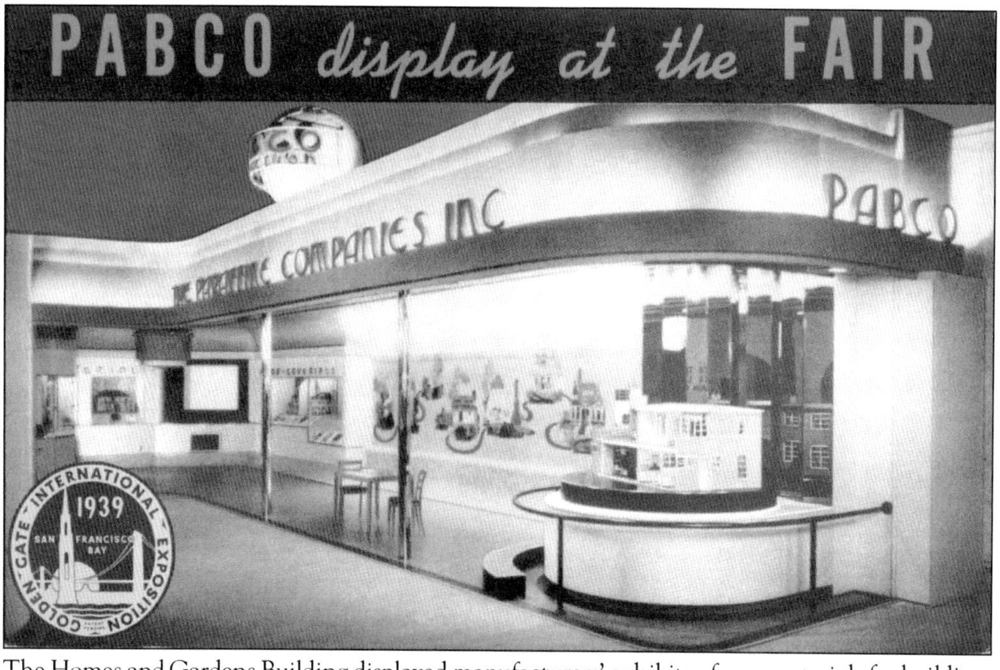

The Homes and Gardens Building displayed manufacturers' exhibits of new materials for building, home decoration, and home furnishings. The Parafine Companies, Inc. (Pabco), specialized in "joy-of-living" floor coverings and paint products showcased in a streamlined modern exhibition space. The Pabco mural, within inlaid linoleum, depicted the evolution of shelter from the days of the cave dwellers to modern-day 1939 California.

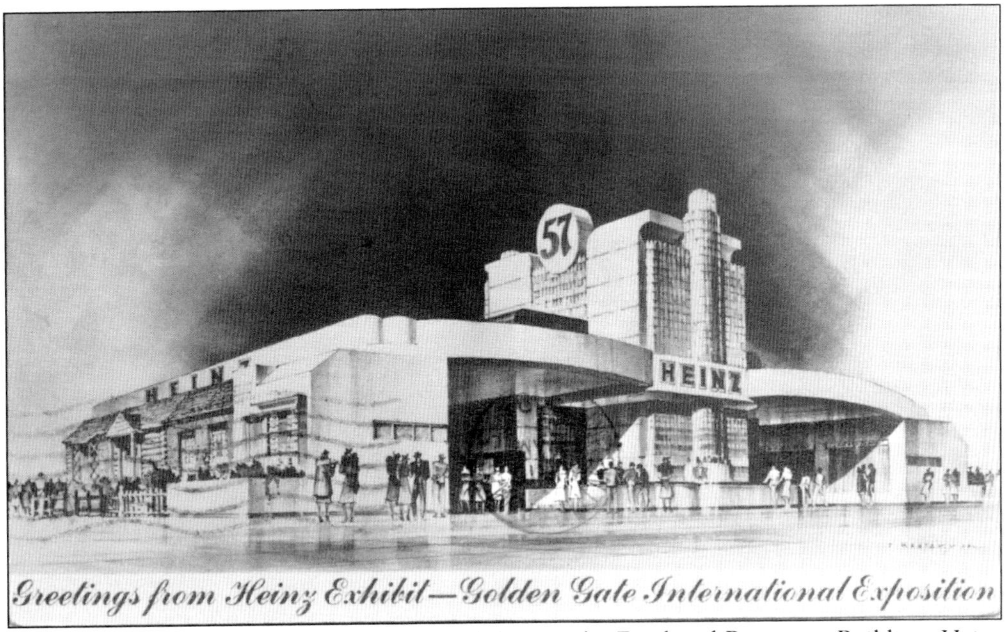

The futuristic Heinz Exhibit was 1 of 34 exhibits in the Food and Beverages Building. Heinz displayed ketchup, tomato juice, chili sauce, canned foods, and soup. Everyone visiting the pavilion, adults and youngsters alike, wanted to walk away with one of Heinz's promotional pickle pins, a tiny green plastic pin in the shape of a pickle.

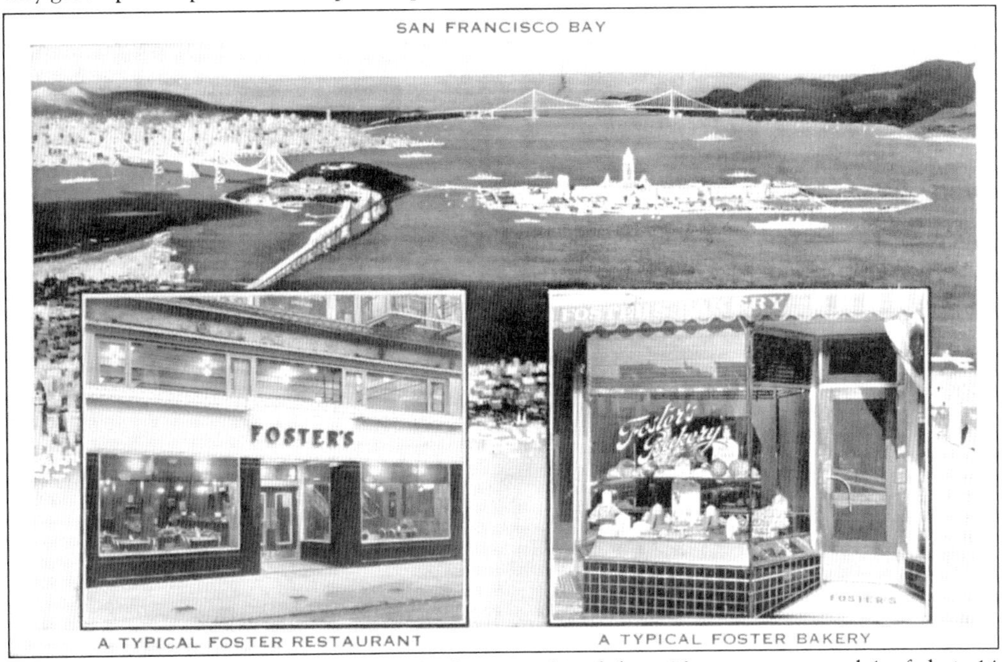

Archie and Lotta Foster (see page 36) had views of 1 of their 23 restaurants and 1 of their 14 bakeries superimposed over a postcard image showing Treasure Island and San Francisco Bay with its new bridges. Businesses throughout the Bay Area displayed photographic prints of Treasure Island and, whenever possible, did what they could to link their businesses to the fair and the two new bridges.

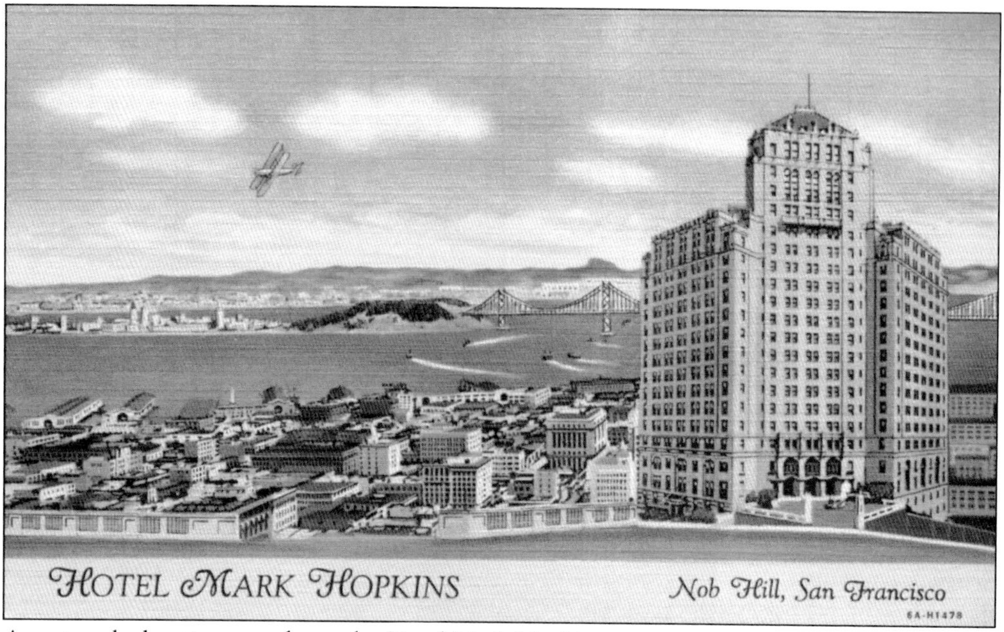

A postcard advertisement shows the Hotel Mark Hopkins in an interesting view with Treasure Island in the background. With fewer visitors then expected, San Francisco hotels stood to lose a great deal of money if the fair didn't reopen for a second year. Hotel proprietors convinced chamber of commerce president Marshall Dill to serve as president of the fair when it reopened for a second year in May 1940.

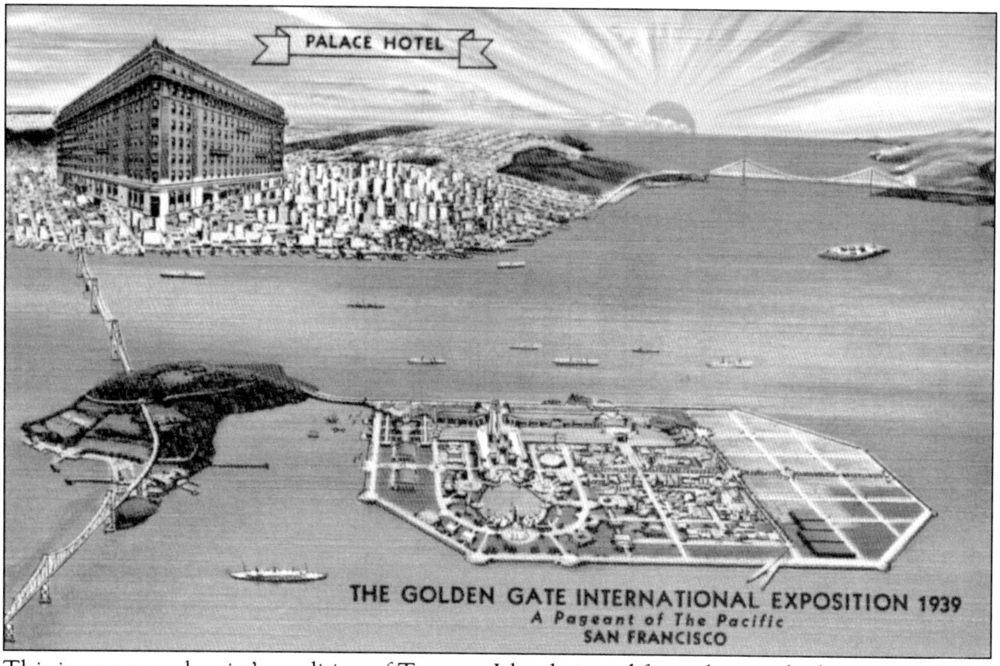

This is an unusual artist's rendition of Treasure Island viewed from the east looking towards the setting sun in the west. The postcard, printed as an advertisement for the Palace Hotel, shows the hotel as a giant landmark in the heart of San Francisco, drawing almost a spiritual connection between the hotel and the exposition.

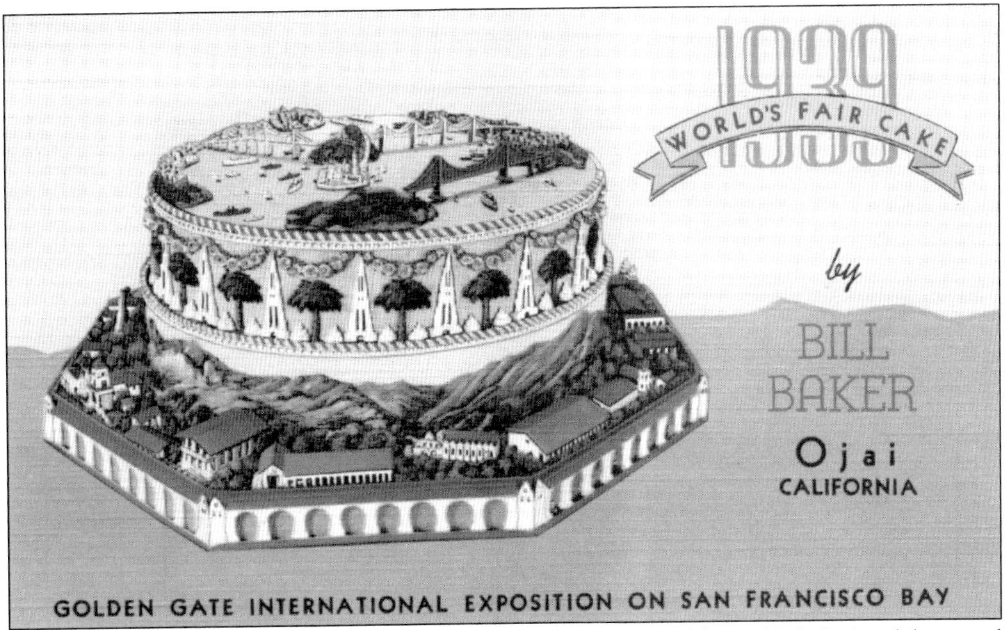

One of the noteworthy achievements at the fair was the 1,000-pound fruitcake, baked and decorated by Bill Baker of the Soya and Lima Bean Bakery in Ojai, California. Chef Baker used 600 eggs, 100 pounds of flour, 200 pounds of raisins, 150 pounds of fruit peel, 75 pounds of cherries, and 10 gallons of wine in making the 5- by 3-foot fruitcake.

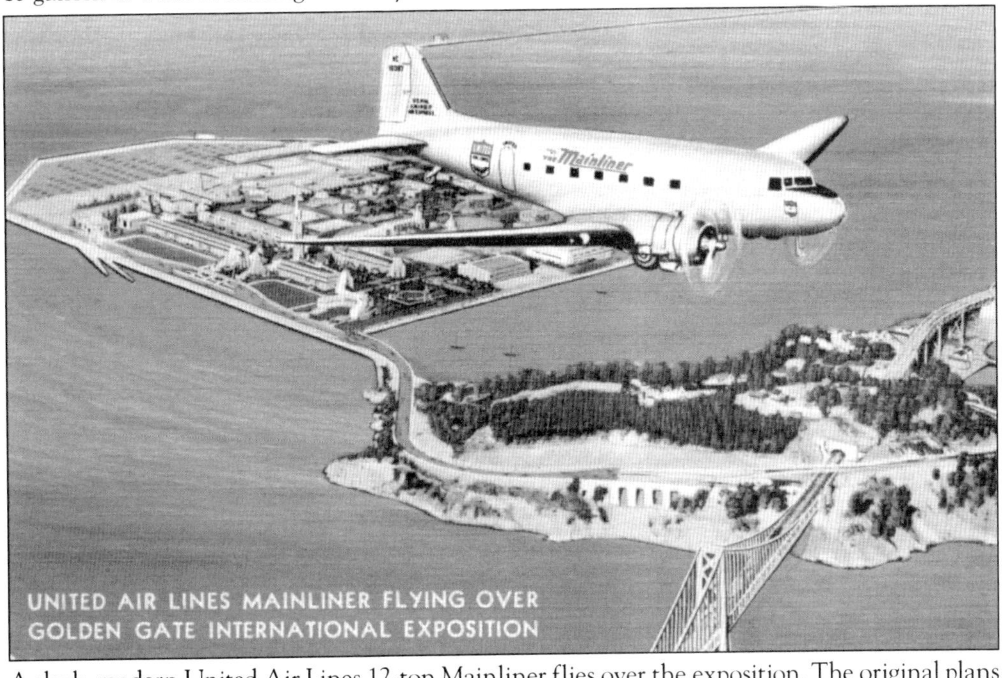

A sleek, modern United Air Lines 12-ton Mainliner flies over the exposition. The original plans called for Treasure Island to become an international airport, but the winds of war brought about changes to those plans when Rear Adm. John W. Greenslade, commandant of the Twelfth Naval District, wrote a letter to Mayor Angelo Rossi requesting that "in a national emergency, the city grant permission to the Navy to use the island."

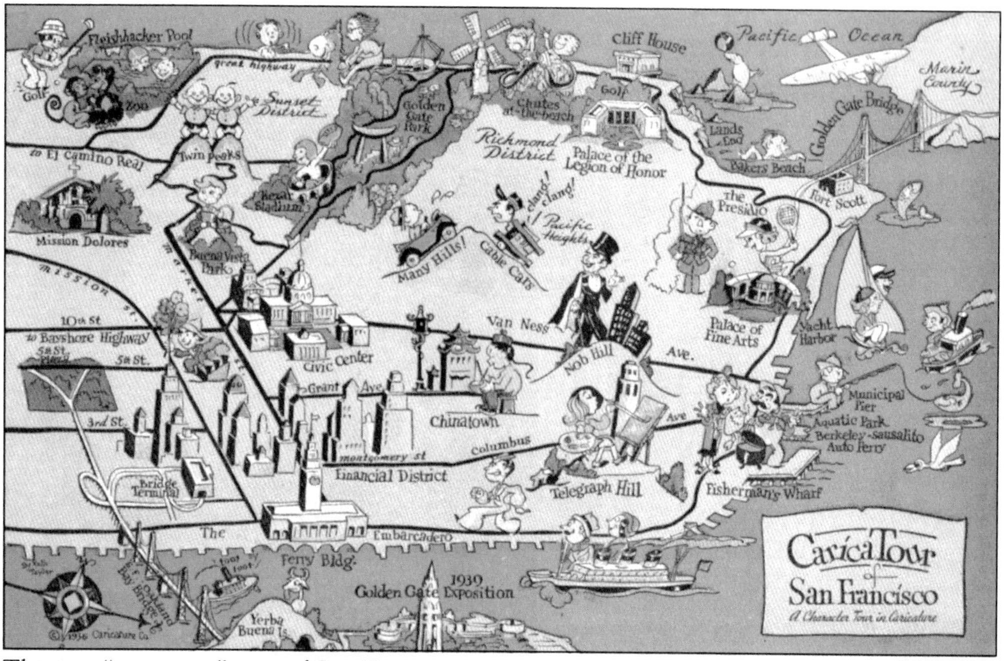

This is a "caricatour" map of San Francisco in 1939. The comic illustration shows caricatures of San Franciscans and many points of interest to be found in the city, including the Golden Gate International Exposition, but one shouldn't try to find the way with this map, as he or she might get lost.

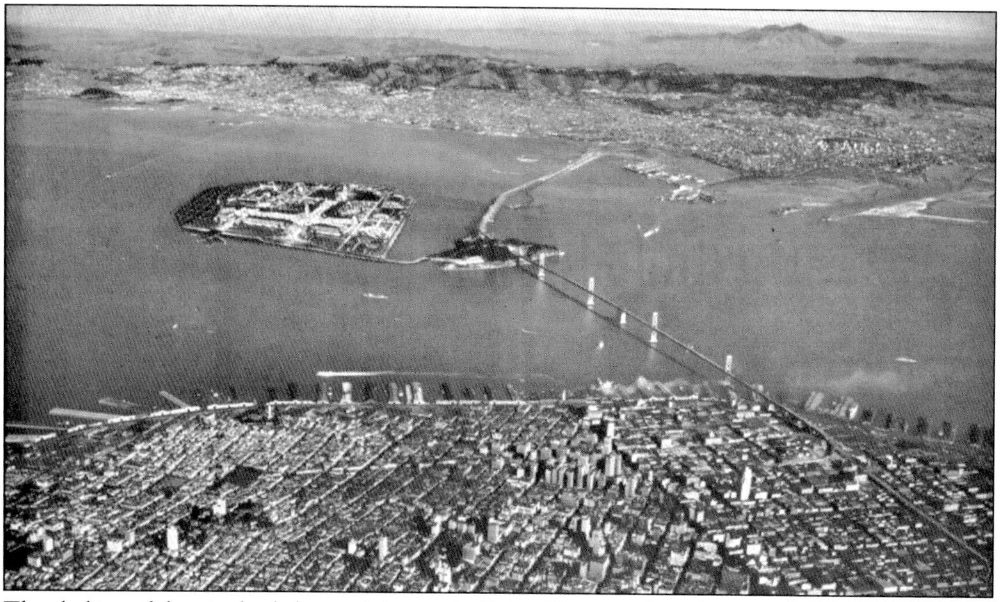

The skyline of the city had changed dramatically in 15 years when this aerial was taken in 1940. With the closing of the World's Fair on Treasure Island, the Art Deco era in San Francisco was coming to an end as well. The exposition officially closed amidst a midnight fireworks display on September 29, 1940. Five months later, on February 28, 1941, the U.S. Navy leased Treasure Island from the City and County of San Francisco. The "pageant of the Pacific" was over, and in 10 months, the United States would be at war.

Ten

PRESERVATION

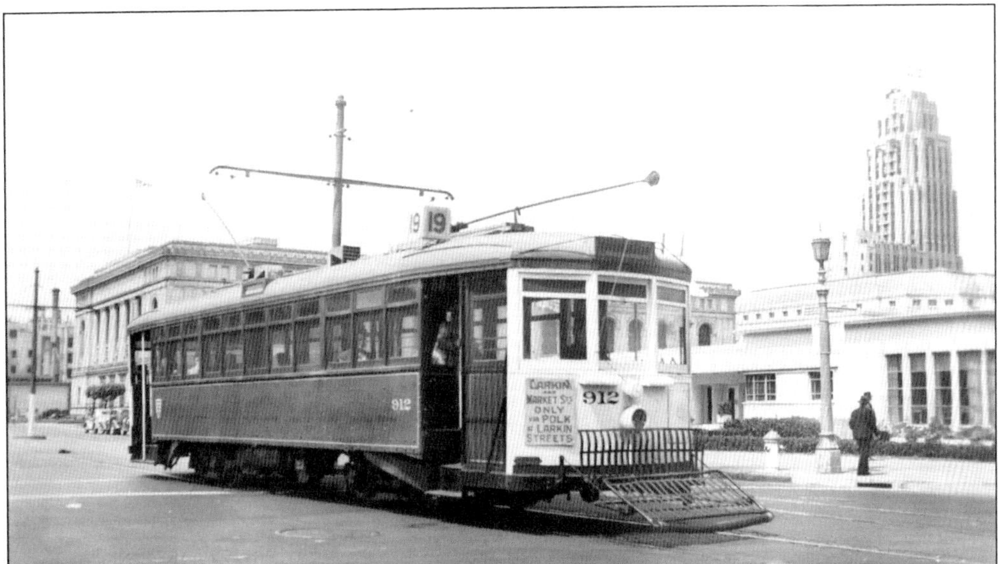

Many San Francisco landmarks of the Art Deco era have either disappeared or have been considerably changed. A look at a 1943 photograph taken at Larkin and Grove Streets provides some idea of the transformations that can occur. The No. 19 Polk streetcar line switched to buses in 1945. George W. Kelham's beaux-arts main San Francisco Public Library has been extensively remodeled as the Asian Art Museum. The William Taylor Hotel now provides housing for Hastings Law School students, and the Hospitality House was demolished in 1992 to make room for the new main San Francisco Public Library.

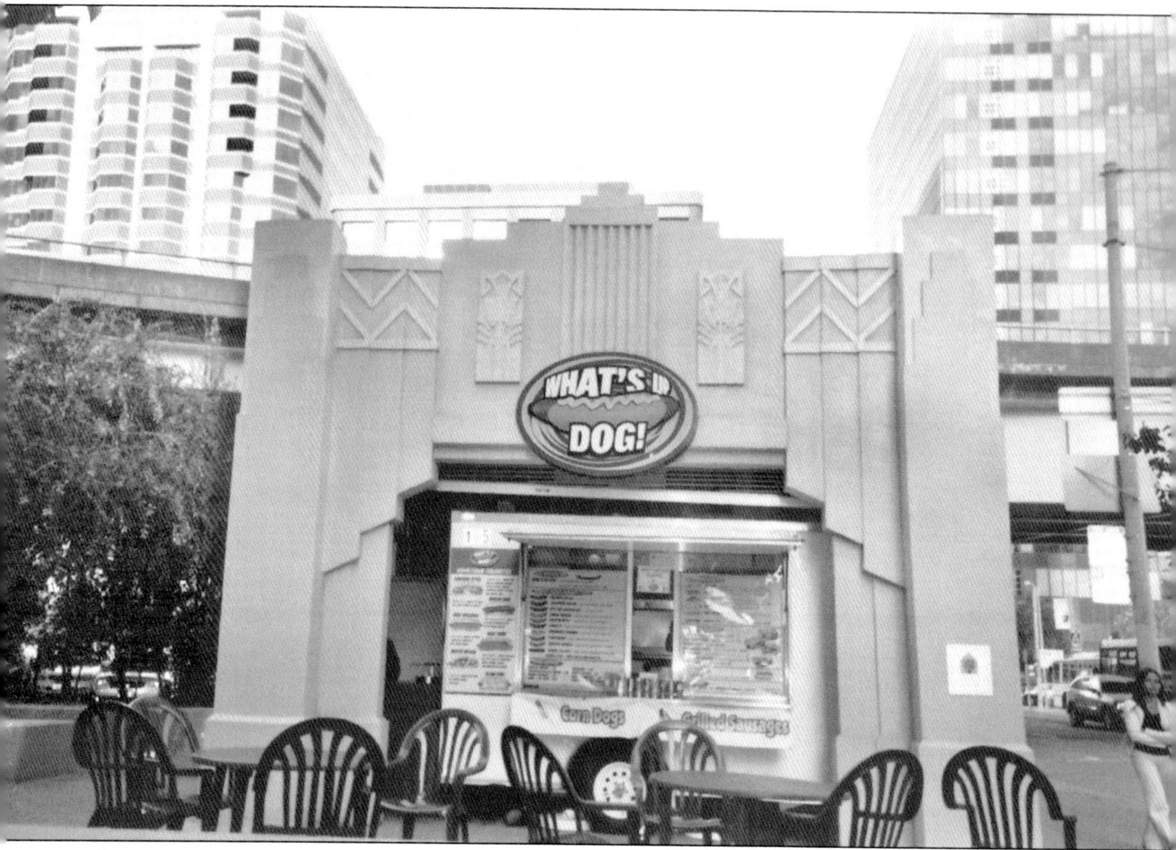

This remnant of a two-building station at the corner of Howard and Beale Streets is now a good example of adaptive reuse. Formerly located at 1501 Pacific Avenue, the original stepped arches and cornice elements reflect a Mayan design influence. Reputable architects for large oil companies often designed gas stations during the period. Frank Lloyd Wright and Norman Bel Geddes are just two of the architects who produced these prototype designs.

Although built in 1927 in a Spanish Colonial Revival style, the current appearance of the former White Motor Car Company at 1500 Mission Street shows the changes made by Henry Gutterson in the mid-1930s. The architect gave the building a distinctly streamlined look with a stepped tower, curved walls, and speed lines in the area above the windows. This kind of remodeling shows how important it was to have a more modern-looking building, particularly for commercial structures.

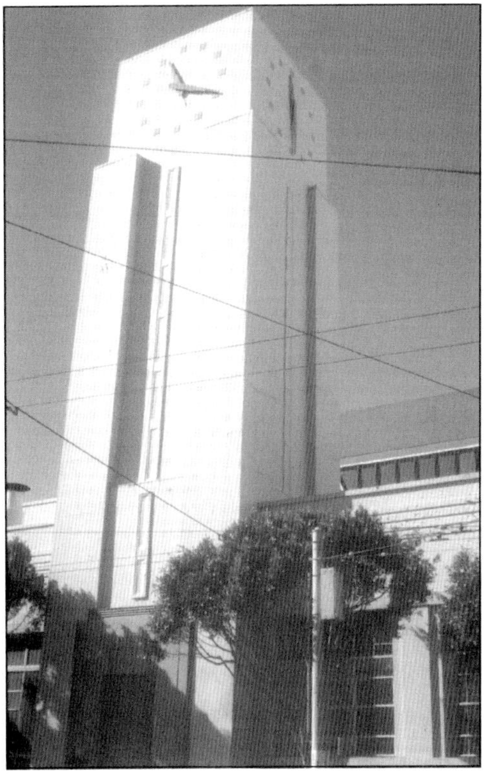

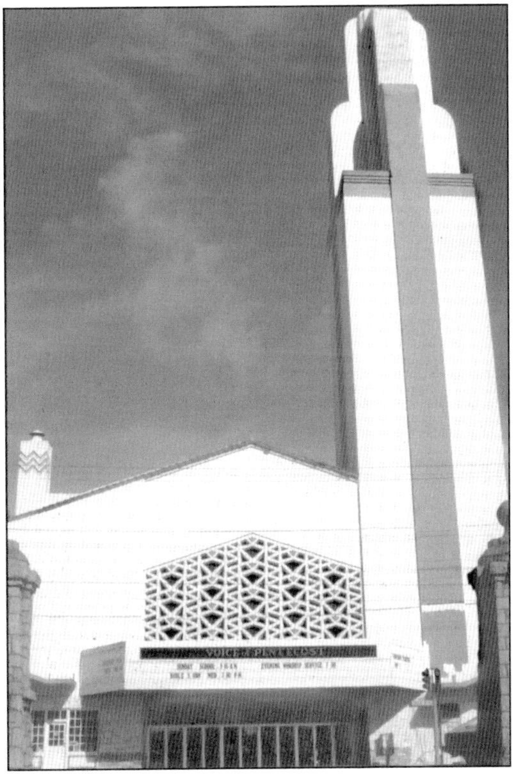

Timothy Pflueger designed the El Rey Theater at 1970 Ocean Avenue in 1931. It is unusual with the tall, stepped vertical tower, which Pflueger had not used in his previous theater designs. The decorative grille over the entry bears some similarity in the angular openings of the Roosevelt Middle School of 1928. It is now adaptively used as a church, which appears compatible with its original use.

Historic Preservation in San Francisco

The preservation of historic Art Deco buildings is subject to the same forces as any other historic resources in the city of San Francisco. There is protective legislation for designated city landmarks, which requires a Certificate of Appropriateness for any work undertaken on the landmark. The work must meet the requirements of the Secretary of the Interior's Standards for the Treatment of Historic Properties and is reviewed by the Landmarks Preservation Advisory Board. The members of the board are appointed by the mayor and serve at his pleasure.

Generally speaking, Art Deco buildings are eligible to be declared landmarks just like any other resource. Some, such as those in the downtown Financial District, are protected by specific legislation for that area. Others in various parts of the city could be part of designated historic districts. These and any historic resources not in such designated areas are subject to the California Environmental Quality Act. This legislation requires the city to consider all of the impacts that could occur to a property either officially recognized as historic or that has been determined to be historic through a city survey listing or research of its history.

If a property is historic, the proponent for a project that would affect this property must develop a project that would not adversely affect the property. If possible, mitigation measures must be developed to minimize harm to the resources. This information is developed for an Environmental Impact Report, which is presented to the public for review and comment.

There are various advocacy groups in the city that monitor the activities affecting historic resources. However they need an informed public to assist in these efforts. The San Francisco Architectural Heritage organization is the leader. Often it works in concert with neighborhood groups or special interest groups, such as the Art Deco Society of California, to ensure the protection of Art Deco resources. The National Trust for Historic Preservation and the California Preservation Foundation also provide technical assistance and sometimes financial support for preservation activities.

The most protection for historic resources is provided by local ordinances. Listing on the National Register of Historic Places, while an honor, does not necessarily protect a historic resource. It does not prevent demolition or alteration unless the project is undertaken, funded, or licensed by a federal agency.

Preservation is a community responsibility based on an informed public. Many of the preservation organizations provide educational programs, lectures, walking tours, and house tours. These activities give the public the opportunity to learn the importance and significance of buildings, neighborhoods, and architects. But they are usually membership organizations, and it is important for them to have this financial support to continue to provide these services. Below is a brief listing of them for the City of San Francisco.

Landmarks Preservation Advisory Board
Mark Luellen,
Preservation Coordinator
Planning Department
1660 Mission Street
San Francisco, CA 94105
415/558-6478

San Francisco Heritage
Charles Chase, Director
2007 Franklin Street
San Francisco, CA 94109
415/441-3000

National Trust for Historic Preservation
Anthea Hartig, Director
5 Third Street, Suite 707
San Francisco, CA 94103
415/956-0610
www.nationaltrust.org

The Art Deco Society of California
The Shell Building
100 Bush Street, Suite 511
San Francisco, CA 94104
415/982-DECO (3326)
www.artdecosociety.org

Market Street Railway
870 Market Street, Suite 803
San Francisco, CA 94102
415/956-0472
www.streetcar.org

California Preservation Foundation
5 Third Street, Suite 424
San Francisco, CA 94103
415/495-0349
www.californiapreservation.org

Bibliography

Bayer, Patricia. *Art Deco Architecture, Design, Decoration and Detail from the Twenties and Thirties.* New York: Thames and Hudson, 1999.

Benton, Charlotte, Tim Benton, and Ghislaine Wood, eds. *Art Deco 1910–1939.* Boston: Bullfinch Press, 2003.

Breeze, Carla. *American Art Deco.* New York: W. W. Norton, 2003.

Brown, Allen. *Golden Gate, the Dramatic Story of the Planning, Building and Operating of the Bridge.* Garden City, NY: Doubleday, 1965.

California's Diamond Jubilee, 1850–1925. San Francisco: E. C. Brown, 1927.

Carpenter, Patricia F., and Paul Totah. *The San Francisco Fair, Treasure Island, 1939–1940.* San Francisco: Scottwall Associates, 1989.

Cohen, Stan. *Wings to the Orient, Pan American Clipper Planes 1935 to 1945.* Missoula, MT: Pictorial Histories Publishing Company, 1990.

Crowe, Michael F. *Deco By The Bay, Art Deco Architecture in the San Francisco Bay Area.* New York: Viking Studio Books, 1995.

Duncan, Alastair. *American Art Deco.* New York: Thames and Hudson, 1999.

———. *Encyclopedia of Art Deco.* New York: Knickerbocker Press, 1998.

Flamm, Jerry. *Good Life in Hard Times, San Francisco in the 20s and 30s.* San Francisco: Chronicle Books, 1999.

———. *Hometown San Francisco, Sunny Jim, Phat Willie, and Dave.* San Francisco: Scottwall Associates, 1994.

Gilliam, Harold. *The San Francisco Experience, the Romantic Lore behind the Fabulous Facade of the Bay Area.* Garden City, NY: Doubleday, 1972.

Hillier, Bevis. *Art Deco of the 20s and 30s.* New York: Schocken Books, 1985.

Jester, Thomas C. *Twentieth-Century Building Materials, History and Conservation.* Washington, D.C.: Archetype Press, 1995.

Lee, Anthony W. *Painting On The Left, Diego Rivera, Radical Politics and San Francisco Public Murals.* Berkeley: University of California Press, 1999.

Neuhaus, Eugen. *The Art of Treasure Island.* Berkeley: University of California Press, 1939.

Pflueger, Milton T. *Time and Tim Remembered.* San Francisco: Pflueger Architects, 1985.

San Francisco Bay Exposition. *Golden Gate International Exposition.* San Francisco: The Crocker Company, 1939.

Short, C. W., and R. Stanley-Brown. *Public Buildings, Architecture Under the Public Works Administration, 1933 to 1939.* Washington, D.C.: U.S. Government Printing Office, 1939.

Siefkin, David. *Meet Me at The St. Francis, the First Seventy-Five Years of a Great San Francisco Hotel (1904–1979).* San Francisco: St. Francis Hotel Corp., 1992.

Strauss, Joseph Baermann and Clifford Emmett Paine. *The Golden Gate Bridge, Report of the Chief Engineer, 50th Anniversary Edition.* San Francisco: Golden Gate Bridge Highway and Transportation District, 1987.

Weber, Eva. *American Art Deco.* Greenwich, CT: Dorset Press, 1985.

Wiley, Peter Booth. *San Francisco, National Trust Guide.* New York: Preservation Press, 2000.